Brave New World: Contexts and Legacies

For Hank and Maggie (J. G.) and little Henry, Orson, and Sienna (N. W.), and their futures.

FOREWORD

Whether Aldous Huxley borrowed his title from *The Tempest* or lifted it from the final stanzas of Kipling's 'The Gods of the Copybook Headings' (1919)—'As it will be in the future, it was at the Birth of Man— | There are only four things certain since Social Progress began:— | That the Dog returns to his Vomit and the Sow returns to her Mire, | And the burnt Fool's bandaged finger goes wabbling back to the Fire; | And that after this is accomplished, and the brave new world begins | When all men are paid for existing and no man must pay for his sins, | As surely as Water will wet us, as surely as Fire will burn, | The Gods of the Copybook Headings with terror and slaughter return!'—it has become irremovably cemented in our culture and indissolubly associated with the author of *Brave New World*.[1]

'Unhesitatingly', Ethel Mannin wrote in January 1931, 'I place Aldous Huxley as the most important, the greatest intellect and the most serious artist of my male contemporaries.'[2] Mannin's comment is an important indication of the kind of esteem in which Huxley was held by many of his peers a year before *Brave New World* was published. Significantly, however, H.G. Wells, the peerless kingpin of futuristic speculation at this time, was not one of Huxley's literary admirers, even though it could be argued that Wells was one of Huxley's guru figures in the late 1920s and especially the early 1930s (following the likes of H.L. Mencken, D.H. Lawrence, and J.W.N. Sullivan, and a little in advance of Gerald Heard) and that Huxley became an ardently Wellsian 'open conspirator' during this period.[3] On 22 July 1929 the economist and political theorist Harold Laski wrote to the American jurist Oliver Wendell Holmes, Jr. about a party he had recently attended. 'The most amusing moment, I think, a fight between Arnold Bennett and H.G. Wells over the merits of Aldous Huxley. H.G. insisted that he [Huxley] committed the first great sin in being unable to tell a story and that he was pretentious. Bennett said he was a great stylist in quest of material. They fought like cats.'[4] When Laski got round to reading *Brave New World* he was suitably receptive to the provocative obscenity of the text, though he prudishly condemned it as 'foul ... like a small boy taking you into a corner to snigger at a bawdy story.'[5]

Given Huxley's keenness on Wells's concept of a world state and a samurai caste system, and their strong agreement on what they saw as the failings of mass democracy, Wells's strident antipathy to the work of his admirer is striking, though Huxley, of course, did famously claim that his book was about 'the horror of the Wellsian utopia and a revolt against it' (*AHL* 348). In turn, this fairly pervasive slant on *Brave New World* was no doubt one of the reasons why Wells argued in a broadcast of December 1938 that:

> so much *Fiction of the Future* degenerates into a rather silly admission of insincerity before the tale is half-way through. The writer's imagination gives *out*, he ceases to feel you can possibly believe in him, and so he begins to grimace and pretend that all along he was only making fun. [...] That is the case, for example, in that incredibly dismal book, Mr Aldous Huxley's *Brave New World*. It becomes at last a sour grimace at human hope. [...] Every developing tendency to which a young man might devote himself is distorted and guyed.[6]

Wyndham Lewis, in similar vein, noted that '"Brave New World" was an unforgivable offence to Progress and to political uplift of every description',[7] while, less huffily but equally dismissively, P.G. Wodehouse remarked in one of his letters that he had 'bought Aldous Huxley's book but simply can't read it. Aren't these stories of the future a bore? The whole point of Huxley is that he can write better about modern life than anybody else, so of course he goes and writes about the future.'[8]

Despite its satirical take on contemporary developments at home and in the USA, Huxley's take on things to come, of course, was the main point of *Brave New World*, and this aspect of the novel was given great emphasis by Chatto & Windus's marketing department. The firm's publicity included a large billboard advertisement in central London and the commission of an arresting dust jacket from Leslie Holland that perfectly captured the global reach of Huxley's visionary World State and the key role of flight in such a dispensation. As a consequence, not long after the novel was published, its title became embedded in the heady language of the advertising industry. 'A world without grime and dirt—without ageing, back-breaking toil', ran an advertisement in the *Daily Mail* in 1933 for domestic electricity installation:

> A world where the years of youth last longer. A new age of light and leisure, of cleanliness and comfort. An age when the touch of a finger commands a help with a hundred hands.
> Not long ago this was a dream. Now it is coming true! The sources of power have been harnessed to hearth and home, to farm and factory. The brave new world is taking shape. The Electrical Age is at hand.[9]

Similarly, a 1936 advertisement in the *Daily Mirror* for the 'Talbot Ten' automobile represented its target woman driver as 'A Questing Modern ... born of this brave new world. In the pursuit of pleasure her car is her boon companion.'[10]

But beyond the use of the novel's title in advertising copy and as a handy catchphrase for anything that might be construed as remotely futuristic or outré, for most of the past 80-odd years Huxley's text has remained in many ways suggestively ambiguous or elusive to readers and critics alike, which is one of its undoubted strengths. It has generally been read as a straightforward dystopia, but there is plenty of evidence to suggest it was absorbed into the anti-utopian tradition all too hastily and it has stubbornly remained there. The novel's reception emphasized this pigeonholing of the book. Rebecca West, in particular, wrote at length about it and with great perception and critical intelligence, while Charlotte Haldane was also astute in her comments on the book, whereas others, such as G.K. Chesterton, assessed *Brave New World* with their habitual limitations very much to the fore.[11]

This present volume represents a major contribution to the debates that have surrounded *Brave New World* during the decades since it was published, focusing on the novel's genealogy, the texts and attitudes it is constructed from, and where its ideological heart lies. This last is a question first addressed by Patrick Parrinder and then handed on from one contributor to the next. Parrinder, for example, alerts us to the 'key role [Huxley] gives to sports and games as factors in social cohesion', and more generally this volume engages in essay after essay with fascinating questions about where consensual cohesion gives way to corporate control and whether individual freedom and the root-and-branch organization of society can ever be compatible. Furthermore, *Brave New World* goads us to probe the nature of governmental power and prompts us to ask where consensus ends and social engineering begins. And while the World State's emphasis on an easeful death is not as abhorrent now as it was in 1932, the termination of its citizens' lives solely in relation to their age and their utility as sources of phosphorus is unlikely to find favour with the majority of the novel's readers. But it does make us think about how euthanasia is a cultural construct rather than simply some vile anathema. We are now beginning to rethink death as we have gradually reconfigured procreation over the past century and I, for one, regard this development as civilized and enlightened rather than utterly abhorrent. But as Parrinder says, the novel's 'greatness' or distinction 'lies in its paradoxes' not its convictions, just as beyond the text one person's commitment to what they regard as progressive ideas is another person's confrontation with a raft of unacceptable principles and prejudices. Likewise, Jonathan Greenberg not only acknowledges the novel's celebrated prescience, but also draws attention to its time-bound blinkeredness—Huxley's 'blind spots'—especially in relation to our sensitivities about race and gender.

Among many other things Huxley was an intellectual magpie and *Brave New World*, like all his novels, lays out the fruits of his wide-ranging plundering (an annotated edition of the novel is sorely needed, just as a proper edition of his entire output would be hugely beneficial to scholars). But it is also a work that effortlessly flies free of its sources and continues to be acclaimed by a diverse community of readers, so this volume of criticism could not be more timely. It brings criticism of the novel up to date, yet it also examines Huxley's key ideas in the light of the values that dominate our own social and personal agendas. Like its original dust jacket, *Brave New World* remains edgy, modernistic, inviting, and quirkily peculiar, and even for those who think themselves fully familiar with it, this collection of essays will underline that there is every reason to read and rethink *Brave New World* afresh.

Worcester College,   Professor David Bradshaw
Oxford University

NOTES

1. R. Kipling, *The Cambridge Edition of the Poems of Rudyard Kipling – Volume II: Collected Poems II*, ed. T. Pinney (Cambridge: Cambridge University Press, 2013), pp. 1393–4.
2. Mannin's opinion is quoted in J. Laver, *Between the Wars* (London: Vista Books, 1961), p. 117.
3. A case is made for the intellectual indebtedness of Huxley to Wells in 'Open Conspirators: Huxley and H.G. Wells 1927–35' (*HH* 31–43).
4. M.D. Howe (ed.), *Holmes-Laski Letters: The Correspondence of Mr. Justice Holmes and Harold J. Laski 1916–1935* (London: Geoffrey Cumberlege and Oxford University Press, 1953), ii, p. 1167.
5. Howe (ed.), *Holmes-Laski Letters*, p. 1364.
6. H.G. Wells, 'Fiction About the Future' (1938), in *H.G. Wells's Literary Criticism*, ed. P. Parrinder and R.M. Philmus (Brighton: Harvester, 1980): pp. 246–51, at p. 248.
7. W. Lewis, *The Letters of Wyndham Lewis*, ed. W.K. Rose (London: Methuen, 1963), p. 226.
8. P.G. Wodehouse, *Yours Plum: The Letters of P.G. Wodehouse*, ed. F. Donaldson (London: Hutchinson, 1990), pp. 186–7.
9. 'The Wizard in the Wall', *Daily Mail* (20 Oct. 1933): 19.
10. 'Talbot "Ten"', *Daily Mirror* (6 May 1936): 10.
11. See D. Watt (ed.), *Aldous Huxley: The Critical Heritage* (London and Boston: Routledge & Kegan Paul: 1975), pp. 197–222.

ACKNOWLEDGEMENTS

The Editors in the first instance thank the late David Bradshaw for giving them the chance to edit this collection of essays. Without his encouragement, geniality, and scholarship, this volume would not have been possible. David died in September, 2016, just as this book was completed; his passing is a great loss to all who benefited from his immense erudition, wisdom, and kindness. The Editors also thank Giana Milazzo for her assistance in preparing the manuscript, and Max Saunders for solving a bibliographical problem. Above all, the Editors thank the contributors for providing such thought-provoking chapters, tolerating innumerable proofing and copy-editing queries, and generally being patient with a drawn-out, labour-intensive assembly and checking process.

Jonathan also thanks the College of Humanities and Social Sciences at Montclair State University for support of this project, Montclair State University for a summer research grant, and the Montclair State Global Education Center and its Director, Marina Cunningham, for funding the travel to the UK that proved essential to his research in its early stages. Giana Milazzo aided in many aspects of his research, identifying valuable primary and critical texts. David Greenberg offered expert assistance with questions of American intellectual history. The keen and curious minds of Montclair State's undergraduates have consistently reminded him what a rich and strange work *Brave New World* is. Lee Behlman, Naomi Liebler, Lucy McDiarmid, and Jeff Miller have offered insight, advice, and support. Finally, he is grateful for the love and encouragement of Megan Blumenreich, Hank Greenberg, and Maggie Greenberg through every stage of the writing and editing of this book.

Nathan also thanks his colleagues in the School of English at the University of Nottingham for making possible such a kind-hearted environment in which to conduct and discuss research. Particular appreciation goes also to Nathan's undergraduate and postgraduate students (past and present), whose insights into the nature of dystopian fiction have shaped his thinking in more ways than he can register here. Alice Reeve-Tucker has been there every step of the way, encouraging him with love and serenity throughout the work that editing a volume of this sort requires. Similar thanks go to Alan, Paulene, Charlie, Jenny, Fred, Joan, and Maureen. As ever, Nathan's friends and all members of the Waddell and Reeve-Tucker clans have been nothing but perceptive, humorous interlocutors.

Spelling in this volume is standardized by chapter and by institutional location of the author: chapters written by US-based scholars use American spelling; chapters written by UK-based scholars use British spelling. Where appropriate, references have been standardized according to entries in David J. Bromer and Shannon Struble, *Aun Aprendo: A Comprehensive Bibliography of the Writings of Aldous Leonard Huxley* (Boston: Bromer Booksellers, 2011).

At Palgrave, Jon and Nathan thank Ben Doyle, April James, and Frances Tye, and at SPi Global, Preethi Agnes.

CONTENTS

NOTES ON THE CONTRIBUTORS

David Bradshaw was Professor of English Literature at the University of Oxford, UK. He was a recognized expert on Aldous Huxley, and wrote several articles on his life and work. He also wrote extensively on twentieth-century literature and culture, focusing in particular on literary modernism, and edited numerous scholarly editions of texts by D.H. Lawrence, Huxley, Evelyn Waugh, and Virginia Woolf.

Laura Frost writes about modern and contemporary literature and culture. She is the author of two books—*Sex Drives: Fantasies of Fascism in Literary Modernism* (2001) and *The Problem With Pleasure: Modernism and Its Discontents* (2013)—and many articles about literature, film, art, and the history of sexuality. Her work has been heard, seen, and/or read at The New York Public Library, on the History Channel, the Discovery Channel, on Chicago Public Radio, on the BBC's 'The World',and in *The San Francisco Chronicle/Examiner, The New Yorker, the Village Voice, Bookforum, The Times Higher Education*, Quartz, *Publishers Weekly*, the *LA Times*, and other academic and general audience venues. She can be reached at laurafrost.info.

Andrzej Gąsiorek is Professor of Twentieth-Century Literature and Head of the English Literature Department at the University of Birmingham, UK. He is the author of *Post-war British Fiction: Realism and After* (1995), *Wyndham Lewis and Modernism* (2004), *J.G. Ballard* (2005), and *A History of Modernist Literature* (2015). He is a co-editor of *T.E. Hulme and the Question of Modernism* (2006), *The Oxford Handbook of Modernisms* (2010), *The Reinvention of the British and Irish Novel, 1880–1940* (2010), *Wyndham Lewis and the Cultures of Modernity* (2011), and *Wyndham Lewis: A Critical Guide* (2015).

Jonathan Greenberg is Professor of English at Montclair State University, USA. He is the author of *Modernism, Satire, and the Novel* (2011) and the forthcoming *Cambridge Introduction to Satire*, as well as numerous articles on twentieth-century British and American literature.

Keith Leslie Johnson is currently Lecturer of English and Media Studies at the College of William & Mary, Williamsburg, VA, USA. He has published essays on Franz Kafka, Samuel Beckett, Aldous Huxley, and other modernist figures. He recently completed a monograph on Czech surrealist Jan Švankmajer and is working on a second book entitled *Ethics After People*.

Aaron Matz is the author of *Satire in an Age of Realism* (2010). He is Associate Professor of English at Scripps College in Claremont, USA.

Jerome Meckier is Professor Emeritus of English at the University of Kentucky, USA. He has written *Aldous Huxley: Satire and Structure* (1969), *Aldous Huxley: Modern Satirical Novelist of Ideas* (2006), and *Aldous Huxley, from Poet to Mystic* (2011). He edited *Critical Essays on Aldous Huxley* (1996) and co-edits the *Aldous Huxley Annual*.

Patrick Parrinder is Emeritus Professor of English at the University of Reading, UK. A Fellow of the English Association, he is a leading authority on H.G. Wells and has edited many of Wells's texts for Penguin Classics. His book *Shadows of the Future: H.G. Wells, Science Fiction and Prophecy* won the 1996 University of California Eaton Award. He is author of *Nation and Novel* (2006) and General Editor of the ongoing 12-volume *Oxford History of the Novel in English*. His most recent book is *Utopian Literature and Science: From the Scientific Revolution to 'Brave New World' and Beyond*, published in 2015 by Palgrave Macmillan.

Claudia Rosenhan is a Teaching Fellow at the University of Edinburgh, UK. Her research interests include identity, language, and culture, especially cultural identity at the beginning of the twentieth century. A further interest is the context of education in early twentieth-century literary works. She has published and presented papers on a range of modernist and Edwardian writers, and is the author of *All Her Faculties: The Representation of the Female Mind in the Twentieth-Century English Novel* (2014).

Carey Snyder is Associate Professor of English at Ohio University, USA. She is the author of *British Fiction and Cross-Cultural Encounters: Ethnographic Modernism from Wells to Woolf* (2008) and the editor of the Broadview Press edition of H.G. Wells's *Ann Veronica* (2015). Her recent essays have appeared in such venues as the *Journal of Modern Periodical Studies* and the collection, *Modernism and Nostalgia* (2013).

Kathryn Southworth is a founding fellow of the English Association. Formerly Head of English and Associate Dean at the University of Wolverhampton, she was Vice Principal at what is now Newman University. At present she is an independent writer and reviewer in London, and a review manager with the Quality Assurance Agency for Higher Education.

Nathan Waddell is an Assistant Professor in the School of English at the University of Nottingham, UK. He is the author of *Modern John Buchan: A Critical Introduction* (2009) and *Modernist Nowheres: Politics and Utopia in Early Modernist Writing, 1900–1920* (Palgrave, 2012). He has co-edited several essay collections, among them *Wyndham Lewis and the Cultures of Modernity* (2011), *Utopianism, Modernism, and Literature in the Twentieth Century* (Palgrave, 2013), and *Wyndham Lewis: A Critical Guide* (2015).

LIST OF ABBREVIATIONS

Texts by Aldous Huxley:

AE   *Ape and Essence* (1948), introd. D. Bradshaw (London: Vintage, 1994).

AHL   *Letters of Aldous Huxley*, ed. G. Smith (London: Chatto & Windus, 1969).

AHSL   *Selected Letters*, ed. J. Sexton (Chicago: Ivan R. Dee, 2007).

BNW   *Brave New World* (1932), introd. M. Atwood and D. Bradshaw (London: Vintage, 2007).

BNWR   *Brave New World Revisited* (1958), introd. D. Bradshaw (London: Vintage, 2004).

CY   *Crome Yellow* (1921), introd. M. Bradbury, biog. introd. D. Bradshaw (London: Vintage, 2004).

EG   *Eyeless in Gaza* (1936), introd. D. Bradshaw (London: Vintage, 1994).

HCE1   *Complete Essays: Volume I, 1920–1925*, ed. R.S. Baker and J. Sexton (Chicago: Ivan R. Dee, 2000).

HCE2   *Complete Essays: Volume II, 1926–1929*, ed. R.S. Baker and J. Sexton (Chicago: Ivan R. Dee, 2000).

HCE3   *Complete Essays: Volume III, 1930–1935*, ed. R.S. Baker and J. Sexton (Chicago: Ivan R. Dee, 2001).

HCE4   *Complete Essays: Volume IV, 1936–1938*, ed. R.S. Baker and J. Sexton (Chicago: Ivan R. Dee, 2001).

HCE5   *Complete Essays: Volume V, 1939–1956*, ed. R.S. Baker and J. Sexton (Chicago: Ivan R. Dee, 2002).

HCE6   *Complete Essays: Volume VI, 1956–1963*, ed. R.S. Baker and J. Sexton (Chicago: Ivan R. Dee, 2002).

HH   *The Hidden Huxley*, ed. D. Bradshaw (London: Faber and Faber, 1994).

I   *Island* (1962), introd. D. Bradshaw (London: Flamingo, 1994).

PCP   *Point Counter Point* (1928; London: Chatto & Windus, 1933).

Texts by Others:

ACM   Donna Haraway, 'A Cyborg Manifesto: Science, Technology, and Socialist-Feminism in the Late Twentieth Century', in S. Stryker and S. Whittle (eds), *The Transgender Studies Reader* (New York: Routledge, 2006), pp. 103–18.

AHU   Theodor W. Adorno, 'Aldous Huxley and Utopia' (1942), in *Prisms*, trans. S. and S. Weber (1955; Cambridge, MA: MIT Press, 1967), pp. 95–118.

CJM   Fay Weldon, *The Cloning of Joanna May* (London: Collins, 1989).

DS   Shulamith Firestone, *The Dialectic of Sex: The Case for Feminist Revolution* (1970; New York: Farrar, Strauss and Giroux, 2003).

E   Samuel Butler, *Erewhon, or Over the Range* (1872), ed. P. Mudford (London: Penguin, 1970).

HSI   Marge Piercy, *He, She and It* (New York: Ballantine Books, 1991).

MAH   Nicholas Murray, *Aldous Huxley: An English Intellectual* (London: Abacus, 2003).

MU   H.G. Wells, *A Modern Utopia* (1905), ed. G. Claeys and P. Parrinder (London: Penguin, 2005).

MW   Charlotte Haldane, *Man's World* (1926; New York: George H. Doran Company, 1927).

LT   Harold Loeb, *Life in a Technocracy: What It Might Be Like* (1933), introd. H.P. Segal (Syracuse, NY: Syracuse University Press).

U   Sir Thomas More, *Utopia* (1516), ed. R. Marius (London: J.M. Dent, 1994).

WFFW   Anthony M. Ludovici, *Lysistrata; or, Woman's Future and Future Woman* (1924; New York: E.P. Dutton, 1925).

WI   Austin Tappan Wright, *Islandia* (1942; New York: Signet, 1958).

WOET   Marge Piercy, *Woman on the Edge of Time* (1976; London: The Women's Press, 1979).

LIST OF FIGURES

CHAPTER 1

Introduction

Jonathan Greenberg and Nathan Waddell

Reconsidering *Brave New World* over 80 years after it was published, it now seems hard to believe that its singularly resourceful author felt while he was writing it that he had 'hardly enough imagination' (*AHL* 348) to do justice to its subject matter. Time would prove Aldous Huxley wrong. *Brave New World* has long been deemed one of the most inventive, enjoyable, multifaceted, and satirically impudent futurological fictions written during the twentieth century. It is a book readers and writers across the world have loved, abhorred, questioned, and imitated, goaded as much by its unforgettable anticipations as by its inevitable blind spots and inconsistencies. *Brave New World* fully deserves the praise of such figures as J.G. Ballard, who in 1998 judged it 'a masterpiece of a novel' that is 'uncannily accurate in its prediction of the society we are now becoming: soma, feelies, test-tube babies.'[1] And the remarkable prescience that Ballard identifies is only one aspect of the book's enduring appeal. While Huxley's prognostic ability continues to astonish new generations of readers, the book also rewards attentive querying of those predictions it makes

J. Greenberg (✉)
Department of English, Montclair State University, Montclair, NJ, USA

N. Waddell
School of English, University of Nottingham, Nottingham, UK

© The Editor(s) (if applicable) and The Author(s) 2016   1
J. Greenberg, N. Waddell (eds.), Brave New World: *Contexts and Legacies*, DOI 10.1057/978-1-137-44541-4_1

which now seem strange, and of the problems it does not manage or even attempt to resolve. In short, *Brave New World* is a profoundly unsettled text. It appears ambivalent—sometimes even confused or confusing— in its attitudes towards power, freedom, and the nature of community. On the one hand it warns against despotism and on the other celebrates intelligent ruling elites. Readers are never quite sure whether it is a satirical swipe at the socio-economic, philosophical, and scientific wrongs, as Huxley saw them, of the 1920s and 1930s, or if it is a fairly candid broadcast of its author's illiberal prejudices. Such contradictions have given the book a life beyond its historical moment. It continues to anger and energize its readers to this day.

To be sure, few readers would deny that the book reflects its author's dismay about technological utopianism, hyper-industrialization, scientific progress, cultural decline, and the increasingly tyrannized subject positions available to human beings in the modern world. But in *Brave New World* Huxley queries, rather than simplistically plugs, his own ideological investments. Numerous scholars have shown that although strong correspondences exist between the opinions Huxley voiced in his non-fictional essays of the 1920s and 1930s and those put forth (explicitly or implicitly) in *Brave New World*, there is no simplistic 'message' to be extracted from the book, as Joseph Conrad would have it, like a nut from its shell.[2] A good example is the book's attitude towards eugenics. Like many thinkers of his time, Huxley wrestled with this problem throughout the 1920s and 1930s, frequently articulating opinions about human life and human rights at a time when, to quote Bradshaw, '[m]any progressives envisaged eugenics as a humanitarian means of fast-forwarding to a better world' (*HH* xv). Hence Robert S. Baker's fair (if guarded) remark that while Huxley never adopted H.G. Wells's 'progressivist faith in science and technology, he did [...] briefly entertain some notions that admittedly raise difficult and salient questions about his own tentative complicity in some of the darker aspects of social engineering.'[3] Readers hoping unproblematically to place *Brave New World* on either side of the debate—as a straightforward attack upon or endorsement of eugenic principles—have a difficult task ahead of them, not least because when Huxley was writing the book he was still grappling with the elementary anxieties upon which the debate itself was founded. What makes the task more difficult still is our own historical distance from Huxley. As Aaron Matz reminds us in his essay on Huxley and reproduction in this volume, the Holocaust forever changed the ethical and political implications of eugenic thinking, making the pre-Second World

War liberal enthusiasm for such bio-engineering appear today disconcerting if not downright outrageous. Such is only one of the many interpretive challenges *Brave New World* puts before its twenty-first-century readers.

Thus if any consensus emerges from the essays assembled in this volume, it is, as Patrick Parrinder suggests in the opening chapter, that the contradictions of Huxley's novel are its greatest strength. It is probably wise to recognize that the novel may irritate some readers with an air of moralizing (what Parrinder calls its 'didacticism'). Despite his quarrels with H.G. Wells, Huxley follows the older writer in unapologetically using fiction as a vehicle for intellectual argument. Yet the discursive or essayistic side of Huxley should not lead us to mischaracterize *Brave New World* as flatly propagandistic or monological. Time and again, the essays in this collection reveal to us a perplexing fictional text that appears multi-sided, contradictory, or dialectical. For Nathan Waddell, the book's openly satirical attack on a technocratic state exists in an unresolved tension with a more subtle insistence on the role of experts and elites in managing modern problems of social and economic organization. For Laura Frost, the sexual traditionalism of *Brave New World* is undermined by a prurient excitement taken in the representation of perpetually youthful, hypersexual bodies—a representation that locates the novel surprisingly near to the sensationalistic mass-cultural entertainments it purports to condemn. For Keith Leslie Johnson, the fantasy of complete human mastery over nature paradoxically reveals that human existence, in the novel's final analysis, is nothing *but* nature. Other contributors find similarly productive tensions in *Brave New World*'s representations of education, islands, competition, the management of human populations, and of course the nature and desirability of utopia itself. It is because of the value of such confusions and ambiguities that Jonathan Greenberg urges readers not to look past anachronistic details of the imagined future (whether card catalogs and telephone books or attitudes on race and gender) for the very reason that these anachronisms tether Huxley's novel to its own 'context' and show us overlooked contradictions in the design of Huxley's imaginary future society.

In subtitling this book 'Contexts and Legacies' we mean to signal that these tensions and paradoxes become most visible when we situate *Brave New World* in a multiplicity of contexts and trace from it a plurality of legacies—many of which have been understudied. Two important, overlapping trajectories to recognize up front are the location of the text in Huxley's *oeuvre* and its placement in relation to the works of his contemporaries. The Orwellian 'context' is important here, providing an enduring critical heritage in which *Brave New World* and *Nineteen Eighty-Four* (1949) are celebrated, rightly, as two of the twentieth century's most perceptive and persuasive investigations of state power and individual dissent. Yet the foregrounding of Orwell with regard to Huxley can disguise other narrative relationships which are no less important and in some cases more interesting. Comparisons between Huxley and the writings of Wells, for instance, let us mark out the influence of a predecessor for whom Huxley had a shifting respect but whose formative stimulus upon *Brave New World* is undeniable. As several commentators have noted, Huxley's World Controllers share many qualities with the Samurai class outlined by Wells in *A Modern Utopia* (1905), the ruling elite whose 'widely sustained activities [...] had shaped and established the World State' (*MU* 176) that Wells's book examines in such detail (see also *HH* 31–43). And behind Wells stands the entire late-Victorian boom of utopian fiction, through which nineteenth-century utilitarianism and technologism, with their faith in science and progress, were articulated (and sometimes subjected to critique).[4] Likewise, tracing links between *Brave New World* and its forerunners in Huxley's own body of work—not only but perhaps especially in his essays of the 1920s and early 1930s, and in his 'discussion novel' *Crome Yellow* (1921), where the Wellsian Mr Scogan discourses on the shape of a future 'Rational State'—helps us to view *Brave New World* less as a one-hit wonder in his career and more as a palimpsestic recapitulation of issues that had concerned him throughout his adult life. Huxley's essays (cited liberally by many of this volume's contributors) reveal the persistence and depth of his intellectual concerns, while *Crome Yellow*, with its over-earnest poet-protagonist Denis Stone, reminds us that Huxley learned early in his career the value of satirizing his own satiric observer—a technique he would use in *Brave New World* to complicate readers' assessments of Bernard Marx and John the Savage.

Prioritizing these particular contexts, however, means downplaying or ignoring others. It is therefore worth insisting here that 'contexts' and 'legacies' are always contingent, and that the terms cast light on and define each other. '[B]eginnings', writes Edward Said, 'have to be made for each project in such a way as to *enable* what follows from them', and the same truth applies to contexts: the choices we make in selecting the contexts in which we situate a work will determine how we view its legacies.[5] And while such a claim may be true to a degree of all literary texts, the future setting and utopian themes of *Brave New World* explicitly foreground the relationship of contexts and legacies—the interplay of pasts, presents, and futures. No one asks whether the world that Virginia Woolf creates in *To the Lighthouse* (1927) has come true; everyone asks this of the reality Huxley constructs in *Brave New World*. That is to say, the comprehensive fictional imagination of a planetary future charges the reader to consider how contemporary developments, even seemingly evanescent fads, may unfold over decades or centuries. At the same time, fantasies of our individual or collective futures—shot through with comic exaggeration or fanciful adornment—can disclose to us our own self-image and our own present in ways that may be unavailable to a more sober or restrained realism.

Certainly the critical heritage of the novel affirms that the selection of different contexts has enabled different generations of readers to interpret the text and its legacies in contrasting ways. For instance, Adorno summarized an enduring tradition of reading *Brave New World* as a critique of consumerism and standardization when he wrote about its 'perception of the universal similarity of everything mass-produced, things as well as human beings', and about Huxley's conviction that under the conditions of capitalism men and women are relentlessly worn down until they become 'deindividualized products of the corporations' absolute power' (*AHU* 98). But although the theoretician Adorno is typically invoked to explain (indeed to critique) Huxley the novelist, Huxley's impact on Adorno and his colleagues was arguably stronger and more direct than is generally acknowledged. In June Deery's words, '[b]efore the Frankfurt School decamped and brought their distrust of mass culture to America in the mid-1930s, Huxley was railing about the central nexus of media/entertainment, consumerism, and social conformity'.[6] Laura Frost's essay in this book reminds us that Adorno—along with Max Horkheimer, Herbert Marcuse, and Bertolt Brecht—took part in a 1942 seminar on Huxley held at the Institute on Social Research in Los Angeles, and that *Brave New World* proved highly provocative to an entire cluster of mid-century 'Freudo-Marxist' thinkers. These thinkers, in other words, constitute not only a context for reading Huxley but also a legacy emerging from his work. There remains much to be explored about Huxley's relation to one of the twentieth century's most significant bodies of social analysis, and while several contributors here sign on to Adorno's criticism of Huxley as insufficiently materialist, Andrzej Gąsiorek's chapter mounts a fierce defence of the novel against what he sees as Adorno's ideological over-reaching.

Probably the only theme in *Brave New World* criticism more prominent than the phenomenon of standardization that occupied both Huxley and his Frankfurt School associates has been that of utopia and totalitarianism. (Utopia and totalitarianism are of course related to standardization in *Brave New World*, but none of the novel's major themes can be fully disentangled from the others.) Social thinkers of the Cold War years, writing in the aftermath of Hitler's and Stalin's atrocities, quite naturally gravitated to the novel's treatment of political and economic structures and to those structures' consequences for the individual subject. The precise relationship between an emancipatory or reformist aspiration to utopia, on the one hand, and the totalitarian nightmare of pervasive state control, on the other, is a vexed question.[7] But however one assesses the progressive and reactionary dimensions of utopia as an ideal, it is clear that the topics of utopia and state power have become so embedded in scholarly treatments of *Brave New World* that no one can imagine them away. As Fredric Jameson has intimated, grouping *Brave New World* with other classic works of the dystopian genre—especially Yevgeny Zamyatin's *We* (1921) and *Nineteen Eighty-Four*—has become almost a critical reflex. (The cultural impact of *Nineteen Eighty-Four* in particular was so great that even Huxley himself was, later in life, frequently compelled to discuss *Brave New World* in relation to its most famous intellectual progeny.) Yet the critical habit of linking Huxley and Orwell—or Zamyatin, Huxley, and Orwell—can prevent us from differentiating these texts adequately. To enshrine what Jameson calls a 'canonical dystopian trilogy' can obscure interpretations of *Brave New World* as 'very much an aristocratic critique of the media and mass culture, rather than of any Orwellian "totalitarianism"'.[8] Generations of readers have interpreted Huxley's text as an out-and-out assault on totalitarian goals, but Huxley himself claimed in his famous 1949 letter to Orwell that *Brave New World* envisaged a future in which totalitarianism would no longer be required. On the contrary, Huxley had in mind a world where the ruling classes have found 'that infant conditioning and narco-hypnosis are more efficient, as instruments of government, than clubs and prisons, and that the lust for power can be just as completely satisfied by suggesting people into loving their servitude as by flogging and kicking them into obedience' (*AHL* 605).

The critics assembled in this book do not ignore concerns about utopia and the authoritarian wrongs to which utopianism can lead, nor do they overlook *Brave New World*'s engagement with questions of individual freedom and the fate of the modern subject. What they do, rather, is seek new angles of approach and root out overlooked details to gain new purchase on these persistent themes. Parrinder, for example, by assembling passing mentions of champion athletes, glamorous celebrities, and professional high-achievers, raises questions about the role of rivalry, competition, and excellence in utopia—questions that turn out to be far from settled in the land of community, identity, and stability. Jerome Meckier, by examining the motif of the island (*locus classicus* of utopia since Thomas More), discovers a surprising proximity between the island's function as a penal colony and its role as a utopian refuge. Could a dystopia's prison somehow turn out to be a utopia? What would that transformation say about utopia as a local rather than a planetary possibility? Claudia Rosenhan narrows in on the particular question of education in utopia and finds intriguing affinities between Huxley and John Dewey in their shared critique of mass education as a force for standardization and social cohesion rather than for individual development and growth. And Nathan Waddell's exploration of the 1930s American Technocracy movement discloses an oft-overlooked economic context for Huxley's utopian musings in which free-market capitalism was widely viewed as a wasteful, inefficient system that had driven the developed world into the dead-end of the Great Depression.

Of course utopia refers not only to a political idea but also to a literary genre, and the question of the genre of *Brave New World* has been yet another recurrent context through which critics have approached the book. Readers continue to puzzle over the matter of whether or not it is a novel, as Ballard at least partially took it to be, or whether it is a literary dystopia, a label to which academics, journalists, and publishers have routinely been drawn, and which Rosenhan, for instance, investigates in her chapter in this volume. Huxley himself never quite settled on a consistent term for the book, calling it a 'comic, or at least satirical, novel about the Future' (*AHL* 351) shortly after he finished writing it; a 'book about the future' (*BNW* xliv) in its 1946 'Foreword'; and in his 1963 essay 'Utopias, Positive and Negative' one of a trio of 'Utopian fantasies', the other two being *Ape and Essence* (1948) and *Island* (1962).[9] Such wavering was not indecision pure and simple. Huxley had written an experimental and in some ways formally wild book that tested his opinions (and the gap between dystopia and utopia) through elliptical narrative forms, conversations between characters, ambiguous imagery, and projections into a future whose dangers are not obviously meant as a 'warning'. For these reasons, *Brave New World* is among the texts Margaret Atwood has used to formulate her concept of the 'ustopia': a word 'combining utopia and dystopia—the imagined perfect society and its opposite—because [...] each contains a latent version of the other.'[10] As in Swift's Country of the Houyhnhnms in Book Four of *Gulliver's Travels* (1726), utopian and dystopian faces of the fictional world can appear and vanish with only the slightest change in perspective.

Such terminological hair-splitting may for some readers seem trivial, but it is a symptom of Huxley's responsiveness to the unsettled contexts in which *Brave New World* first made its way. If we do take *Brave New World* as in some sense a dystopian fiction, then its legacy takes shape in a well-established canonical line ranging from the 'canonical dystopian trilogy' Jameson mentions through (inter alia) Anthony Burgess's *A Clockwork Orange* (1962) and Margaret Atwood's *The Handmaid's Tale* (1985). Yet putting these canonical texts aside can open critical space to consider another fertile but neglected context through which to explore *Brave New World*: the rich body of science-fictional and dystopian texts produced by women writers before and between the World Wars. Charlotte Perkins Gilman's *Herland* (1915), Charlotte Haldane's *Man's World* (1926), Naomi Mitchison's *We Have Been Warned* (1935), and Katharine Burdekin's *Swastika Night* (1937), for example, should all be seen as important, albeit quite different, counterpart texts to *Brave New World*, whose utopia foregrounds men's over women's experience.[11] On another track, the Ministry of Brains in Rose Macaulay's *What Not* (1918) antedates by some margin Huxley's World State, which so famously manufactures people (in descending order of intelligence) as Alphas, Betas, Gammas, Deltas, and Epsilons. In *What Not* the Ministry ranks human beings as As, Bs, or Cs, encouraging those with more brainpower to couple with those with less 'in proportion as they seemed favourable or otherwise to the propagation of intelligence in the next generation'; newspapers call for the elimination of 'the old and the middle-aged'; and the intelligentsia anxiously debates questions of heredity, 'that force so inadequately reckoned with, which moulds the generations.'[12] Huxley himself appears in Katharine Burdekin's *Proud Man* (1934), an undeservedly little-read text in which an ideally evolved humanity of the future travels back in time to inspect the 'subhuman' creatures of the 1930s. For Burdekin, Huxley's work was a necessary foil against which to explore 'men and women as they actually [are]' and to theorize the utopian 'change in their characters which must come about if they [are] brought up in a totally different way.'[13]

Yet even to put forth these novels as a neglected 'context' for *Brave New World* is to suggest, misleadingly, a Huxleyan nucleus around which intriguing but problematically 'secondary' narratives rotate. A more apt metaphor might imagine *Brave New World* as part of a web or network of influence and inheritance which ultimately stretches quite far away from its author's immediate concerns, even if specific instances of homage remain identifiable within it. Similarly, we can find affinities to, or even 'legacies' of, *Brave New World* in many later dystopian novels, but we must acknowledge these texts' own narrative, imaginative, and stylistic innovations if we are not to reduce them to mere 'inheritors' of Huxleyan emphases. We do not need to pretend that *Brave New World* is anything but a tour de force to accept that it is not so much the centre of a network as it is a prominent node within a set of discussions about issues that concerned writers long before Huxley himself, and that continue to occupy novelists even now.

However, once we accept this qualification of the notion of a Huxleyan legacy, we can find meaningful echoes of his work across the landscape of contemporary literature. For instance, Joe Haldeman's *The Forever War* (1974)—in which the narrator utters 'O brave new world' at the prospect of an accelerated gestation chamber—demonstrates how a later writer can appropriate Huxley's text, and its Shakespearean antecedents, in different historical moments (here the closing stages of America's involvement in the Vietnam War).[14] P.D. James's *The Children of Men* (1992) similarly invokes *Brave New World* through intertextual means: the sudden, inexplicable infertility pandemic of its imagined future occurs in a world where golf is the national pastime, pornography centres keep bodies 'occupied' and minds 'quiescent', and eugenic ideas refuse to go away; there is even at one point a reference to *The Tempest*.[15] In his near future satire *Super Sad True Love Story* (2010), Gary Shteyngart conjures a post-9/11 dystopia where fascism is on the rise under the Orwellian name of the Bipartisan Party, but where the sexual culture is pure Huxley. Orgies are common social events; mobile devices display the relative 'fuckability' of all the customers in a bar; exhibitionist young women wear transparent 'onionskin' jeans and clothes whose brand names (AssLuxury, JuicyPussy) indicate a vulgar coarsening of public discourse. Will Self's phantasmagoric comedy *Great Apes* (1997) creates a mirror-universe—not precisely a dystopia—in which evolved, literate chimps have become the dominant species, and humans a brutish cousin-species confined to zoos and African reserves. This alternate universe is, like Huxley's, a 'satirical trope' for defamiliarizing the known world and exploring human sexuality.[16] In the public and polygamous mating habits of the super-evolved chimps, Self insists upon our ineradicable animality, and in his jokes about the sexual games of chimpanzee young he alludes to the uninhibited erotic play of the children in Huxley's World State.

The dystopian, near-future, and alternate-universe subgenres continue to thrive, and the roll call of esteemed authors who have penned them continues to grow—Angela Carter, J.M. Coetzee, Maggie Gee, Kazuo Ishiguro, Cormac McCarthy, China Miéville, and David Mitchell are only a few. But while Huxley's legacies routinely show up on the short lists for the Man Booker Prize and National Book Award, they cannot be confined there. For as Jonathan Greenberg points out in his chapter, it is a telling irony that the very genre Huxley helped to elevate is now routinely repurposed by the same mass entertainments that he satirized so cuttingly in his representation of the feelies. Huxley's fictional model for imagining the future has penetrated every corner of popular culture. And a similar irony resides in the strategies used to sell *Brave New World*, its vision of consumerism run riot itself consumed by audiences increasingly plagued by capitalist excess. If *Brave New World* is a dystopia, as it is commonly said to be, then it is a dystopia whose popularity helps it to contribute, however self-critically, to the same lust for profit that the text—whose future world runs on '[s]elf-indulgence up to the very limits imposed by hygiene and economics' (*BNW* 209)—so memorably explores.

Even within a framework of utopian and dystopian fiction it is clear that shifting contexts yield shifting legacies. Kathryn Southworth's essay demonstrates that when we situate *Brave New World* in the context of the debates about motherhood and reproduction that took place in the *To-day and To-morrow* pamphlets of the 1920s and early 1930s—many of them written by members of Huxley's own circle—then we begin to see that a long line of women writers have developed core elements of Huxley's text in ways he could not have foreseen. Works such as Joanna Russ's *The Female Man* (1975) and Marge Piercy's *Woman on the Edge of Time* (1976) and *He, She and It* (1991) embrace 'the liberating potential of technology' (rather than its disciplinary or repressive potential) in ways consistent with the work of the feminist theorists Shulamith Firestone and Donna Haraway. Perhaps even more surprisingly, Laura Frost's contribution suggests that if we place *Brave New World* in the context of Wilhelm Reich's 1930s anti-fascist psychoanalytic writings on sexual liberation and bodily pleasure, then we can find a Huxleyan legacy in Roger Vadim's cult film *Barbarella: Queen of the Galaxy* (1968) or even in the softcore parody film *Flesh Gordon* (1974), both of which amplify 'the playful, campy, and bawdy notes' that Huxley's novel sounds but that his readers often fail to hear. Campy and cartoonish as they may be, these films express 'the century's continuing preoccupation with the socio-political function of pleasure' and articulate 'the utopic hedonism' of the same counterculture that landed Huxley on the cover of *Sgt. Pepper's Lonely Hearts Club Band* (1967). Like the feminist science fiction of the era, low-budget cinema rediscovers the utopian or emancipatory possibilities of technological innovation.

Yet utopia and dystopia are far from the only generic contexts in which to understand this anomalous work. What would it mean to consider *Brave New World* as a comedy of manners, a satire on the young, idle, and promiscuous? What if we follow *Crome Yellow*'s Scogan in taking sex to be 'one of the few permanently and everlastingly amusing subjects that exist' (*CY* 79)? Huxley himself clearly thought that the book could be approached in this way. His rewriting of *Brave New World* as a musical comedy in the mid-1950s indicates its humorous potential, but also highlights the pressure between tragedy and light-heartedness from which comedy as a genre is inseparable.[17] As Carey Snyder shows in her contribution to this volume, nowhere is that tension more intriguing than in the context of certain periodicals—*Vanity Fair* in particular, and the glossy, 'smart' print culture it embodies—to which *Brave New World*, with its representation of a society that is 'overly *somatic*—all body and no mind', can be interpreted as a complex response. Snyder helps us to shift our gaze away from typical Cold War concerns about state power, economic organization, and technological progress onto Jazz Age discourse surrounding a gossip-hungry youth culture and an increasingly mass mediated public sphere. In so doing, we might note surprising Huxleyan correlations not only to our own celebrity-besotted moment but also to the early Evelyn Waugh, whose *Vile Bodies* (1930) explicitly occurs in the 'near future', in a time when 'existing social tendencies have become more marked.'[18] Both texts capitalize upon Ronald Firbank's formal experiments with decontextualized dialogue and continue his interest in the hedonistic clowning of his peers. Moreover, both texts set upon the implications of an infantile modernity in which youth and its subcultures have become false idols, that 'formidable decadence', to quote Wyndham Lewis, 'in which "Youth" becomes a thing that-can-never-grow-up, is regarded as an end-in-itself—something entirely cut off from life: a strictly *useless beauty*.'[19] *Brave New World* pushes such decadence to extremes just as preposterous as those in Firbank and Waugh. The World State's puerile citizens may in different ways be 'lustrous with youth' (*BNW* 120), but their freshness is both an affectionate joshing on Huxley's part and a dour indictment of the individuals to which they presumably allude—namely the Bright Young People and their imitators.

Virtually all of these themes (state power, sexual freedom, reproductive technologies) coalesce in questions of bioethics, biopolitics, and ecocriticism. Several of the essays in this book address these topics front and centre. Huxley's World State, as Parrinder notes, carefully manages the human organism from its artificial conception all the way through to its gently euthanized death—and even beyond death, since the ever-efficient World State harvests the corpses for phosphorous. Matz, setting *Brave New World* beside *Point Counter Point* (1928), finds in this phosphorous recovery not only the sacrilegious instrumentalization of the body that readers generally take it for, but also a link to an environmentally conscientious Huxley who sounded warning bells on the consumption of fossil fuels over 80 years ago. As Matz notes, the Huxley who frets over the wasteful consumption of resources and the explosion of a voracious global population often seems to regard 'the creation of people as an ethical quandary in its own right.' The World State, moreover, regulates not only human life but the entire natural world (which infants are conditioned, through electroshock treatments, to abhor). Both Gąsiorek and Johnson take up the philosophical and political consequences of a world where humans are reduced (to quote Gąsiorek) to 'pure corporeality', where 'Nature' (in Johnson's words) is 'conceived as [merely] resources to be managed'. Indeed, both contributors recognize the menacing legacy of such utilitarianism, yet come to different conclusions about it. Whereas Gąsiorek opposes the Brave New World's utilitarianism to a humanist ethics grounded in the Romantic category of the sublime (notably dramatized in Bernard's wish to view from on high the moonlight on the English Channel), Johnson sees that same utilitarianism as an inevitable consequence of humanism rather than its rejection, and seeks instead a non-anthropocentric or post-humanist ethical relation to all life. These diverging interpretive possibilities are symptomatic of our own critical moment, for the essays collected in this volume, like other recent work on Huxley, tend to complicate or unsettle received readings of *Brave New World* rather than shore up knowledge or clear away moments of doubt.

But that is only to say that we, as Huxley's readers, can never extricate ourselves from the critical concerns of the present, even if those concerns often double back to the issues which troubled Huxley in the early 1930s and to the pressures which have determined the reception of *Brave New*

World ever since. If today's scholars tend to accentuate the inconsistencies and productive tensions within *Brave New World*, in one sense all this does is take us back to the Huxley who in 'Vulgarity in Literature' (1930) defended 'the lively, the mixed, and the incomplete in art' and (against many of his modernist contemporaries) regarded 'the classical discipline, with its insistence on elimination, concentration, [and] simplification, as [...] essentially an escape from, a getting out of, the greatest difficulty— which is to render adequately, in terms of literature, that infinitely complex and mysterious thing, actual reality' (*HCE3* 27–8). With such a statement in mind, it is hard not to conclude that when we note the 'ambiguities' of *Brave New World* we are simply affirming what Huxley himself always acknowledged the text to be: a partial, self-querying, contentious investigation of those phenomena which troubled him most, enlivened by healthy doses of fantasy, outrage, and humour. Huxley's 'actual reality' is no longer precisely *our* reality, but the fact that *Brave New World* still seems pressingly relevant to twenty-first-century audiences is perhaps the clearest sign of how fully Huxley registered the problems of a modernity we still struggle to understand.

NOTES

1. S. Sellars and D. O'Hara (eds), *Extreme Metaphors: Selected Interviews with J.G. Ballard, 1967–2008* (London: Fourth Estate, 2012), p. 359.
2. Influential accounts of *Brave New World* in this respect include, among many others: R.S. Baker, *Brave New World: History, Science, and Dystopia* (Boston: Twayne, 1990); S. Bedford, *Aldous Huxley: A Biography* (Chicago: Ivan R. Dee, 2002); J. Deery, *Aldous Huxley and the Mysticism of Science* (New York: St. Martin's Press, 1996); P. Firchow, *Aldous Huxley, Satirist and Novelist* (Minneapolis: University of Minnesota Press, 1972); L. Frost, *The Problem with Pleasure: Modernism and its Discontents* (New York: Columbia University Press, 2013); E. Gottlieb, *Dystopian Fiction East and West: Universe of Terror and Trial* (Montreal: McGill-Queen's University Press, 2001); D.G. Izzo and K. Kirkpatrick (eds), *Huxley's 'Brave New World': Essays* (Jefferson, NC: McFarland, 2008); and J. Meckier, *Aldous Huxley: Satire and Structure* (London: Chatto & Windus, 1969). See also *The Hidden Huxley*, ed. D. Bradshaw (London: Faber and Faber, 1994); R.S. Baker's and J. Sexton's editorial work for the Huxley *Complete Essays* volumes; and the essays published in *The Aldous Huxley Annual: A Journal of Twentieth-Century Thought and Beyond*, edited by B. Nugel and J. Meckier.

3. R.S. Baker, 'Aldous Huxley: History and Science between the Wars', *CLIO: A Journal of Literature, History, and the Philosophy of History*, 25.3 (1996): 293–300, at 298.
4. See M. Beaumont, *Utopia, Ltd.: Ideologies of Social Dreaming in England 1870–1900* (Leiden: Brill, 2005).
5. E. Said, *Orientalism* (New York: Random House, 1978), p. 16.
6. J. Deery, '*Brave New World*, the Sequel: Huxley and Contemporary Film', in P.E. Firchow and H.J. Real (eds), *The Perennial Satirist: Essays in Honour of Bernfried Nugel* (Münster: Lit Verlag, 2005): pp. 183–200, at p. 183.
7. For an illuminating discussion of this problem, see V. Geoghegan, *Utopianism and Marxism* (London: Methuen, 1987), pp. 1–7.
8. F. Jameson, *Archaeologies of the Future: The Desire Called Utopia and Other Science Fictions* (New York: Verso, 2005), p. 202, n. 36.
9. A. Huxley, 'Utopias, Positive and Negative' (1963), ed. J. Sexton, *Aldous Huxley Annual*, 1 (2001): 1–5, at 1.
10. M. Atwood, *In Other Worlds: SF and the Human Imagination* (London: Virago, 2011), p. 66.
11. D. Seed, 'Aldous Huxley: *Brave New World*', in D. Seed (ed.), *A Companion to Science Fiction* (Oxford: Blackwell, 2008): pp. 477–88, at p. 484.
12. R. Macaulay, *What Not: A Prophetic Comedy* (London: Constable and Company, 1918), pp. 12, 69, and 94. See also A. Crawford, *Paradise Pursued: The Novels of Rose Macaulay* (Madison, NJ: Fairleigh Dickinson University Press, 1995), p. 61.
13. K. Burdekin, *Proud Man* (1934), ed. D. Patai (New York: The Feminist Press, 1993), p. 226. See also E. English, *Lesbian Modernism: Censorship, Sexuality, and Genre Fiction* (Edinburgh: Edinburgh University Press, 2014).
14. J. Haldeman, *The Forever War* (1974), introd. A. Roberts (London: Gollancz, 2009), p. 169.
15. P.D. James, *The Children of Men* (1992; London: Faber and Faber, 2010), pp. 9, 146, 236 and 148. Other Huxleyan links include the fact that one of the main characters in James's text, Xan Lyppiatt, attended Balliol College, Oxford, as Huxley himself did, and shares a surname with Huxley's Casimir Lypiatt, the artist in *Antic Hay* (1923).
16. W. Self, *Great Apes* (New York: Grove, 1997), p. 404.
17. See A. Huxley, '*Brave New World*: A Musical Comedy' (1956), ed. B. Nugel, *Aldous Huxley Annual*, 3 (2003): 33–128.
18. E. Waugh, *Vile Bodies* (Boston: Little, Brown & Company, 1930), n.p.
19. W. Lewis, *Doom of Youth* (London: Chatto & Windus, 1932), p. 20.

CHAPTER 2

Brave New World as a Modern Utopia

Patrick Parrinder

In his book *Utopia and Anti-Utopia in Modern Times* (1987), Krishan Kumar wrote that 'Fundamentally, although he was at his sparkling best as an anti-utopian satirist, Huxley was a utopian'. Later, Kumar adds that 'Like almost no other modern utopia or anti-utopia, neither Wells's nor Orwell's, [*Brave New World*] has the exact feel of today'.[1] These observations suggest the close and often paradoxical relationship between utopia and anti-utopia, a point to which I shall return. They also suggest just why Huxley's novel continues to fascinate us. If in 1987, and also in the early twenty-first century, *Brave New World* has, in some senses, 'the exact feel of today', this is the sign of a multi-faceted work that continues to reveal new aspects to different generations of readers, and indeed to the same reader at different times.

In the summer of 2012, 80 years after the publication of *Brave New World*, the Olympic and Paralympic Games were held in London. Revisiting Huxley's novel during this event and subsequently, I have been struck by an element of Huxley's foresight that few, if any, previous critics have mentioned: the key role that he gives to sports and games as factors in social cohesion. In the New World, sports, and especially sports which involve elaborate apparatus, are seen, first of all, as an economic benefit: the Director of Hatcheries for Central London explains that sport

P. Parrinder (✉)
Department of English, University of Reading (Emeritus), Reading, UK

© The Editor(s) (if applicable) and The Author(s) 2016
J. Greenberg, N. Waddell (eds.), Brave New World: *Contexts and Legacies*, DOI 10.1057/978-1-137-44541-4_2

is preferable to horticulture or country walks because 'A love of nature keeps no factories busy' (*BNW* 18). But their chief function, it seems, is to help maintain the levels of communal excitement and euphoria that are also provided by universal sexual promiscuity and addiction to the drug *soma*. First work, then sport, then courtship and sex is the New Worlders' daily routine, and, since at least the first two activities involve communal showers and changes of clothes, it is significant that the main characters are introduced through a series of brief scenes in the men's and women's changing rooms at the Hatchery Centre. One of the main official goals of today's Olympic and Paralympic movements—to extend active participation in sport to nearly everyone—has, apparently, been achieved. At the same time, the prominence of sport in Huxley's vision of the future raises questions that we do not often hear asked about *Brave New World*.

In sport there are winners and losers, not, as in Huxley's twenty-sixth century, a system of castes within which 'everyone belongs to everyone else' (*BNW* 34). In amateur sports it may, of course, be said that winning or losing does not matter. Possibly this is true of the 'two thousand Beta-Minus mixed doubles' (*BNW* 53) games taking place at Shepherd's Bush while Henry Foster and Lenina Crowne make their way to the Obstacle Golf courses at Stoke Poges, but not all sport in the New World is like this. Helmholtz Watson is a former Escalator-Squash champion, Bernard Marx goes with Lenina to the Women's Heavyweight Wrestling Championship in Amsterdam, and Linda spends her dying moments in a London hospital watching the South American Riemann-Surface Tennis Championship on her bedside television. This precisely anticipates our own culture of televised spectator sport, and of sporting celebrity as the preserve of a tiny elite, suggesting a future that is very much closer than Huxley's twenty-sixth century. The prominence of sport in the novel highlights the paradoxes of a New World that in some respects resembles twenty-first century capitalism, while in other respects representing a vision of the future that (for better or worse) the twenty-first century has left behind: a future with a centralized economy, no profiteering, no private enterprise, and no separate national or regional cultures within the global state.

Defining the Modern Utopia

In a much-quoted letter in 1931, Huxley described the book he was working on as 'a novel about the future—on the horror of the Wellsian utopia and a revolt against it' (*AHL* 348). The reference here is both to a particular book—H.G. Wells's *A Modern Utopia* (1905)—and to the Wellsian ideal of an enlightened socialist future fuelled by industrial progress and the new knowledge offered by sociology, social psychology, and biotechnology.[2] Huxley's was not the first of what we may call the modern anti-utopias, since that distinction belongs to E.M. Forster's short story 'The Machine Stops' (1909) and to Yevgeny Zamyatin's *We* (1920–1921), which had appeared in English translation in 1924.[3] But Huxley did more than any other novelist to discredit the Wellsian modern utopia. The atmosphere of his New World, and its motto of 'COMMUNITY, IDENTITY, STABILITY', are echoed, to take just one example, in the closing lines of John Betjeman's 'The Planster's Vision' (1945), attacking the new socialist government that had just been elected in Britain:

I have a Vision of the Future, chum,
   The workers' flats in fields of soya beans
      Tower up like silver pencils, score on score:
And Surging Millions hear the Challenge come
   From microphones in communal canteens
      'No Right! No Wrong! All's perfect, evermore!'[4]

Of course Huxley's argument was not just with Wells, since he was satirizing both the behaviourist psychology and assembly-line production techniques pioneered in the USA, and the scientific-industrial utopia supposedly in the process of construction in the Soviet Union. In any case, the first significant 'modern utopia' in English had been published to huge acclaim 17 years before Wells's *A Modern Utopia*; this was *Looking Backward: 2000–1887* (1888), by the American socialist Edward Bellamy. It was Bellamy, rather than Wells, who did most to reshape the earlier conventions of the utopian genre. Here it will be convenient to distinguish between three different aspects of utopian narrative—the framework, the utopian creed, and the representation of utopian experience—since modern utopias beginning with *Looking Backward* differ from their predecessors in all three aspects.

In its narrative framework, *Looking Backward* stands in sharp contrast to two of its best-known immediate predecessors, Edward Bulwer Lytton's *The Coming Race* (1871) and Samuel Butler's *Erewhon* (1872). (The fact that each of these works is primarily a satirical anti-utopia reinforces but does not account for this basic contrast.) *The Coming Race* tells of the accidental discovery of a teeming underground world, while

Erewhon is an isolated civilization on the far side of a hitherto unpenetrated antipodean mountain range. Bellamy's Julian West, however, travels not in space but in time, falling asleep in the Boston of his day and waking up 100 years in the future. The society of *Looking Backward* is not a fantastic, topsy-turvy creation like those of Lytton and Butler but the embodiment of a future political constitution that the author is urging us to work towards. Similarly, Huxley treats his imagined society (most obviously in his subsequent essay collection *Brave New World Revisited*, published in 1958) not as a mere satire but as the more or less inevitable shape of things to come (*BNWR* 43–4).[5] *Brave New World*, like Wells's utopia and Bellamy's future Boston, is a global community or part of one; no longer a remote and isolated enclave modelled on the traditional utopian island, but a typical part of future metropolitan society. (The same is true of *Nineteen Eighty-Four* (1949) even though the world there is divided between three contending superpowers.) All these books from *Looking Backward* onwards are representations of technological modernity and, partly because of this, they portray societies still in the process of construction and change. The modern utopia, as Wells influentially outlined, is not static but kinetic, not a 'balance of happiness won for ever against the forces of unrest and disorder that inhere in things' but 'a hopeful stage leading to a long ascent of stages' (*MU* 11).[6] In *Brave New World*, despite the fact that 'stability' is one of the New World's declared aims, genetic research into human reproduction is still going on and the Bokanovsky Process is still being perfected.[7] There is social experimentation, too. Mustapha Mond, the World Controller may describe all scientific discovery as 'potentially subversive' (*BNW* 154), but he has no qualms about setting up a mini-social experiment when he allows his people free access to John the Savage.

Not only is the framework of the modern utopia global, futuristic, and technological, but it is also one of political society as an end in itself, not as a means towards some spiritual or other-worldly goal. The modern utopia is utilitarian, not millenarian. This point is made explicitly by Mustapha Mond in his scene with John the Savage when he reads out the words of Cardinal Newman—'We are God's property' (*BNW* 205)—only to wave them instantly aside. God, he says, is a remnant of '"pre-modern times"' (*BNW* 206); '"God isn't compatible with machinery and scientific medicine and universal happiness"' (*BNW* 207). And God is indeed absent from all the major modern utopias and anti-utopias, including *Brave New World*, *Nineteen Eighty-Four*, and Zamyatin's *We*, even though these societies rely on synthetic, substitute religions such as the worship of 'Our Ford' to help maintain social solidarity.[8]

The sense in which, for all its deep and sometimes fanatical hostility to utopia, dystopia or anti-utopia should be regarded as a subdivision of the utopian genre is nowhere clearer than when we move from the narrative framework to the utopian creed. Didacticism is a quality shared by utopias and anti-utopias, many of which contain long passages of abstract exposition which impatient readers have been known to skip. Samuel Butler's 'The Book of the Machines' and Orwell's interpolated essay on 'The Theory and Practice of Oligarchical Collectivism' (during the reading of which his heroine Julia falls asleep) identify *Erewhon* and *Nineteen Eighty-Four* as vehicles of utopian ideas and, indeed, as fictions rather less subtly constructed than is suggested by the Wellsian ideal of a 'shot-silk texture between philosophical discussion on the one hand and imaginative narrative on the other' (*MU* 6). In all utopian novels, however, the creed is woven into the story as well as being—as in the two examples just given—more or less blatantly separable from it. In both *Nineteen Eighty-Four* and *Brave New World* there is, too, an evident discrepancy between the society's formal guiding principles and the actual beliefs and practices that allow it to function. For example, the names of the three great organs of bureaucracy in *Nineteen Eighty-Four*—the Ministries of Truth, Love, and Plenty—stand in stark opposition to the perceived reality in which every official of the bureaucracy has been terrorized by the conviction that 'Big Brother is watching you'. Similarly, Huxley's formal creed of 'COMMUNITY, IDENTITY, STABILITY' (evidently an updating of the motto of the French Revolution) bears no obvious relation to the New Worlders' actual preoccupations with personal satisfaction and instant gratification. As Henry tells Lenina—and, since '[t]hey had heard the words repeated a hundred and fifty times every night for twelve years', Lenina promptly repeats them—'"everybody's happy now"' (*BNW* 65). Huxley here gives a new twist to the greatest-happiness principle underlying the utilitarianism of *Looking Backward* and other modern utopias. If happiness is now an official, collective goal, then what matters is not that people are authentically, spontaneously happy, but that they think they are. From this follows the strained, artificial quality of utopian happiness, which might be summed up in another slogan vaguely reminiscent of the Trinitarian formulas of the Christian scriptures: not 'faith, hope, and love' or, quite, T.S. Eliot's 'Birth, and copulation, and death', but a version of Eliot's triplet embellished by the utopian prefix eu-: euphoria, eugenics, and euthanasia.[9]

Euphoria, Eugenics, Euthanasia

The three terms indicate Huxley's perception that a modern utopia is based on universal mobilization, collectivization, loss of individuality, and a boundless faith in the progressive effects of biotechnology, scientific psychology, and scientific medicine. Euphoria, in its original sense as a 'state of well-being', is the manifest condition of the people of both Bellamy's twenty-first century and Huxley's twenty-sixth century. Eugenics and euthanasia are also present in Bellamy's Boston, though understandably less emphasized. Huxley's satire brings them to the fore, with its scenes set in the London Hatchery and Conditioning Centre and the Park Lane Hospital for the Dying. In more general terms, the people of both Huxley's and Bellamy's utopias may be said to have mastered the 'art of pursuing life with happiness as the ultimate goal', which is the dictionary definition of another, rather less familiar eu-word derived from the Greek: eudemonics. Accidentally or not, the term eudemonics reminds us of the Faustian or devil's pact that utopia involves, a pact that is heavily hinted at in Chapter XVII of *Brave New World*, where John the Savage interrogates Mustapha Mond about the new civilization's denial of God. (Mond has a collection of sacred texts, which he keeps locked up and dismisses as 'pornographic old books' (*BNW* 204), but, as we have seen, he also has Newman's theology at his fingertips.)

If there is a devil's pact in *Looking Backward*, it does not take the form of hostility to traditional religion. Indeed, the nearest equivalent in Bellamy's novel to Orwell's excerpt from 'The Theory and Practice of Oligarchical Collectivism' is the 5000-word Sunday sermon to which we are treated in Chapter 26.[10] Rather, the devil's pact in *Looking Backward* lies in Bellamy's solution to the labour problem of the nineteenth century, his creation of an Industrial Army based on universal conscription. Bellamy was writing two decades after the end of the American Civil War, a war that was won after immense sacrifices by the world's first modern conscript army. Our suspicion that the Industrial Army is a Faustian necessity rather than a glorious feature of the future socialist utopia arises, in part, from the fact that none of the future citizens named and portrayed in *Looking Backward* actually belongs to it. Dr Leete is a retired medical doctor, hence a member of a reserved profession; his wife's 'maternal duties' mean that she is excused; and his daughter Edith, presumed to be under 21, has yet to be conscripted.[11] Bellamy tells us a great deal about the mobilized labour force but gives us no direct experience of it whatever. Instead, as most recent critics of *Looking Backward* have noted, his is a utopia of universal consumption and not of production. *Brave New World* is another utopia of consumption, so much so that what Mustapha Mond calls 'the conscription of consumption' (*BNW* 42) is part of official policy. Bernard, an educational psychologist, and Lenina, a lab technician, are only very briefly seen at their respective places of work. During their leisure hours, the New Worlders are encouraged to maintain a state of ecstatic euphoria through the constant use of *soma*, as well as by participating in programmed entertainments such as the feelies. At monthly intervals they are forced to undergo treatment with 'Violent Passion Surrogate'. As Mond explains, '"We flood the whole system with adrenalin. It's the complete physiological equivalent of fear and rage"' (*BNW* 211). Huxley's depiction of a pharmaceutically managed euphoria is but one example of his determination to base his utopia on medical intervention taken to extremes.

Eugenics was present in utopia long before the word itself was invented by Francis Galton in 1883, five years before the publication of *Looking Backward*. Beauty as well as contentment is the sign of utopia, since the inhabitants are invariably described as being healthier and better-looking than the non-utopian human average. Various explanations are given for this, but one element is the regulation and control of sex and marriage, such as we find in both Plato's *Republic* and Thomas More's *Utopia*. Unhealthy and ill-favoured people are gradually 'bred out' of the human stock. The utopian tradition has many precedents for the 'scientific' eugenics of Galton and his followers, and indeed Galton himself wrote an unpublished utopian novel called *Kantsaywhere*.[12] What is most unusual in *Brave New World* is that (as Huxley himself later observed) both eugenics and dysgenics are fundamental to the social order.[13] The Bokanovsky Process of cloning outlined at the beginning of the novel is used to construct a slave state in which healthy and good-looking Alpha individuals rule over the mass-produced lower castes, whose intelligence and physique have been systematically stunted. Not even dissidents such as Bernard Marx and Helmholtz Watson seem to find the use of genetic engineering to produce Epsilon semi-morons objectionable. The Gammas, Deltas, and Epsilons are Huxley's version of Bellamy's Industrial Army, seen, as in Bellamy, from a position both high up in and slightly aloof from the social pyramid. The cost of dysgenic social stratification appears towards the end of the novel when a group of Deltas runs amok at the Park Lane Hospital and the riot police, 'goggle-eyed and swine-snouted in their gas-masks'

(*BNW* 188), are instantly summoned. This is the only time we actually see these paramilitary thugs—they are not, apparently, called in to control the orgiastic crowds thronging around the Savage's watchtower at the end of the novel—but their prompt arrival at the hospital suggests they are kept on constant standby.

If life in *Brave New World* begins with eugenics and dysgenics, it ends with euthanasia in its primary sense of 'a gentle and easy death'. Early in the novel, as Henry Foster flies with Lenina over the Slough Crematorium, their helicopter is tossed upwards by a column of hot air. The 'squirt of hot gas' is caused by some human being's final disappearance. Henry feels melancholy for an instant, but then recalls that '"there's one thing we can be certain of; whoever he may have been, he was happy when he was alive"' (*BNW* 65). As Bernard Marx puts it, the New World offers '"Youth almost unimpaired until sixty, and then, crack! the end"' (*BNW* 95). The process of making death easy and gentle begins with the 'Death Conditioning' of infants and the abolition of bereavement; it ends in the perfumed atmosphere of the Galloping Senility ward in the Park Lane Hospital, '"something between a first-class hotel and a feely-palace"' according to the nurse (*BNW* 174). How far the elderly are helped to die quickly is left undisclosed, except in the scene where Linda persuades the doctor to increase her *soma* ration even though he knows that it will '"finish her off in a month or two"' (*BNW* 134). When the doctor's prophecy is fulfilled, the nurse looks on John's exhibition of grief as a 'disgusting outcry—as though death were something terrible, as though any one mattered as much as all that!' (*BNW* 181). In *Brave New World* euthanasia (both in the sense of an easy death, and of helping on such a death) is supposedly an aid to happiness or euphoria, but like the use of *soma* it exemplifies the systematic suppression of spontaneous emotion and individual feeling.

Shakespeare, Helmholtz Watson, and the Expulsion of the Poets

After the framework and the utopian creed, the third narrative aspect to be considered is the representation of utopian experience, including both the experiences of daily life and the characteristic plot devices and outcomes of utopian novels. The key fact of daily life in *Brave New World* is its infantile banality, about which Bernard, Helmholtz, John, and Mustapha Mond all have their say. These four males singled out for their critical awareness are set off against the stereotypically unreflecting females Lenina and Linda, and the rest of the supporting cast. The range of characters in *Brave New World* (there are more characters here than in most utopias) results from Huxley's combination of two narrative models, that of the utopia in which a naïve visitor is shown around by an experienced guide, and the dystopia centring on the developing awareness of one or more dissident intellectuals, and leading to a one-on-one confrontation with authority. The utopian narrative model derives from Thomas More, while the dystopian model (based in part on the early Wells) comes to fruition in Zamyatin's *We* and later in *Nineteen Eighty-Four*.[14] In *Brave New World* we also have a doubling of the visitor-and-guide plot, first in the tour of the Hatchery and Conditioning Centre laid on for a group of new students (whose ignorance and innocence are so great that it seems all memory of their own conditioning must have been expunged), and secondly in John the Savage's introduction to civilization. In the meantime, however, Bernard Marx has been shown expressing his discontent and then taking Lenina to the Savage Reservation of Malpais, a venture beyond the formal confines of his society, just as Zamyatin's D-503 breaks through the city walls and Winston Smith takes Julia for a day out in the countryside. John, the noble savage reared in Malpais on the plays of Shakespeare, is certainly an unusual variation on the standard utopian visitor such as Bellamy's Julian West. Unlike West and his many avatars, John is not the narrator of his experiences, nor can we identify with him as an emissary from our own familiar world. Similarly, Bernard Marx, the novel's comic anti-hero, is both more and less than the usual dissident intellectual torn by conflicting impulses between rebellion and conformity. He is 'not Prince Hamlet, nor was meant to be'—in some ways he is more like Malvolio.[15] Although he is portrayed as an intellectual, Bernard lacks the keenly inquiring mind of D-503 or Winston Smith, and his desire to understand his society is all too easily satisfied. In his role as unfocused malcontent, he perhaps anticipates the anti-heroism of the postwar Angry Young Men, and like Jim Dixon in Kingsley Amis's *Lucky Jim* (1954) he is much more fortunate than he deserves, though he would never admit it. Sympathetic yet also somewhat detestable—his friend Helmholtz Watson characteristically wishes that 'Bernard would show a little more pride' (*BNW* 61)—he reminds us, too, of Amis's well-known verse line about 'Our own nasty defeats, nastier victories'.[16]

John the Savage differs from the traditional visitor in that he finds the allure of utopian civilization all too easily resistible; but he *is* like the visitor in countless utopian romances, including *Looking Backward*, in that he falls in love with a utopian female. John's experience of love, however, seems calculated to illustrate the basic premise of the New World that sexuality (like all behaviour) is determined by childhood conditioning. Traumatized by his mother's promiscuity and his own outcast status in Malpais, John is in some respects a more lurid version of the sex-hating small boy seen by the party of students at the beginning of the novel— the boy who, reduced to tears by a slightly older and more precocious little girl, is sent for an urgent psychological check-up '"Just to see if anything's at all abnormal"' (*BNW* 26). But what redeems John, though it also makes him somewhat absurd, is his discovery of Shakespeare and his ability to identify his own emotional torments with those of Shakespeare's tragic heroes. John's Shakespeareanism suggests that he has less in common with Bernard Marx, who befriends him and brings him back to civilization, than with the novel's second dissident character, the 'emotional engineer' Helmholtz Watson.

Helmholtz, a lecturer at the 'College of Emotional Engineering (Department of Writing)', is a composer of feely scenarios and 'hypnopaedic rhymes' (*BNW* 57). His one openly dissident act is to read out his own verses on solitude (doggerel though they are) to his students, but this is enough to establish him as the symbolic figure of the poet in utopia, the poet regarded as a subversive presence and a potential corrupter of the city's youth. (In this he is like R-19 in *We* and Orwell's character Ampleforth, the translator of Kipling's poems into Newspeak who is imprisoned because the only rhyme he can find for 'rod' is the one beginning with 'G'.) John and Helmholtz '[take] to one another at once' (*BNW* 159), even though Helmholtz is reduced to uncontrollable laughter when John reads a favourite passage from *Romeo and Juliet* 'with an intense and quivering passion' (*BNW* 160). What Helmholtz cannot deny, after all, is that Shakespeare was a '"marvellous propaganda technician"' (*BNW* 161).

To the extent that the modern dystopias of Zamyatin, Huxley, and Orwell are still imprisoning or expelling their poets, they look back to the foundational discussion in Plato's *Republic*, but with this difference: there is no longer the sibling rivalry between poetry and philosophy that figures so strongly in Plato's dialogue. (It was, after all, his master Socrates and not the unruly poets whom the Athenian state had condemned to death for corrupting youth.) In the modern dystopia, all forms of the critical intellect are suspect, as Mustapha Mond—a modern equivalent, perhaps, of Plato's philosopher-king—freely acknowledges; and when we see Mond exercising his role as literary censor, it is not a volume of poems but 'A New Theory of Biology' that he decides to suppress (*BNW* 154). Yet the poets and artists retain their status as Socratic gadflies, although—like R-19 in *We* and Ampleforth in *Nineteen Eighty-Four*—Helmholtz is a subsidiary character in *Brave New World* and his importance is easily over-looked.[17] Krishan Kumar, for example, opines that 'Huxley shows us little meaning or significance in his revolt. From the first time that we encounter Helmholtz to his final departure for the island, he remains frozen in his development. [...] [As a rebel] he remains impotent, and is unlikely to influence anyone by his verses in praise of solitude'.[18] Kumar seems strangely unaware of the role of the poet both in anti-utopia and in actual twentieth-century totalitarian societies.

Where Kumar is perhaps partially right is in detecting that Helmholtz is not essentially changed by his encounters with John and with Shakespeare's poetry. He has no need to be, since he already shares Huxley's own sense of the power of words, and of the New World's determination both to harness and suppress that power. The twenty-sixth century civilization is effectively built on words, since the formulas inculcated by sleep conditioning penetrate every aspect of daily life. Yet Helmholtz also perceives that words have the potential to overturn society, if only that potential could be tapped. Words to him are '"like X-rays, if you use them properly—they'll go through anything. You read and you're pierced. That's one of the things I try to teach my students—how to write piercingly."' But to write piercingly you must have real emotions to write about, not '"an article about a Community Sing, or the latest improvement in scent organs"' (*BNW* 60). Shakespeare was able to be a great poet because '"he had so many insane, excruciating things to get excited about"' (*BNW* 161). Helmholtz's understanding of how the New World has squandered and perverted the power of words makes his eventual expulsion (and perhaps also that of his friend Bernard) inevitable.

Aldous Huxley, writing in 1932, can hardly have foreseen the extent of Stalin's vast 'Gulag archipelago', yet one of the most remarkable features of *Brave New World* is the necessity of its mechanism of social expulsion, which is potentially aimed at every member of the intellectual elite. Mustapha Mond would have been sent to an island had he not chosen to become World Controller instead. Alphas cannot be cloned; as the Provost of Eton says, his school '"is reserved exclusively for upper-caste boys and girls. One egg, one adult"' (*BNW* 140). Since they are not conformists by nature (or rather biotechnology), they are expected to make what the Director of Hatcheries calls a 'special effort' to conform (*BNW* 84). But most apparently fall short, as Mustapha Mond's cynical observation suggests: "'It's lucky [...] that there are such a lot of islands in the world. I don't know what we should do without them. Put you all in the lethal chamber, I suppose'" (*BNW* 201). He then offers Helmholtz a choice of climatic conditions, and Helmholtz memorably asks to be banished to an island with a thoroughly bad climate. It will bring more out of him and enable him to write better—a sentiment that the World Controller instantly understands and respects. This, too, tells us something about the nature of the modern utopia.

The Moral Equivalent of War

We saw earlier that there are professional sportsmen and sportswomen in *Brave New World* and that sport involves both winners and losers. Competition is not quite dead in this society even though 'everyone belongs to everyone else' and certain forms of rivalry, particularly sexual rivalry, have been relegated to pathology. It is true that caste membership, at least for the Alphas and Betas, provides one of the main outlets for self-satisfaction and the feeling of superiority over others. But Bernard Marx is not necessarily alone either in his irritable stirrings of sexual possessiveness or, more importantly, in his chip-on-the-shoulder sense of social envy. There are plum jobs to be had in the New World, not only that of World Controller but the Director of Hatcheries, the Provost of Eton, and the Arch-Community-Songster of Canterbury. There is also a culture of sought-after celebrity, as Bernard discovers when he becomes the guardian of the Savage and finds himself hailed as a 'person of outstanding importance' (*BNW* 135). When, after this, he falls from grace, his one-time admirers are 'furious at having been tricked into behaving politely to this insignificant fellow with the unsavoury reputation and the heretical opinions. The higher their position in the hierarchy, the deeper their resentment' (*BNW* 151). The New World's equality within castes is no more than a façade.

This rather modest display of one-upmanship is not enough, however, to dislodge George Orwell's critique of *Brave New World*, made in his 1946 review of Zamyatin's *We*: 'In Huxley's book [...] [t]here is no power hunger, no sadism, no hardness of any kind. Those at the top have no strong motive for staying at the top, and though everyone is happy in a vacuous way, life has become so pointless that it is difficult to believe that such a society could endure'.[19] Orwell's was hardly a new observation, since it closely resembles the disillusionment with the New World expressed by John the Savage. Moreover, perhaps unknowingly, Orwell was repeating a commonplace of social psychology famously expressed by the philosopher William James, a friend of Wells and a contemporary of Edward Bellamy. James wrote in 1906 that society had to find some means of expressing what he called humanity's 'ideals of hardihood' and 'innate pugnacity' without the mass killing and mechanized destruction involved in the modern warfare that began with the American Civil War. In any plausible utopia there must be what he called a 'moral equivalent of war'.[20] In historical terms, James's essay coincided not only with the first faltering steps towards a legal framework for international peace but with the establishment of such familiar quasi-military institutions as the Salvation Army, the Boy Scouts, and indeed the Olympic Games. The search for a moral equivalent of war is also manifest in every modern utopia beginning with Bellamy and his Industrial Army.[21] Huxley knew and admired the work of William James, whose *Varieties of Religious Experience* (1902) is on Mustapha Mond's bookshelf; and he would soon expound the idea of a 'moral equivalent of war' in the *Encyclopædia of Pacifism* that the Peace Pledge Union published under his 'editorship' (in fact, he wrote most or all of it) in 1937.[22] The same idea is present in both *Brave New World* and his later utopia *Island* (1962), but, as Orwell points out, in *Brave New World* it is officially disavowed. This is why, for example, Lenina finds John's compulsion to prove his hardihood for her benefit simply incomprehensible. Later, Mustapha Mond tells John that '"civilization has absolutely no need of nobility or heroism. These things are symptoms of political inefficiency. Conditions have got to be thoroughly unstable before the occasion can arise"' (*BNW* 209). While we have no reason to doubt Mond's sincerity, what he says is not wholly true of the world over which he presides.

For one thing, Mond himself is an exception to the utopian principles he so lucidly outlines, since in his lonely role as World Controller, in which he is forced to suppress everything he knows to be truly valuable, there is something perversely heroic. He at least could surely appreciate Helmholtz's poem on solitude. It may be said that things are made easy for him since he is allowed to be the intellectual master of all he surveys. For the ordinary citizens, nobility and heroism are supplied vicariously at the feelies and in the form of the 'Violent Passion Surrogate' already mentioned. The pornographic feely 'Three Weeks in a Helicopter', for example, features a 'gigantic Negro' suffering from concussion who develops an 'exclusive and maniacal passion' (*BNW* 146) for the heroine. Propriety is eventually restored when he is 'packed off to an Adult Re-conditioning Centre' (*BNW* 147). Since the feelies have to be filmed, and the televised sporting events must actually be staged, it is not the case that the testing ordeals that John and Helmholtz desire are totally absent. For example, right at the end of the novel we meet the unlikely figure of Darwin Bonaparte, 'the feely Corporation's most expert big-game photographer' who is prepared to spend 72 hours in acute physical discomfort in order to get a shot of the whip-wielding Savage (*BNW* 223). The infantile comfort of the many depends on the willingness of a few technical specialists to undergo at least moderate danger and hardship. Mustapha Mond does not mention this feature of the New World, but the novel ends with a riotous orgy that calls the whole pharmaceutically imposed order into question.

Did Huxley mean to anticipate the social breakdown that Orwell, for one, thought *Brave New World* must lead to? It is hard to say. If—arguably, at least—the greatness of Huxley's novel lies in its paradoxes, then the final paradox of this deeply utopian anti-utopia is its author's sometimes flawed understanding of what he had written. For example, he wrote in *Brave New World Revisited* (1958) that 'the twenty-first century, I suppose, will be the era of World Controllers, the scientific caste system and Brave New World' (*BNWR* 35), and he could not have been more wrong. He had failed to see that by 1958 the modern utopia, as I have outlined it, was already slipping into the past. Yet in other respects *Brave New World* continues to anticipate the twenty-first century, and if its future citizens have yet to find a satisfactory moral equivalent of war, so, all too distressingly, have we.

NOTES

1. K. Kumar, *Utopia and Anti-Utopia in Modern Times* (Oxford: Blackwell, 1987), p. 226 and p. 266.
2. Much of Wells's later writing sets out this vision of utopia (or progress towards it). Particularly relevant to Huxley in 1931–1932 may have been the concluding sections of *The Work, Wealth and Happiness of Mankind* (1931), and of *The Science of Life* by H.G. Wells with Julian Huxley and G.P. Wells (1930).

3. See M.R. Hillegas, *The Future as Nightmare: H.G. Wells and the Anti-Utopians* (New York: Oxford University Press, 1967).
4. J. Betjeman, *Collected Poems*, introd. The Earl of Birkenhead (London: John Murray, 1958), p. 120.
5. See below, p. 28.
6. See also J.S. Partington, 'The Death of the Static: H.G. Wells and the Kinetic Utopia', *Utopian Studies*, 11.2 (2000): 96–111.
7. One inevitable side effect of the Bokanovsky Process is population growth. Since this can only be speeded up by further developments in 'Bokanovskification', the New World must rely on limitless economic expansion to maintain its social 'stability'. This problem is never acknowledged in *Brave New World*.
8. There are signs, though, of other-worldly religion returning in what may be loosely called the postmodern utopia, a kind of future society that is no longer global in scope or technologically advanced, such as that envisaged by Margaret Atwood in *The Handmaid's Tale* (1985).
9. T.S. Eliot, 'Fragment of an Agon' (1927), in *The Complete Poems and Plays* (London: Faber and Faber, 1969), pp. 121–6, at p. 122.
10. E. Bellamy, *Looking Backward: 2000–1887* (1888), ed. M. Beaumont (Oxford: Oxford University Press, 2007), pp. 160–71.
11. Bellamy, *Looking Backward 2000–1887*, p. 150.
12. See P. Parrinder, 'Eugenics and Utopia: Sexual Selection from Galton to Morris', *Utopian Studies*, 8.2 (1997): 1–12.
13. Huxley wrote: 'In the Brave New World of my phantasy, eugenics and dysgenics were practised systematically' (*BNWR* 19).
14. George Orwell greatly admired Wells's *When the Sleeper Wakes* (1899; revised as *The Sleeper Awakes*, 1910), while Zamyatin, who translated many of Wells's novels into Russian, may have been particularly influenced by Wells's novella 'A Story of the Days to Come', collected in *Tales of Space and Time* (1899).
15. T.S. Eliot, 'The Love Song of J. Alfred Prufrock' (1915), in *The Complete Poems and Plays*, pp. 13–17, at p. 16.
16. K. Amis, 'Dirty Story' (1980), in *Collected Poems 1944–1979* (Harmondsworth: Penguin), pp. 26–7, at p. 27.
17. In Wells's utopian film *Things to Come* (1936), the artist Theotocopulos does take the leading dissident role; but his function, rather like that of the 'Obstinate Refusers' in William Morris's *News from Nowhere* (1890), is to represent a critical opposition that is both tolerated and righteously swept aside.
18. Kumar, *Utopia and Anti-Utopia*, pp. 279–80.
19. G. Orwell, 'Review [of We by E.I. Zamyatin]' (1946), in *The Collected Essays, Journalism and Letters—Volume 4: In Front of Your Nose 1945–1950*, ed. S. Orwell and I. Angus (London: Penguin, 1970), pp. 95–9, at p. 97.

20. W. James, 'The Moral Equivalent of War' (1910), in *Memories and Studies* (New York: Longmans, Green, and Co., 1911), pp. 265–96, at p. 276 and p. 269.
21. See P. Parrinder, 'War is Peace: Conscription and Mobilization in the Modern Utopia', in D. Seed (ed.), *Future Wars: The Anticipations and the Fears* (Liverpool: Liverpool University Press, 2012), pp. 50–65.
22. 'Moral Equivalent of War', in A. Huxley (ed.), *An Encyclopaedia of Pacifism* (London: Chatto & Windus, 1937), pp. 69–72.

CHAPTER 3

Signs of the T: Aldous Huxley, High Art, and American Technocracy

Nathan Waddell

Although the question of Aldous Huxley's attitude towards the state systems depicted in *Brave New World* (1932) remains the stuff of fierce debate, the technocratic features of that state have long been recognized by scholars, students, and general readers alike. Indeed, *Brave New World* is often grouped with *Nineteen Eighty-Four* (1949) as one of the twentieth century's most compelling representations of 'the threat posed by technocracy and totalitarianism to civil society', Huxley's grey future reminding its readers of the power of technology and the allure it holds for those who seek to use technical expertise for political goals.[1] As this quotation indicates, scholars tend to interpret this future as a scenario depicting the systematic and objectionable purging of individual liberty. Evelyn Cobley, for instance, writing about *Brave New World* in relation to the Ford Motor Company, proposes that Huxley's text 'associates the assembly line with the utopian dream of the perfect society that devolves into the dystopian nightmare of the totalitarian state.'[2] Technocracy—rule or government by a class of technical specialists—is in these terms an object of Huxley's satire, something the text queries rather than celebrates. And yet at other

N. Waddell (✉)
School of English, University of Nottingham, Nottingham, UK

© The Editor(s) (if applicable) and The Author(s) 2016
J. Greenberg, N. Waddell (eds.), Brave New World: *Contexts and Legacies*, DOI 10.1057/978-1-137-44541-4_3

times Huxley's support for illiberal sentiments comes to the fore. Hence David Bradshaw's claim that for 'all its hideousness, the hierarchical, aseptic, colour-coded world of A.F. 632 is not aeons away from the scientific utopia Huxley was promoting elsewhere before, during and after he wrote *Brave New World* in 1931' (*BNW* xxii). This approach foregrounds the text's ambivalence. It asks us to decide whether Huxley's apparent mockery of a politics based on scientific knowledge co-exists with an approval of technocratic authority. In other words, different readings of Huxley's account of technocracy diverge on the nature of his response to technocracy, yet agree that a response exists. *Brave New World* may analyse technocracy this way or that. Analyse technocracy, however, the text unarguably and unforgettably does.

The purpose of this chapter is to re-contextualize that analysis in relation to a little-studied corpus of historical materials, specifically by comparing *Brave New World* with Harold Loeb's *Life in a Technocracy: What It Might Be Like* (1933), one of the most fascinating documents to emerge from the early 1930s American Technocracy movement and an important inter-war statement of utopian principles. The 'soundly scientific' goal of American Technocracy, as H.G. Wells put it in *The Shape of Things to Come* (1933), was 'to restate economics on a purely physical basis' and to implement 'a new social order in which social and economic life was to be treated as an energy system controlled by "experts".'[3] Following the movement's fragmenting into opposed factions in January 1933, Loeb's *Life in a Technocracy*—a discursive 'fantasy', as he called it—drew up one version of that system in which the arts played a central role.[4] Against Loeb stood Howard Scott, the engineer around whom the movement first coalesced in New York in 1919. Throughout the 1930s Scott and his allies, including the scientist M. King Hubbert, outlined an anti-aesthetic political system that saw the arts as a wasteful continuation of the capitalism that Technocracy sought to dethrone.[5] Whereas Loeb was a committed supporter of the arts, a defender of Western cultural history, and a founder of the little magazine *Broom: An International Magazine of the Arts* (1921–4), Scott claimed that 'European culture and traditions [had] nothing of worth-while importance to offer America in [the] twilight period preceding the dawn of a new era.'[6] The pamphlet *Technocracy: Some Questions Answered* (1934), which carried an enthusiastic 'Foreword' by Hubbert, stopped short of criticizing artists in this way, but noticeably did not include them among the 'intelligent, functionally capable' people engaged in 'socially useful' occupations whom American Technocracy welcomed with open arms.[7] Loeb's distinctiveness as a contrasting Technocratic voice is well established, particularly as one who provides a liberal perspective in contrast to Scott, Hubbert, and those with similarly anti-aesthetic tendencies, but the broad connections between *Brave New World* and *Life in a Technocracy* have yet to be uncovered.[8]

Although it is a commonplace that Huxley took a qualified interest in technocratic ideas—among them scientific managerialism, Fordian industrialism, eugenicism, and Wellsian socialism—before, during, and after the composition of *Brave New World*, placing his work specifically in relation to the American Technocracy movement allows us to formulate a new perspective on the tension between art and technocratic control that Loeb and Huxley diagnosed as a key problem of post-Fordian modernity. *Brave New World* conceives the relationship between technology and the arts relationally. It suggests that if the machine age tends to subordinate aesthetic beauty to rhetorics of efficiency and central planning, such rhetorics may also be a necessary counterpart to more creative spaces hived off from, yet at the mercy of, technocratic systems (as those who are exiled to Iceland and elsewhere prove). *Life in a Technocracy* takes a comparable line, imagining technocracy as a means with which to make the arts flourish and thus to create a society that would transform 'the gusto of competition inherent in man' into regenerative 'life values' (*LT* 169). That viewpoint put Loeb at odds with Scott and brought him close to the Huxley who suggested in 'Pascal', published in *Do What You Will* (1929), that the 'fine arts and the arts of life have flourished most luxuriantly in those societies in which a very sharp distinction was drawn between mechanic and liberal occupations' (*HCE2* 369), a view that pithily anticipates the corporatist viewpoint elaborated more fully in *Life in a Technocracy*.

By the time Huxley made this remark he had long doubted the 'mechanic' as a criterion for socio-political engineering. In a 1926 letter to John St. Loe Strachey, for instance, he outlined his anxieties regarding the 'prestige of science' and the concomitant view that 'the measurable', rather than qualitative, 'aspect of the world is [its] total reality' (*AHSL* 186). Huxley had also by this point established many of his concerns about the ever-more rationalized qualities of machine-age society and the purpose of art within it. When he wrote *Brave New World* his disquiet at such issues was still evident. Yet he had also become convinced that the ethic of the machine called democracy into question. At this point in time, Huxley openly favoured caste-based social models that preserved intellectual aristocracies and embraced autocratic governance, and was increasingly drawn to eugenics (see *HH* vii–xxiii). He suggested in 'Machinery, Psychology, and Politics' (1929) that the age of the machine demanded an efficient 'factory-like political organization', but he remained uncertain about the long-term effects of such proposals upon 'the psychology of the individual human being' (*HCE3* 220), and, consequently, upon the creative spirit. Huxley was similarly torn about science, which after the Wall Street Crash he was keen to see 'applied by humanists' (*HCE3* 155), as he put it in 'Science and Civilization' (1932), in order to bring civilization back from the brink of chaos, even though he suspected that science was more likely to be used by 'economists' to standardize the world and 'to train up a race [...] of perfect mass-producers and mass-consumers' than it was to be used to create a 'deliberately progressive' society, 'consciously tending towards the realization of the highest human aspirations' (*HCE3* 150). *Brave New World* dramatizes these antagonisms: it charts the systematic purging of finely wrought aesthetic forms in a society where benevolent dictatorship has generated political stability by jettisoning the 'waste' of art and liberal democracy, and by limiting the use of science to functional applications as opposed to the pursuit of knowledge for its own sake. As a fictional narrative, therefore, the text is profoundly unresolved. Indeed, the text's formal contradictions imply that *Brave New World* designates the high arts as a source of value, and this gesture, as I will show, registers Huxley's closeness to Loeb's account of technocracy, a philosophy from which many modern commentators would want to distance him.

In the World State, A.F. 632, high art is an awkward, unwanted reminder of 'gratuitous' (*BNW* 18), non-utilitarian culture. Particular versions of sociopolitical stability and happiness that limit the prominence and attractiveness of such culture have been facilitated by machine systems, consumerism, anti-individualism, and mass entertainment. Under this post-Fordian regime, what used to be called high art—here symbolic of the judicious, rational, yet tortured world of the creative mind—has been replaced with cultural forms that satisfy the lustful needs of the glands, and which call to mind Huxley's deep-rooted concerns, to quote him in 'The Outlook for American Culture: Some Reflections in a Machine Age' (1927), about 'go[ing] the American way' (*HCE3* 185). Where technocracy seeks efficiency and permanence, high art, at least in the eyes of Mustapha Mond, creates disorganization and chaos. For the intelligent, observant Mond, high art is a symptom of an unstable, self-destructive past that has been superseded by the better future of sex and steel. Ancient Egyptian, Harappan, Semitic, Greek, and Roman sculpture and architecture; continental philosophy; English literature; European classical music—all such forms have in A.F. 632 become the victims of anti-historical imperatives. Unlike the socialist future of *News from Nowhere* (1890), where the healing potential of art has been channelled into the labour of 'every man who produces', in the World State to create artistically is to interfere with the technocratic principles that make citizens 'sane, virtuous, [and] happy' (*BNW* 35), even if such sanity, virtue, and happiness come at the cost of many individuals' psychological uniqueness.[9] 'Gratuitous' art is a danger, a source of personal expression that threatens the standardizing logics of collective life. As such it must be destroyed, concealed, or adapted to other purposes. New, functional things are better than old, beautiful things, bluntly put, despite the fact that from its title onwards *Brave New World* heralds the moral relevance of old things—Shakespeare, in this case—as a possible counter to the techno-cratic undertakings that have so drastically transformed humankind.

How we understand Huxley's attitude towards these complexities depends in large part on how we approach the text's account of the cultural forms produced under technocracy and the high art to which certain characters, such as Mond, oppose it. And as with much else in *Brave New World*, here ambiguities proliferate. Mond states that the price paid for stability in A.F. 632 is the loss of all those cathedrals, Renaissance plays, requiems, and symphonies (*BNW* 29) that Mond himself seems to respect, but which, like the philosophical, religious, and historical tomes kept in the cabinet in his study, are forms of 'smut' (*BNW* 207) that must be hidden from a world with rather different scruples. Theoretical science has suffered the same fate, its abstractions jettisoned in favour of disciplines fixed on 'the most immediate problems of the moment' (*BNW* 200). Utility has taken the place of beauty, commercialism has deposed individualism, and here *Brave New World* arguably channels the Huxley who in 1930 bemoaned the influence of American culture upon its European counterparts, the latter falling prey, in his view, to the former's standardizing advance. Indeed, the 'religious respect for culture' that Huxley sought to save from an 'age of abounding rubbish' (*HCE3* 49) parallels Mond's dutiful preservation of high culture, both Huxley and Mond amounting in this regard to cognoscenti finding solace in art forms inaccessible to the common run of people. This is the reading of *Brave New World* offered by John Carey, who argues that the text implies 'that mass happiness is inherently inferior. Only the solitary individual can experience happiness that is significant or profound.'[10] The physical remnants of high art are locked away to contain their harmful teachings and thereby to maintain the hierarchies upon which social stability depends, those same hierarchies rendering high art unintelligible in an ahistorical society in which most people feed on entertainments that do little to challenge the mind. Only an aristocratic World Controller such as Mond has the necessary refinement to appreciate truth, beauty, and knowledge. Yet this very privileging of a certain kind of culture makes more noticeable the value of the high art that is not to be had. And in this respect the text queries the function of imagination and creativity in a world in which high art is dangerous enough to be put under lock and key but not so threatening as to be altogether obliterated.

So while on the one hand *Brave New World* presents an elitist viewpoint—high art is a thing of the past, opposed to modern mass entertainments, and can be treasured only by those intelligent enough to appreciate it—on the other it defensively suggests that under technocracy the fate of high art is to be something that can only be understood, but never openly revered, by a self-interested minority. High art is a sign of privilege (the elite lording it over the masses from their technocratic bastions) in the first instance, and a sign of besiegement (the elite being *displaced* by the masses) in the second. The only other option the text explores is for those who enjoy high culture or pure intellectualism, such as Helmholtz Watson, to be contained as exiles in places where the World State's priorities have been abandoned and people maintain civilization in less regimented ways (see *BNW* 209). Mond, as a former, 'pretty good' (*BNW* 198) physicist who once questioned the dominant theories upon which science rests, represents the type of inquisitive mind interested in things for their own sake. In this sense he is an envoy of the realm of pure creativity, that place where things are made or explored with no subsequent goal in mind other than to relish the creative act itself. Yet rather than enjoy such things in the margins, or in exile, Mond chooses to serve the World State as one of its controllers, and therefore to safeguard the world's collective, technocratic happiness despite the fact that such public loyalty negates his private contentment. Hence when Mond affectionately recalls his time as a physicist he sighs repeatedly at the memory (*BNW* 199–200), his attachment to the culture of the past echoing his fondness for his scientific training and the intellectual autonomy it facilitated.

Mond's predicament focalizes the text's broader investigation of the relationship between high art, 'pure' imagination, and technocracy. Of course, Huxley's response to technocracy can, as we have seen, be construed divergently. *Brave New World* satirizes but is also something of a billet-doux for technocracy, a system of government to which Huxley was in many ways attracted during the text's composition. However, *Brave New World* seems less undecided when it addresses, implicitly or otherwise, the value of high art in the face of technological modernity. In the World State the language of Shakespeare is firmly out of place, its profound sense of difference confusing and ostracizing John the Savage, rather than helping him decode his surroundings. In this way the text invites us to debate whether Shakespeare has any relevance at the end of a modernity featuring 'the full flush of scientific utopia', and, if we think he does, to ask: 'To whom does he speak?'[11] But even if *Brave New World* investigates the relevance of Shakespeare in a future that seemingly has no use for Renaissance-era moralities, the text nevertheless *invests* in Shakespeare as an allusive resource (or artistic point of comparison). Huxley thereby very clearly signals Shakespeare's appositeness as a cultural cipher with which to conceptualize the nature and potential problems of technocracy, despite the fact that the narrative queries, at the diegetic level of its story, the reliability of a Shakespearean moral compass. More interestingly, the very ambivalence of *Brave New World* on the matter of technocratic value might itself be read as a counter to technocratic utilitarianism, the lack of a snappily quotable moral message going against technocracy's striving for usefulness, and matching Shakespeare's lack of moral tub-thumping in his plays (a characteristic for which they are so often revered).

Or consider the role played by classical music, which in the World State appears to have been 'whisk[ed]' (*BNW* 29) into oblivion by those who, like Mond, have accepted the Fordian logics that proscribe its existence. Classical music is 'bunk', nonsense, incomprehensible to a world that no longer has any use for it. Synthetic music machines and scent organs manufacture the indulgences that classical compositions once facilitated, their imitation melodies 'reassuringly' (*BNW* 97) calming and 'delightfully refreshing' (*BNW* 145) their audiences rather than evoking a problematic but superseded cultural yesteryear. Jazz provides similar fulfilments, the synthetic music played by Calvin Stopes and his Sixteen Sexophonists at the Westminster Abbey Cabaret exemplifying Huxley's aversion to what in 'Silence is Golden' (1929) he saw as jazz's 'loud vulgarity of brassy guffaw and caterwauling sentiment' (*HCE2* 20). Yet by means of a very precise linguistic strategy *Brave New World* contradicts, and implicitly rejects, such destructive 'whisking', again disclosing a tension between the diegetic and extra-diegetic levels of the text. When at the level of narrative plotting classical music is ostensibly sidelined, Huxley reintroduces classical musical terminology at the level of narrative vocabulary. As a result, he locates synthetic and olfactory 'music' in historical and lexical contexts that re-authorize the high artistic past at exactly those moments when it seems most thoroughly obscured. In the cabaret scene the gradual sounding of an erotically charged chord takes the form of 'a *diminuendo* sliding gradually, through quarter tones, down, down' (*BNW* 66), whereas later in the text a fragrant 'Herbal *Capriccio*' conveys its aromas with 'rippling *arpeggios* of thyme and lavender' (*BNW* 145, emphases added). Shortly afterwards a music machine emits a high note far above the most extreme capacities of the human voice, thereby diminishing the achievement of even Lucrezia Aguiari, who once famously impressed Leopold Mozart with her vocal dexterity (*BNW* 145). History is in such moments anything but 'bunk', anything but erased by the modern machineries with which it is said to have been replaced. Indeed, these formal conflicts foreground classical music and its vocabularies even as *Brave New World* registers their absence 'within' the story, repossessing high art from the technocratic doctrines that elsewhere claim its desuetude.

All of which is to say that the relationship between high art and technocracy in *Brave New World* is fraught with complexity, and that the connections between Huxley's thoughts on culture and society and the values he explored in this text are far from straightforward. What seems clear, however, is that in the late 1920s and early 1930s Huxley was disturbed by the influence of the machine upon humanity in the postwar period, and that he was uncertain about what sort of role the creative individual might meaningfully play in a post-Fordian epoch. As Huxley's essay 'The Outlook for American Culture' demonstrates, he accepted the labour-saving benefits of the machine yet bemoaned the fact that a more leisured age meant a more passive, increasingly standardized, more easily manipulated, and generally less cultured world. During the Depression these problems had become even more distinct. As Huxley wrote in 'The Victory of Art over Humanity' (1931), the 'tragedy of the machine' was that it had liberated the world from 'the intolerable load of mere drudgery' while simultaneously depriving 'the overwhelming majority of men and women of the possibility, the very hope, of even the most modest creative activity' (*HCE3* 282). Humanity had become its own rival, 'staggering under the blows received in the course of this disastrous conflict with the organized forces of its own intelligence' (*HCE3* 283). *Brave New World* adopts a conflicted position in response to this scenario. Depending on how one reads the text (and here I am simplifying things somewhat), Huxley either seems to be satirizing such a predicament as a questioner of hierarchical models of society, inviting his readers to free themselves from the standardizing effects of the machine age in the process; or to be outlining a technocratic, profoundly hierarchical, and nerve-jangling solution to that same quandary in which, within certain predetermined limits, and to return again to 'The Outlook for American Culture', 'men and women are guaranteed a decent human existence' and 'are given every opportunity to develop such talents as they possess, and where those with the greatest talent rule' (*HCE3* 192). Yet however one reads *Brave New World*, in 1931 Huxley suggested that the solution to a disorganized, progressively more anarchic civilization lay in a centrally planned 'world-wide adjustment of production to consumption [...]—in a word, a general agreement to make some universally valid sense out of our babel of separate and private achievements' (*HCE3* 285).

An 'adjustment' along these lines was exactly what American Technocracy promised to bring about in Depression-era America. Although the idea of technocracy can claim a lineage going back several centuries, the first stirrings of the American Technocracy movement occurred circa 1919 in New York's Greenwich Village, where Loeb happened to live in a flat above Scott.[12] That year, influenced by Thorstein Veblen's progressive economics and the scientific management philosophies associated with such figures as Frederick Taylor and Henry Laurence Gantt, Howard Scott established the Technical Alliance, whose purpose was to compile 'a mammoth statistical survey of energy sources in North America' that would identify causes of inefficiency in the industrial sector and project the impact of waste upon national living standards.[13] Other members of the Alliance included Charles Steinmetz, the head of the research laboratory at General Electric; Alice Burrows, deputy director of the US Department of Education; and Veblen, whose ideas formed the foundation upon which Scott developed his analysis of America's industrial problems. Among the groups who became interested in Scott's activities were the Industrial Workers of the World, the so-called 'Wobblies', who employed him as their research director from 1920 until 1921, and under whose auspices he published articles exploring the links between industrialism, society, and machinic thought. He claimed that society could be better understood (and improved) by rooting social policy in measurements of energy usage rather than in capitalistic production for profit. The Technical Alliance dissipated in 1921, but the policies it advanced would return to public view in 1932 when Scott, in league with Walter Rautenstrauch (the chairman of Columbia University's Department of Industrial Engineering), Dal Hitchcock, Frederick L. Ackerman, M. King Hubbert, and others, formed the Committee on Technocracy, whose goal was to address 'the inability of businessmen to curb their quest for profit in the interest of social harmony' and to empower engineers to 'take up the responsibility of reorganizing supply and demand.'[14]

The Committee on Technocracy lasted until January 1933, by which time it had claimed that the socio-economic planning of the day was backward-looking and unsatisfactorily scientific. More precisely, the Committee urged that the links between the market, labour, and social change should be understood quantitatively by charting patterns of energy consumption rather than by debating supposedly antiquated 'principles of right, equity, propriety, duty, belief and taste as stabilized in the days of the handicraft guilds of Central Europe.'[15] Scott's ambition was to look past such archaic standards, as he saw them, in order to locate what he thought was a more clear-sighted and more equitable set of attitudes towards labour and social structures. He stated that the Committee offered 'no solution' to America's economic crises, but nevertheless proposed that the way forward lay in abandoning the price-system, with its concomitant 'wish-fulfilling thought and romantic concepts of value', which would be replaced by a physicalist account of wealth as a conversion of 'available energy into use-forms and services.'[16] Put another way, energy consumption—rather than monetary exchange—was to become the basic measure of labour interactions, which would be reduced to a minimum. Such claims were inseparable from the Committee's insistence that American society was inadequately calibrated to the labour-saving potential of modern industrial machines, whose deployment, for Scott and his allies, proliferated rather than eliminated waste, increased rather than reduced unemployment, and threatened a catastrophe that would dwarf the upheavals wrought by the Wall Street Crash. The answer was to calibrate technology more precisely in line with human needs and, so the logic implied, to place an engineering class in charge of the American nation, whose ailments would be cured by scientific judgement.[17]

Many commentators agreed that the Technocrats had identified several highly important problems. Scott certainly found his admirers. Theodore Dreiser, for instance, wrote in a 1932 letter to Scott that there was 'something amazingly iron and powerful' about him, and that he gave Dreiser 'the feeling of a titan made of bronze.'[18] At the same time, a substantial body of critics, including Ford Madox Ford and H.L. Mencken, formed around the movement and around Scott in particular.[19] Attacks on Technocracy at this early stage ranged from accusations of unoriginality— Scott's opposition to the price system, for instance, left him open to the charge that he had plagiarized the bulk of Technocracy from Frederick Soddy's *Wealth, Virtual Wealth, and Debt* (1926)—to more straightforwardly satirical claims that the movement's ideas were indecipherable.[20] Before long, filmmakers began ridiculing Technocracy in such films as Charles Lamont's *Techno-Crazy* and the W.C. Fields comedy *International House* (both 1933). Gordon Phillips, appearing as 'Lucio' in *The Manchester Guardian* in January 1933, wrote in his comic poem 'Abracadabra' that it 'would be hypocrisy' to say he understood the 'finer shades of meaning | In this term so newly heard', and saluted Technocracy 'as one leaning | On another bright boss-word!'[21] Understanding the movement's 'finer shades of meaning' was made even more problematic when Scott attempted to silence his critics in a radio speech but instead delivered 'a rambling, confusing, and most uninspiring address'.[22] Scott's performance prompted Rautenstrauch to leave the Committee on Technocracy and was a factor in the movement's splitting into two opposed factions. The first group, the Continental Committee on Technocracy, was initially loyal to Scott but in time came to be dominated by Loeb, who published *Life in a Technocracy* in 1933 (having written it three years beforehand).[23] Scott formed Technocracy, Inc. in March 1933, at which point this branch of the movement started to adopt the grey-toned partisan regalia that later in the 1930s adorned its offices and many of its publications, giving it a paramilitary, quasi-fascist temperament, an attitude aided by the fact that Scott opened and closed its meetings with a gesture based on the hand salute used by the American armed forces.[24]

Huxley had long been interested in comparable symbols of office, as his depictions of Everard Webley and the Brotherhood of British Freemen in *Point Counter Point* (1928) attest. From this perspective, it's not surprising that the civilization depicted in *Brave New World* has its fair share of official cryptograms and state-sanctioned gesticulations, including the 'signs of the T'—variously an emblem of maleness, a salute, a zipper fastening, a book stamp, and a representation of triumphant technocracy—that comprise many of its ceremonial appurtenances. One of the first qualities of Huxley's World State to be emphasized is its greyness. The very first line of the book introduces us to the Central London Hatchery, a 'squat grey building of only thirty-four storeys' (*BNW* 1), and subsequently we learn about the grey clothing worn by Alpha children (*BNW* 22) and the 'blank grey eyes' (*BNW* 56) of the attendants who take care of Bernard's plane. Indeed, we might add the text's emphasis on monochromatic self-fashioning to the list of Technocratic idiosyncrasies that Roger Luckhurst has argued *Brave New World* seems improbably to predict, along with Scott's gradual drift towards authoritarianism and his interest in Pavlovian behavioural conditioning.[25] By the end of the 1930s Technocracy, Inc. had been permeated by '[a] uniform gray', its pamphlets adopting the colour and individual members painting their automobiles in its tones, while '[g]ray [...] double-breasted suits, worn over gray shirts with blue neckties appeared in increasing numbers after 1937.'[26] Long before that time, Huxley had magnificently imagined a triumphant, monotone technocracy that critics would eventually see as having foreshadowed American Technocracy, warts and all.[27]

However we construe the role of technocracy in general in *Brave New World*—as an object of satire or as something of which Huxley for a time questioningly approved, or both—the commitment to high art disclosed by the text's structural contradictions makes for a revealing comparison with *Life in a Technocracy*, in which Loeb insisted that the 'highest type of work' is 'the creative' (*LT* 58); argued that the 'control of anything of the appeal of which is subjective, such as the theater, or painting, should not be entrusted to the state' (*LT* 127); and contemplated a utopian (albeit improbable) future wherein the artistic imagination has become so fully integrated into socio-economic life that the life of the artist (as a discrete specialism) would be no longer necessary (*LT* 169). While Loeb insisted that *Life in a Technocracy* amounted to 'merely a tentative sketch of the new heaven or ideal state' (*LT* 192) that might be adopted by America to solve its economic and industrial problems, nevertheless he clearly hoped to use the text to convey his support for government by technical specialists and to oppose Scott's rejection of culture. Loeb wrote in *The Way It Was* (1959) that Scott 'disparaged the arts and expected technical men to take charge of society when the price system collapsed.'[28] *Life in a Technocracy*, by contrast, reconciles art and technocracy in a way that preserves the former within a technocratic future. Loeb's fortunate position as a 'wealthy man of leisure' had a role to play here, but *Life in a Technocracy* can be read as a sincere effort to outline a technocratic vision of society within which the arts play a distinctive, 'uplift[ing]' (*LT* 141) part.[29] Loeb thus differed from Scott, who stated that 'useless art forms' could be supplied by machine-produced replacements (another link to

Huxley's World State, in which music is created synthetically), and echoed Huxley's contemporaneous commitment to the high arts within the scope of a wider, yet shortlived, attraction to technocratic principles, a position with which the latter wrestled throughout his work of the late 1920s and early 1930s, and above all in *Brave New World*.[30]

Loeb followed Scott by maintaining that capitalism should 'make way for a more efficient and more just system of distribution' (*LT* 30), one that would drop the profit motive, adopt a universal unit of work (the erg), force industry to utilize fully the principles of science, and eliminate the injustice of accidental and hereditary privilege.[31] The system Loeb had in mind would divide itself between a technocratic industrial infrastructure, on the one hand, and a sphere within which man's creative urges could be 'deflected to the production of non-essentials' (*LT* 52), on the other— the latter being dependent on, but not coterminous with, the industrial sectors that would allow its existence. Such a framework would force all citizens to work for a minimum of 16 hours per week (just as Scott had suggested; see *LT* 37 and 62), and give them a guaranteed income and satisfy their material wants and needs (*LT* 84), in exchange for 'ample scope' (*LT* 60) to pursue self-bettering activities without allowing any one person to 'acquire more goods than everyone is entitled to' (*LT* 64). Certain individuals within the system would, on top of their minimum working week, opt to devote themselves to improving the industrial infrastructure. Others, by contrast, would be 'marvelously released' (*LT* 69) to 'seek self-realization outside the producing system' (*LT* 64) via imaginative and artistic efforts. The goal was to 'utilize man's egoism for getting the necessary productive work done, and his vanity for continuing the experimentation required if the technique of living is to go on developing' (*LT* 71).

Art in such a utopia of plenty would enjoy government protection but remain free from state control (*LT* 127). Its function would be to allow citizens to express themselves unhindered by capitalist logics ('the outrageous Mysticism of Money'; *LT* 138). Loeb acknowledged that capitalism generated art, but he was far from sanguine about the long-term benefits of such cultural and architectural forms as 'metropolises, jazz, advertisements, success epics, girl shows, comic strips, sporting pages, the movies, [and] the talkies' on the grounds that he deemed capitalism 'a hothouse' that 'fosters growth' while producing fruit that 'lacks taste' (*LT* 133). Although Loeb contended that the capitalist era had made possible innovations, such as the cinema and radio, that could be counted among 'the greatest boons' (*LT* 134) ever given to humanity, he argued that capitalism itself was not 'conducive to a good life' and thus that it was incapable of enabling 'expressions' that 'satisfy' (*LT* 137). Indeed, he is likely to have had Huxley (and figures like him) in mind when he wrote that lowbrow arts were 'sweeping across the world to the bewilderment and lament of every conservative disciple of the older cultures' (*LT* 130). Implicitly addressing such disciples, Loeb assured his readers that via technocracy modern artists would find 'other ideals to vaunt' (*LT* 141) than those encouraged by capitalist protocols, and that artworks 'of the older cultures' would be preserved by the state (*LT* 129). The result would be a social edifice committed to spirit- and life-affirming values rather than to profit motives, and a world enriched by the best art of modernity and antiquity combined.

Put like this, *Life in a Technocracy* answered a range of Huxleyan anxieties, in particular his concerns in 'Machinery, Psychology, and Politics' about the subordination of artistic innovation to rationalizing tenets and the difficulties simultaneously involved in accepting 'the ethic of the machine' (*HCE3* 220), seeking 'the material advantages which accrue to those living in a mechanized world', and protecting the mental benefits of the pre-mechanical past (*HCE3* 221). In other respects, however, *Life in a Technocracy* differs substantially from the account of the future articulated in *Brave New World* and from the views about sociopolitical reform Huxley articulated in the years surrounding its publication. The most obvious difference is textural. *Life in a Technocracy* is a polemic; *Brave New World* is a literary fiction. Loeb's opinions are easily read off the page; Huxley's, by contrast, even when his opinions seem straightforwardly 'present' in *Brave New World*, are nevertheless problematized by its literariness, the text only ever yielding its ideological freight reluctantly, if at all. Even if *Life in a Technocracy* seems to parrot the narrative content of *Brave New World* in numerous ways—for example, as if to echo the sports-mad inhabitants of the World State, Loeb predicts that '[d]uring the first century of technocracy, sport will probably flourish as it never has before' (*LT* 128)—the consumerist World State could not be any more distinct from Loeb's technocracy, in which the 'anti-social incentive called profit would be abolished' (*LT* 131) and ending would most certainly not be better than mending (see *BNW* 42), and where no one would desire 'to replenish their equipment frequently and to expend it continuously' (*LT* 121).[32]

Even more significantly, whereas Huxley argued in 'The Outlook for American Culture' that the ideal state 'is one in which there is a material democracy controlled by an aristocracy of intellect' (*HCE3* 192), Loeb disagreed with 'the system invented by the thinkers of conservative India, a system of stratified castes and wholesale renunciations', favouring instead a framework that would depend on 'specialization of function' yet enable individuals to possess 'equal and absolute economic security' rather than feel 'resigned to the lot into which [they] may be born' (*LT* 174).[33] On this central point Loeb and Huxley were fundamentally opposed, Huxley countering Loeb's liberal perspective with writings calling for a 'revolt against political democracy' (*HCE3* 191) and for power 'concentrated in the hands of intelligent and active oligarchies' (*HCE3* 192), two inclinations represented and arguably extolled in *Brave New World*. Likewise, Huxley and Loeb took very different stances on the problem of eugenics. Huxley later claimed in 'What is Happening to Our Population?' (1934) that 'a nation in which the number of halfwits is steadily growing is a nation whose potential efficiency is being steadily impaired' (*HCE3* 400), thereby echoing the more uncompromising rhetorics of productivity used by Scott and reiterating the eugenicism of the World State. Loeb went in a different direction, stating that 'breeding with specific individuals for specific purposes' would not be contemplated without a 'superman' to 'supervise the job', even though he felt that a technocratic abandoning of 'the false ideals promulgated by late social eras' would 'produce a race of man superior in quality to any [then] known on earth' (*LT* 178). Yet Huxley's commitment to the high arts—to what Loeb called those expressions 'fraught with meaning, the only meaning that matters' (*LT* 167)— aligns him with a technocratic defence of the aesthetic, in spite of the fact that Huxley was not committed to the specific form of technocracy that Loeb defended in *Life in a Technocracy* and elsewhere.

And this leads me to repeat my fundamental point: namely, that Huxley's potential compatibility with Loeb not only establishes a parallel with the American Technocracy movement in particular, but also shows yet again how Huxley's interest in 'technocratic control over reproduction and social reform in the early 1930s' locates *Brave New World* in exactly those contexts from which commentators such as Niethammer have sought to distance it.[34] More recently, Ronald T. Sion has argued that 'of all the major commentators on the modern threat of technocratic arrogance, Huxley remains perhaps the most widely read and influential.'[35]

This is undoubtedly true. It is also the case, however, that Huxley remains perhaps the most influentially *ambivalent* critic of technocracy, arrogant or otherwise, and that there are intriguing connections between his views on the links between art and technocracy and those espoused by Loeb (thereby forcing us to place historically his commentaries on 'the modern threat of technocratic arrogance' with greater care). Consider Huxley's and Loeb's views regarding those who choose, or are forced, to live outside technocratic systems. Loeb notes that 'a few zealots' may decide to end their contract with technocracy (*LT* 40) and the 'two main categories' (*LT* 60) of self-realization—scientific and imaginative—it facilitates. Doing so, however, would mean 'living by Stone Age standards except for borrowed tools and gifts, [and] would be disagreeable for most people' (*LT* 40). Leaving technocracy in Loeb's account means leaving the system as a whole. In *Brave New World*, by contrast, independence is available to those who '"have got too self-consciously individual to fit into community-life"' (*BNW* 200), as Mond puts it; is not unpleasant (though it appears so in prospect); and structurally supports the technocracy to which it is notionally opposed. The exile that Bernard Marx and Helmholtz Watson face represents not exile from the World State per se but signifies another form of containment *within* it, and which is, presumably, still within the power of the World State as a governing agency. Artistic freedom is for Loeb a product of the system. For Huxley, artistic freedom comes about *despite* the system. Yet in both instances technocracy facilitates a realm in which imagination (and presumably the creation and enjoyment of high art) is possible, and in this sense the reciprocal distinction 'between mechanic and liberal occupations' that *Brave New World* examines approximates at least in part to the bond eulogized by *Life in a Technocracy*.

It's worth reiterating that Loeb and Huxley wrote in very different ways, and that *Brave New World* could hardly be called a sociopolitical manifesto in the way that *Life in a Technocracy* more easily can be, despite Loeb's insistence that the text was meant as a rough outline of a possible future. Huxley described *Brave New World* in a 1931 letter to G. Wilson Knight as 'a Swiftian novel about the Future' that would delineate the 'strange and appalling effects on feeling, "instinct" and general *weltanschauung* of the application of psychological, physiological and mechanical knowledge to the fundamentals of human life' (*AHL* 353), so it would be a strange reading indeed that sought uncomplicatedly to equate the text with a technocratic account of the human condition when technocracy is one of the very phenomena that *Brave*

New World satirizes. *Brave New World* is certainly more nuanced in its questioning attitude towards technocracy than such texts as Michael Arlen's *Man's Mortality* (1933), in which technocratic systems that seek '*to dragoon the nations of the world into a colossal scheme of tidiness*' are rebuked more candidly.[36] What is intriguing here is that in *Brave New World*, a text routinely characterized as one of the twentieth century's most powerful invectives against technocratic thinking, we find a relationship between artistic-intellectual creativity and technocracy within whose terms the former can be preserved, rather than annihilated, by the latter.

A brief comparison of Huxley's writings with those of the American Technocrats shows from a new angle how *Brave New World* appeared in the midst of an international debate regarding the roles played by technology and by non-utilitarian high art in sociopolitical life, and that the similarities between Huxley's and Loeb's interventions into this debate—between their respective 'signs of the T', in effect—should prompt us more precisely to discuss *Brave New World* in relation to the American cultural-historical contexts with which it resonates. Despite Huxley's well-known concerns about Americanization, and notwithstanding their incorporation into *Brave New World*, the parallels between Huxley and Loeb suggest a more complex cultural-historical state of affairs than has hitherto been acknowledged. Given the timings, Huxley is unlikely to have based *Brave New World* on the activities of the American Technocrats in particular (though we know he corresponded with Loeb in the early 1920s), but it seems that he wrote the text partially to find some way to reconcile his interest in technocracy with his commitment to, and desire to preserve, the high arts from the more reductively quantitative ideologies of the period.[37] Huxley certainly didn't think that history was bunk. But like Loeb he would have disagreed with Scott regarding art's role in modernity, and thus would have relished the ending of Phillips's assault on Scott in 'Abracadabra':

> Technocracy! Technocracy!
>   A horrid doubt breaks in;
> For verbal aristocracy
>   Sometimes has humbler kin.
> Is there, by chance, distillable,
>   If down, its weight were shrunk,
> That baleful monosyllable
>   The older, brisker 'bunk'?[38]

Notes

1. L. Niethammer, *Posthistoire: Has History Come to an End?*, trans. P. Camiller (London: Verso, 1992), p. 33.
2. E. Cobley, *Modernism and the Culture of Efficiency: Ideology and Fiction* (Toronto: University of Toronto Press, 2009), p. 11. For an excellent overview of the Fordian sources for *Brave New World*, see J. Meckier, 'Debunking Our Ford: *My Life and Work* and *Brave New World*', *South Atlantic Quarterly*, 78 (Autumn 1979): 448–59.
3. H.G. Wells, *The Shape of Things to Come* (1933), ed. P. Parrinder (London: Penguin, 2005), pp. 262–3.
4. H. Loeb, *Full Production without War* (Princeton: Princeton University Press, 1946), p. vii.
5. W.E. Akin, *Technocracy and the American Dream: The Technocrat Movement, 1900–1941* (Berkeley, CA: University of California Press, 1977), p. 146.
6. H. Scott et al., *Introduction to Technocracy* (New York: John Day, 1933), p. 43.
7. M. Adamson and R.I. Moore, *Technocracy: Some Questions Answered* (New York: Technocracy Inc., 1934), p. 15.
8. For an account of Loeb and *Life in a Technocracy*, see H.P. Segal, *Technological Utopianism in American Culture* (Chicago: University of Chicago Press, 1985), pp. 141–5.
9. W. Morris, *News from Nowhere* (1890), in '*News from Nowhere*' and Other Writings, ed. C. Wilmer (London: Penguin, 2004), pp. 41–228, at 160.
10. J. Carey, *The Intellectuals and the Masses: Pride and Prejudice among the Literary Intelligentsia, 1880–1939* (London: Faber and Faber, 1992), p. 88.
11. P. Smethurst, '"O brave new world that has no poets in it": Shakespeare and Scientific Utopia in *Brave New World*', in D.G. Izzo and K. Kirkpatrick (eds), *Huxley's 'Brave New World': Essays* (Jefferson, NC: McFarland, 2008), pp. 96–106, at p. 100.
12. For this lineage, see J. Meynaud, *Technocracy* (1964), trans. P. Barnes (New York: The Free Press, 1968), pp. 194–206.
13. Akin, *Technocracy and the American Dream*, p. ix. The rest of this paragraph is indebted to Akin's study.
14. G. Slade, *Made to Break: Technology and Obsolescence in America* (Cambridge, MA: Harvard University Press, 2006), p. 69 and p. 70.
15. Scott et al., *Introduction*, p. 12.
16. Scott et al., *Introduction*, pp. 48, 46, and 47.
17. For a more nuanced discussion of the Committee's claims see Akin, *Technocracy and the American Dream*, pp. 64–79.
18. Dreiser to Scott (29 Sep. 1932), Theodore Dreiser Collection, 1897–1983 (number 4604), Division of Rare and Manuscript Collections, Cornell University Library.

19. For Ford's attacks on the American Technocrats, see my 'Technocracy and the Fordian Arts: America, *The American Mercury*, and Music in the 1930s', in S. Haslam and S. O'Malley (eds), *Ford Madox Ford and America* (Amsterdam: Rodopi, 2012), pp. 167–80. For Mencken's views see 'Old Dr. Scott's Bile Beans', *The American Mercury* (Apr. 1933): 505–7.
20. See 'Technocracy Idea is Old, says Soddy', *The New York Times* (8 Jan. 1933): 23.
21. 'Lucio' [G. Phillips], 'Abracadabra', *The Manchester Guardian* (14 Jan. 1933): 9.
22. H.P. Segal, *Recasting The Machine Age: Henry Ford's Village Industries* (Amherst: University of Massachusetts Press, 2005), p. 102.
23. See Segal, *Technological Utopianism*, p. 141.
24. H. Elsner, Jr., *The Technocrats: Prophets of Automation* (Syracuse, NY: Syracuse University Press, 1967), pp. 95–6. A key Technocratic symbol was the *yīnyáng* monad, which epitomized Scott's drive to create harmony out of chaos.
25. R. Luckhurst, *Science Fiction* (Cambridge: Polity, 2005), p. 69.
26. Elsner, Jr., *The Technocrats*, p. 95.
27. See Akin, *Technocracy and the American Dream*, p. 148 and p. 166. See also J. Essid, 'No God but Electricity: American Literature and Technological Enthusiasm in the Electrical Age, 1893–1939', unpublished PhD thesis (Indiana University, 1993), p. 256.
28. H. Loeb, *The Way It Was* (New York: Criterion Books, 1959), p. 12.
29. L. Surette, *Pound in Purgatory: From Economic Radicalism to Anti-Semitism* (Urbana and Chicago: University of Illinois Press, 1999), p. 210.
30. Akin, *Technocracy and the American Dream*, p. 146.
31. Loeb outlines these points in Chap. II of *Life in a Technocracy*, 'The Escape'.
32. For more on sport in *Brave New World* see Parrinder's essay in this volume (Chap. 2).
33. D.L. Higdon explores the influence of the Indian 'system of stratified castes' upon *Brave New World* in *Wandering into 'Brave New World'* (Amsterdam and New York: Rodopi, 2013), pp. 44–58.
34. J. Woiak, 'Designing a Brave New World: Eugenics, Politics, and Fiction', *The Public Historian*, 29.3 (Summer 2007): 105–29, at 128.
35. R.T. Sion, *Aldous Huxley and the Search for Meaning: A Study of the Eleven Novels* (Jefferson, NC: McFarland, 2010), p. 204.
36. M. Arlen, *Man's Mortality: A Story* (London: William Heinemann, 1933), p. ix.
37. The Huxley-Loeb correspondence is archived at Princeton University. Given Bernard Marx's surname, one wonders whether Huxley had heard of Guido Marx, an early associate of Scott in New York (see Akin, *Technocracy and the American Dream*, p. 23 and p. 32).
38. 'Lucio', 'Abracadabra', 9.

CHAPTER 4

'That Learning Were Such a Filthy Thing': Education, Literacy and Social Control in Huxley's *Brave New World*

Claudia Rosenhan

Aldous Huxley's continuing relevance to our current world is periodically questioned, as, for example, in John Derbyshire's appraisal, in which he dismisses Huxley's social and political writing as dull and uninspiring.[1] While such a verdict may arguably be upheld in parts for Huxley's wider *oeuvre*, the prescience of *Brave New World* (1932) with regard to our modern life is acknowledged even by an ungracious reviewer such as Derbyshire, who sees in its infantile hedonism a reflection of our own current Western 'embourgeoisement'.[2] Beyond the familiar scenarios of sanctioned sexual and chemical ecstasy and rampant consumerism embedded in the 'culture industry' of the World State lies, however, Huxley's serious concern for one key aspect of the Enlightenment project that underpins utopianism and, by implication, satires on utopianism: education. This chapter investigates Huxley's various critiques of formal education and mass literacy, disclosed here in his satire on different pedagogical discourses that reveal the frequently normative orientation of utopian societies. This criticism is

C. Rosenhan (✉)
Moray House School of Education, University of Edinburgh, Edinburgh, UK

© The Editor(s) (if applicable) and The Author(s) 2016
J. Greenberg, N. Waddell (eds.), Brave New World: *Contexts and Legacies*, DOI 10.1057/978-1-137-44541-4_4

also encoded in *Brave New World*'s didactic parallels in Shakespeare's *The Tempest*, in which Prospero takes on the role of master educator.

Brave New World is often perceived as a 'predictive dystopia', a category with which critics generally associate the foreshadowing of ominous aspects of modernity taken to its logical conclusion.[3] The salient differences between, for example, an Orwellian and a Huxleyan future lie in the fact that the naked exercise of power in the former has been substituted with the internalization of hierarchical relations via pedagogical practices in the latter. Recent essays have determined that Huxley's novel portrays a world that has been pacified by educational conditioning into a state of apathy and ignorance.[4] The citizens of the Brave New World are educated into their social function without much chance of escape, yet the point is that no one really wants to escape. They are, as Huxley says in his 1946 foreword to the novel, educated to 'love their servitude' (*BNW* xlvii). The cause of their anodyne contentment is state-regulated character formation via prenatal manipulation and postnatal conditioning, perhaps a natural progression of the original utopian concept of the wholesale improvability of humankind through formal education.

In Howard Segal's basic but comprehensive overview of utopian writing, the nature of utopia has been, overall, determined by the will to a radical improvement of society, a will that was initially accompanied by a fervent belief in the value of human rational thought, and later in the efficacy of scientific and technological advancement.[5] Although utopias are often based on radically different scenarios, they all put a premium on education as a means to shape people according to the prevailing ideology.[6] Michael Peters and John Freeman-Moir agree that utopias 'can be thought of as fundamentally educational', and that education 'is intrinsically connected with utopia'.[7] Northrop Frye had earlier established that utopias habitually 'depend on education for their permanent establishment'; the literary convention of utopian writing is for him a 'by-product of a systematic view of education'.[8] In the utopian blueprint for a better society, education is often the linchpin of its stability and order, as it ingrains rules that are followed by an enlightened citizenry without the need for further reform.[9] A key aspect of all utopian thinking is, therefore, the conscious rational design of its social and pedagogical rituals and institutions. This rational design is evident in all canonical utopias and dystopias. The eponymous society of Thomas More's *Utopia* (1516), for example, is a homogeneous, conflict-free state in which the values and dispositions of its citizens have been moulded through universal education.

Swift's depiction of the rational state of the Houyhnhnms is, instead, subversive in its depiction of a collective rather than individual identity. As Mark Olsson shows, Huxley's satirical drive aims similarly to expose such human cosmoplasticism, the wilful shaping of collective destinies, as a 'fatal conceit'.[10] In his foreword to *Brave New World*, therefore, Huxley ironically hails the successes of the world's educators, who have instead caused the destructive cataclysm of the recent World War that has (mis) shaped human destiny (*BNW* xlvii–xlviii).

Jerome Meckier has surveyed the intellectual seedbeds of Huxley's essayistic output in the 1920s that were to sprout into the 'eugenic nightmare' and 'lowbrow paradise' that is the World State of *Brave New World*.[11] He has also shown how Huxley's preface to J.H. Burns's *A Vision of Education* (1928) voices his critical perspective on utopian pedagogical tendencies that will inevitably result in 'mediocrity and sameness'.[12] Huxley is clearly very knowledgeable about the utopian tradition, and *Brave New World* can be interpreted as a satiric comment on the pedagogic ideas that were frequently promulgated in classic utopian texts. For example, he takes to the extreme Plato's distrust of family life in the *Republic* by dispensing with parenthood altogether. The World State is now the supreme controller of children's generation, acculturation, and education. Similarly, Huxley debunks the common utopian dream of an increased leisure time spent in pursuit of self-education—put forward, for example, in Thomas More's *Utopia*—and shows people instead in pursuit of puerile entertainment and *soma* holidays. Trust in indefinite scientific progress, championed, for instance, in Francis Bacon's *The New Atlantis*, is discredited by the anthrax bombs that necessitated the substitution of happiness for truth in the World State (*BNW* 201). Yet it is not just a mechanistic view of an ideal society that is under attack. Huxley equally disparages ideals of a simplified, natural life, expressed, for example, in William Morris's *News from Nowhere* (1890), through John's bathetic attempt to escape into the Surrey wilderness. However, as Sydney Thompson indicates in his comment on *Brave New World*, Huxley 'is at bottom less interested in lampooning someone or something for the mere sake of it'.[13] Instead his satire strikes at the heart of Huxley's concerns with education. As I have demonstrated, Huxley retained a lifelong interest in educational systems, especially their sociopolitical function, and this chapter refocuses Huxley's general critical stance towards popular, homogeneous education on to its literary expression in a utopian context.[14]

Popular education was, of course, a utopian scheme in itself. Huxley notes in 'The Idea of Equality' (1927) how it had come to be regarded as the central formative influence on people and as the only viable explanation for existing inequalities (*HCE2* 155). Utopianism was, in effect, a radical call for social justice through social control, in which popular education took centre stage. Many eighteenth- and nineteenth-century political and social reformers believed that all members of society could be educated for a rational life, and this idea of the perfectibility of mankind as a way to radically transform social and political reality and create a new community was based on notions of the indefinite malleability of a child's character. This notion, alluding to Locke's understanding of the mind as a *tabula rasa*, is summed up by Joseph Priestley as 'Education ... *makes the man*'.[15] In his 1927 essay 'Education', Huxley, however, argues that this behaviourist theory exercises a continued 'baneful influence' on educational schemes (*HCE2* 194). He frequently speaks out against what he later called the 'blank page of pure potentiality' ('Where Do You Live?', 1956; *HCE6* 175) and the prominence it affords to nurture over nature. By refusing to acknowledge our Hobbesian universe, reformers were, according to Huxley, taken in by a facile view of human nature ('On Grace', 1931; *HCE3* 119).

Hence, in *Proper Studies* (1927) Huxley sets out to repudiate what he calls the 'entirely false conception' of individual human nature. Since he asserts that social institutions must be in harmony with individual human nature, he predicts that '[i]nstitutions which deny the facts of human nature either break down more or less violently, or else decay gradually into ineffectiveness' ('Measurable and Unmeasurable', 1927; *HCE2* 146). In *Brave New World*, these dangers are averted by the fact that human nature is now made to fit the institutions—not vice versa.[16] The utopian belief in the possibility of human improvement is here satirically inverted as 'arrested development'.[17] When the measure of man becomes only his 'socially valuable abilities' ('Education', 1927; *HCE2* 216), and the babies in the Brave New World are decanted as fully socialized humans, subjugated to man-made conditioning that 'nature is powerless to put asunder' (*BNW* 17), then such guaranteed outcomes of education lend themselves to a satiric deconstruction of education as a warping of human nature.

Huxley's critique is not unprecedented. According to John Dewey, education is the 'sum total of processes by which a community or social group [...] transmits its acquired powers and aims with a view to securing its own continued existence and growth'.[18] Thus formal schooling cannot shake off its connotations with state-controlled character formation. Joseph Lancaster's nineteenth-century monitorial schools were, for example, applauded for the way 'a thousand children collected from the streets were reduced "to the most perfect order, and training [*sic*] to habits of subordination and usefulness"'.[19] This way, children would 'know their place' and not strive to rise up against their betters. Popular education, like utopian education, was therefore conceived to be universal, continuous, and holistic, shaping humankind from birth to death in all areas of their lives.[20] However, from the outset such aims were assessed critically. For example, William Godwin stipulated in *The Enquirer* that 'All education is despotism', even if such education originates from a paternalistic strain.[21] Hence, Dewey's assessment above is predicated on the commonality of interests that are evenly distributed in a democracy. When special interests dominate, education becomes skewed. Therefore, in Chapter 22 of Samuel Butler's *Erewhon* (1872), the narrator encounters Professor Worldly Wisdom, who imparts: '"Our duty is to ensure that [students] shall think as we do"' (*E* 189); that is, befitting Butler's satiric intent, with the utmost vagueness and 'unreason'. From a posthumanist perspective Giorgio Agamben notes that education, in its first instance, destroys a child's individual potential.[22] Huxley had already realized that 'the ends which the individual sets himself to attain' are, in fact, manipulated through education ('Varieties of Intelligence', 1927; *HCE2* 192).

Huxley's stance is that the decline of democracy in the 1930s is directly connected to the introduction of compulsory state education ('Education', 1937; *HCE4* 269–70), because it has 'exposed millions, hitherto immune, to the influence of organized lying and the allurements of incessant, imbecile, and debasing distractions' ('Politics and Religion', 1941; *HCE5* 12). *Brave New World* illustrates this critique, because it shows how education creates an uncritical mass-consumerist populace that is easy to manipulate (see *Science, Liberty and Peace*, 1946; *HCE5* 273–4).[23] Huxley's implicit appraisal of institutionalized education as universal regimentation, championing normative habits of punctuality, obedience, militarism, and industry, denies the possibility of a Freirean pedagogy of freedom. This pessimism about the benefits of a national education system is satirically heightened in his ridiculing of the static and stratified society of the World State, showing 'thousands' of minds subordinated into usefulness by an education that has rooted them into their place in society. Also, the notion that better educated workmen make better workers (a point espoused, for example, in Edward Bellamy's *Looking Backward: 2000–1887* of 1888) is disavowed. Early fears that popular education would risk 'elevating, by an indiscriminate education, the minds of those doomed to the drudgery of daily labour, above their condition, and thereby rendering them discontented and unhappy in their lot' are squashed in *Brave New World* by the daily *soma* rations, as well as by the prenatal conditioning that makes everyone suited only for their predestined labours.[24] The pernicious regimentation of children's education to a state ideology is shown to its logical end in the way the centralized power of the World Controllers perpetuates narrow bases of learning suitable for a particular caste, all with the goal of 'COMMUNITY, IDENTITY, STABILITY' (*BNW* 1) in mind. Discipline and control seem to be the educational orthodoxy of the Brave New World, and the World State assumes a hegemonic, deterministic, and paralysing role in terms of the unitary and total extent of its influence. All external danger has been eliminated and internal dissent neutralized, thus grotesquely fulfilling the initial intentions and aspirations of the champions of popular education. Yet Huxley was clearly utopian in his own thinking on formalized education, and his critique must therefore be regarded as specific rather than general.

A specific utopian pedagogical discourse explored by Huxley in *Brave New World* is psychological, relating to cognitive learning processes as well as learning behaviours informed by technology. Given that science, technology, and education are normally seen to go hand in hand as progressive influences upon human development, it is often hoped by educationalists that instructional technology can take over from traditional sociocultural approaches to education, especially in terms of the democratization of education.[25] Hypnopaedia is an early approach in this arena. But as reports (from as recently as 2003) into the way sleep facilitates learning testify, hypnopaedia has an enduring attraction within the scientific community.[26] Its endorsement as pedagogy, however, says little about the quality of the learning that is achieved.[27] It is satirized in *Brave New World* as the 'greatest moralizing and socializing force of all time' (*BNW* 23), because it is, in fact, unsuited for intellectual education. Nevertheless, D.W. Surry and J.D. Farquhar unfairly paint Huxley as a technophobe, since he often champions new technological inventions, such as the radio, as pedagogical tools.[28] Instead he warns against the possibility of the misappropriation of such technology by dictators, expressly because 'hypnopaedia actually works' (*BNWR* 119).

Hypnopaedia is a niche aspect of educational neuroscience or neuroeducation, which is currently hailed as an interdisciplinary breakthrough in the investigation of brain development and learning. This endorsement, despite persistent warnings of facile 'neuromyths', nevertheless attests to the enduring interest of scientists in exploiting the physiology of the brain in order to attain better learning outcomes.[29] In 1927 Huxley had similarly hoped that reductive cognitive science would be replaced by a new 'psychological realism' in education ('The Outlook for American Culture: Some Reflections in a Machine Age', 1927; *HCE3* 193), by which he meant 'simply applied psychology, applied heredity and applied psycho-physiology' ('Education', 1932; *HCE3* 350). In *Brave New World* this thought is satirically evaluated through Huxley's dysgenic vision of children inescapably designed for their future fates, or through the more conservative pedagogy of behavioural conditioning. As Mustapha Mond illustrates, conditioning leaves the people '[s] till inside a bottle—an invisible bottle of infantile and embryonic fixations' (*BNW* 196), the bottle's size being determined merely by difference in caste. Hence Alphas can make choices and bear responsibilities, yet they are still conditioned into 'infantile decorum' (*BNW* 85). Conditioning children to think and behave in particular ways is still often considered acceptable or even desirable in current pedagogical literature, where learning is explained with reference to non-reflective states.[30] B.F. Skinner's *Walden Two* (1948) goes further, describing conditioning as a positive force that allows people to do what they want to do, rather than forcing them to do what they do not want to do. The Director of Hatcheries in *Brave New World* similarly equates the secret of happiness with the fact that conditioning makes 'people like their unescapable social destiny' (*BNW* 12). Yet this benign perspective is deconstructed by Huxley's scenario of electroshocking toddlers into hating nature and books, thus raising the spectre of an Orwellian setup that satirically undermines the benevolent claims for behaviourism.

Features of hypnopaedia and conditioning are also evident in *Brave New World*'s Shakespearean parallel, *The Tempest*. Not only did the play provide Huxley with the title of his novel, but *The Tempest* is considered an early utopian blueprint, opening with a society in dissolution and closing with social harmony reinstated.[31] Furthermore, throughout the play pedagogical practices are evident. Shakespeare wrote during a 'period of educational revolution' in the wake of the Reformation and increased literacy, and Prospero, depicted as a 'figure of English sovereignty who shapes [...] his subjects through a pedagogical process', is reminiscent, perhaps, of Henry VIII's earlier reformist pedagogical zeal during the dissolution period.[32] In Act I, Prospero, therefore, introduces himself as a schoolmaster (I.ii) and, as Alan Carey-Webb further notes, 'puts knowledge into the services of his political power' through re-educating his subjects.[33] More to the point, Prospero instructs Ariel to fill the island with noises (II.i and III.ii) to stupefy the island population using effects similar to the hypnopaedic susurrations in *Brave New World*. These 'words without reason' (*BNW* 23) condition the Brave New Worlders in both communities into voluntarily yielding to the greater powers of the 'controller'. Prospero's spectacle of thunder and lightning, moreover, reminds one of the electroshocks used to frighten the babies in *Brave New World* into submission.

While H.G. Wells praised Pavlov's *Conditioned Reflexes* (1927) for replacing evolution as the driving force of human improvement with social engineering, Huxley believed that the mind is an organic whole whose essence cannot be isolated in this way ('Varieties of Intelligence'; *HCE2* 181).[34] In his view, human learning should not be reduced to a fixed mechanical system, but should be considered in all its plasticity. This belief in human aspiration is embedded in the traditional liberal view of education, a view which constitutes a disinterested inquiry into the nature of being human. Huxley deplored that by the 1930s, students enter 'the world, highly expert in their particular job, but knowing very little about anything else and having no integrating principle in terms of which they can arrange and give significance to such knowledge as they may subsequently acquire' ('Education', 1937; *HCE4* 276). This view of 'expert-idiocy' is, for example, obliquely referenced in Linda's justification that 'it wasn't [her] business to know' things beyond her Beta caste status (*BNW* 105). Huxley considers a rounded humanistic education to be under attack by technocrats, and that students go to universities only because the pragmatics of the job market demand it.[35] However, Huxley also agrees that the liberal ideal should not be elevated to a universal ideal, because a liberal education is not for the many whose, in Caliban's words, 'foreheads [are] villainous low' (*The Tempest* IV.i.249).[36] Huxley ostensibly champions the humanistic endeavour of education that informed early pioneers such as Godwin and Wollstonecraft, yet he is, in fact, deeply sceptical of the democratic value of book learning that is at the core of the liberal tradition.

Prospero is a scholar who trains and manipulates others by wielding the power of his books, which are 'dukedom large enough' (I.ii.110); he has occupied himself exclusively with the liberal arts, 'those being all my study' (I.ii.74). Mustapha Mond is similarly the ultimate controller of books, a figure who censors dangerous ideas but secretes a stash of forbidden literature, perhaps the 'best which has been thought and said', in his own safe (*BNW* 203). Reading the best of that which has been thought and said, according to Huxley's ancestor Matthew Arnold, will serve to educate the whole person. Godwin likewise noted that books 'are the depositary of every thing that is most honourable to man'.[37] Huxley, however, asserted that '[c]ulture is not derived from the reading of *books*— but from thorough and intensive reading of *good* books' ('Reading, the New Vice', 1930; *HCE3* 48). Because of this limitation, even his sane utopia in *Island* (1962) considers most literature incompatible with an ideal society.[38] Book learning in *Brave New World* is, therefore, excluded from the syllabi of the indoctrination centres that even elite schools such as Eton College have become. While the individuality of the Eton pupils makes education, according to the Provost, more challenging, they are not encouraged to read books. The idea of 'book learning' not just for the elite but operationalized through mass literacy, is, consequently, utterly negated in the World State, which has eliminated all but functional literacy.[39] In fact, utopian ideas of solitary reading as an improvement of the mind are frequently debunked by Huxley's satiric sending-up of educational institutions.

These institutions, the sports venues, feelies, and community services, exist to enhance the regimentation of the populace in *Brave New World*. Huxley's satire alludes here to the heightened social intercourse advocated by many utopian societies, and to the educational motive of increased leisure.[40] Many utopian experiments have faltered, however, because of the shattered dream of a leisured life spent in noble pursuits. This dream was that the pleasure sought by its citizens was the pleasure of learning.[41] However, as intimated in *Brave New World*, increased leisure more often than not leads to an increase in recreational drug use and sexual libertinism. Huxley thus frequently punctures the utopian aspiration of unlimited leisure for the masses, because it is limited by what he terms the 'law of diminishing returns' ('Boundaries of Utopia', 1931; *HCE3* 127). The dreamed-of orderly life carved out of the capitulation of man's disorderly nature to a higher ideal is denigrated by the realities of human selfishness, especially in matters of sex.[42] Caliban, who was instructed by Miranda, but who 'any print of goodness wilt not take, | Being capable of all ill' (I.ii.352–3), is the perfect example of these utopian failures of human perfectibility. In Huxley's view, 'no amount of education or good government will make men completely virtuous and reasonable, or abolish their animal instincts' ('The Future of the Past', 1927; *HCE2* 93). Hence his satirical solution in *Brave New World* is one of passions satisfied rather than deferred.

Reading is no longer deemed pleasurable in the World State, but Helmholtz Watson acknowledges Shakespeare as a great emotional engineer whose craft validates the State's promotion of art as 'practically nothing but pure sensation' (*BNW* 194). Watson, himself a lecturer at the College of Emotional Engineering, nonetheless feels the increasing dissociation of meaning and language in his own propagandist slogans and rhymes, and he begins to query whether it is possible to say 'something about nothing' (*BNW* 60). Writing becomes problematic when 'there's nothing to say' (*BNW* 194) and thus he runs into difficulties by trying to use his own writings on solitude to coax his students into 'feeling as [he'd] felt when [he] wrote the rhymes' (*BNW* 157). While he attributes to words the power to condition, they are, in fact, equally dangerous as deconditioning factors. Overall, conditioning seems rather more unstable than the political needs of the World Controllers would wish it to be. Several instances in the novel are recorded in which conditioning is undone in an instant, and this is given as the reason why literature must be censored. Shakespeare's words in fact have, therefore, a colossal deconditioning effect on Watson, who must now be exiled to his own island. The function of the imaginative as educating reason and individuality is, nevertheless, only open to a minority. Overall the liberal educational discourse in *Brave New World* has failed, endorsing Plato's warning in *The Republic* against the falseness of literature.

The advocacy of literacy as liberating human reason, is, in any case, not automatic in utopian thought. Morris famously relegated the reading of books in *News from Nowhere* to a childish stage in human development when children would pick up books 'lying about' in much the same way John found his tattered version of Shakespeare on the reservation. However, while Morris's children would soon lose interest in reading, John's education is totally predicated on this mysteriously surviving edition, that awoke his sense of self through words.[43] John is, therefore, an inverted Caliban, a keen scholar who falls for the 'terrible, beautiful magic' of words (*BNW* 114). The key to John's downfall is that these words do not have any more meaning than the hypnopaedic slogans of the Brave New World. The narrator emphasizes again and again that John does not fully understand words, either because they are spoken in the Indian languages or in the archaic Shakespearean idiom. Even Linda's 'childish rhymes' become, after her death, 'magically strange and mysterious' (*BNW* 176). John lives in a poeticized world in which words 'rolled through his mind; rumbled, like talking thunder' (*BNW* 114), a situation that provides a corrective to the implied benefits of the literary canon for broadening a person's outlook.[44] Despite John's consolation through literacy ('But I can read [...] and they can't'; *BNW* 112), his reading is 'almost masturbatory'.[45] He is given voice through Shakespeare, but he also loses the critical distance between fiction and reality.[46] John is, in fact, 'functionally illiterate'.[47] Huxley stated that in the early 1930s the mind was in danger of being paralysed by the vast amount of printed material in existence ('Too Many Books', 1932; *HCE3* 88–9), and he drew on this point when in *Beyond the Mexique Bay* (1934) he emphasized that a love for reading cannot make up for a lack of understanding (*HCE3* 578 and 602).

The meaning of words is a frequent preoccupation of utopian writers, and dystopias are, according to David W. Sisk, identifiable through their accounts of forcibly narrowed language that represses free thought and communication.[48] It is therefore no surprise that the World State has stripped language of its connotative and imaginative qualities, thus denying its populace access to complete systems of knowledge.[49] Thomas Horan points out that Huxley is always fully conscious of the connection between thought, behaviour, and language.[50] Caliban famously accuses Miranda: 'You taught me language, and my profit on't | Is I know how to curse' (*The Tempest* I.ii.365). While Caliban's new articulation of his state of mind lacks transformative power, language in the final chapters of *Brave New World* deteriorates more and more into a powerful 'curse', with John's incantation of 'strumpet' and the chanted repetition of 'We—want—whip' that encourages John's frenzy in a way that elucidates the power of propaganda. John's understanding of words comprises a false consciousness due to his lack of critical literacy, which leads to the final chastisement of Lenina, the ensuing orgy, and the destruction of John himself; it adumbrates Huxley's eventual understanding of the dangerous consequences of words applied under the rule of propagandists, and that education must be charged with having facilitated such pseudo-knowledge of the world, related through 'words' (see 'Can We Be Well-Educated?', 1956; *HCE6* 206, and 'The Education of an Amphibian', 1956; *HCE5* 199).[51]

The disruption between knowledge and language became more prevalent in the 1930s and spawned a number of commentaries on the propagandistic breakdown of word-meaning and its replacement with pure emotion.[52] Huxley also criticizes such dangerous distortions of meaning, and he advocates the teaching of the art of dissociating ideas from language as an offset to them, while noting that such teaching 'in schools under direct state control is, of course, almost infinitely improbable'

('Education', 1937; *HCE4* 292). In *Brave New World*, however, the endless audio and televisual sounds of the World State have dissociated meaning and language to an extent that, to adapt Marshall McLuhan, the medium becomes the message. Hence the synthetic music box entitled 'The Voice of Reason' (*BNW* 188), brought in to quell the Delta unrest at the hospital, works not by verbalized 'reason' but by appeals to hypnopaedic slogans learned non-reflectively during thousands of hours of conditioning. This 'synthesis between technology and social life' enables media to engulf the populace with sounds and images that uphold conformity by replacing meaning with well-being.[53]

A familiar conservative critique of the modern, media-driven society is that it causes intellectual and moral enfeeblement.[54] Neil Postman, for instance, likens the mind-numbing effects of television to a form of *soma*.[55] He also argues that the didactic instrumentalization of entertainment is the death knell to any pedagogical aspirations of media, as it provides merely vicarious experiences. Hence Prospero's words—'Our revels now are ended. These our actors' (IV.i.148)—which point to how visual spectacle is often intended to be educational, but must be revealed as such. While Prospero is successful in teaching a lesson through pageant, Postman argues instead that television instils in children a 'wrong' habitus of learning, citing Dewey's idea that education is not about content but about enhancing learning 'by doing'.

Huxley was an enthusiastic supporter of the Dalton Plan because it presented a similar shift in emphasis from *what* is learned to *how* the learning process is handled ('How Should Men Be Educated?', 1926; *HCE2* 75, and 'Education', 1927; *HCE2* 212–30).[56] In 1932 he sent his son Matthew to Dartington Hall School, a progressive co-educational boarding school that offered a curriculum based on Tagore's and Dewey's educational plans, emphasizing 'cooperation, tolerance, persuasion, and loving understanding' rather than indoctrination and punishment.[57] At Dartington, formal classroom activity was eschewed for experiential education, as children tacitly learned through physical integration into the practices of the estate, a definition that matches the traditional notion of apprenticeship. The constraints of traditional understandings of artisanal 'apprenticeship', indicated in John's schooling by old Mitsima in *Brave New World*, is thus expanded by reference to experiential learning through which the 'crooked parody' of John's first lesson eventually grows into the masterly skill of fashioning bow and arrows to hunt. Elizabeth Spiller reminds us that *The Tempest* also reflects the nexus of 'knowledge practice' and scientific knowledge derived from experimental discovery, the latter being the basis for academic knowledge.[58] The older notion of knowledge as a practice, 'a way of doing or making that becomes a form of knowing', is not far off from Dewey's learning-by-doing approach, but it does not, in Huxley's eyes, go far enough. His ideal practical education must also cater for the 'not-selves', our spiritual and vegetative soul (see 'The Education of an Amphibian', 1956; *HCE5* 197–208).

Another kind of experiential education in *Brave New World* is therefore enacted as ethnography, looking in the myths and rituals of other cultures for a tacit performance of human knowledge. This ethnographical discourse is satirically inverted, as the savage reservation, a facet of the 'surrounding primitive world', is used at Eton as an educational tool to highlight oppositions between it and the mores of the Brave New World (and by implication endorsing the latter).[59] Schools, of course, have always been pitched as islands of civilization in a rustic world, especially in a colonial context. Huxley, for example, references here the educational and ethnographical tourism that was in vogue in early twentieth-century America, and Carey Snyder points out that Huxley was well versed in the ethnographical literature of that time.[60] The film showing native penitents thus represents a 'mock ethnography of modern society' in which ethnicity is consumed as spectacle. At the same time, Huxley shows how the nihilistic urges of 'civilized' humanity in the puerile and similarly irrational tribal rites of the orgy-porgy turn the colonial gaze upon itself.

Karl Mannheim, in *Ideology and Utopia* (1929), refers to utopia's 'transcendent' appeal to shatter the 'previous unambiguity of norms and interpretations' as part of the Enlightenment project.[61] Harold Schneiderman, in his recent introduction to Huxley's *Ends and Means* (1937), highlights the 'close intellectual bond' between the two thinkers, though it is unclear if Huxley had read Mannheim in the original German before the English translation in 1936.[62] In any case, he would have greeted Mannheim's idea about the need for new utopian thought in education with critical appreciation. While education is frequently perceived as 'one of the great instrumentalities of progress', dynamically fostering the impulse for growth, transformation, and mobility, in *Brave New World* Huxley mainly highlights its conformist roots.[63] The new educationalists, who cherish utopianism's orientation towards iconoclasm and the human capacity to imagine a better world, cannot (yet) provide a counterbalance to the inertia and lack of tension that is inherent in *Brave New World*'s motto: 'COMMUNITY, IDENTITY, STABILITY'.[64] Nevertheless, Huxley's hopeful exhortation that teachers, by building 'up in the minds of their charges a habit of resistance to suggestion' ('Education', 1937; *HCE4* 288), might instruct children to rely on their own resources and resist external stimulation for a totalitarian cause, means that *Brave New World* was not Huxley's last word on education.

Huxley's many suggestions for non-competitive, stimulating, holistic, individual, and non-verbal teaching have been realized in some way or another in our current education system, albeit often only in niche areas. When it comes to education, it seems, the old 'folkloristic' beliefs have proven surprisingly resilient, to the extent that parents will often ask for the more conservative educational 'banking' approach, in which knowledge is 'deposited' into the minds of their children. Politicians will recurrently endorse the traditional classroom disciplines that, it is believed, will make society safer and saner. A test-oriented 'knowledge economy' model of education is still prevalent in Western societies, notwithstanding a tradition of over 150 years of progressive educational theories. A simple correlation between classroom discipline and social stability, is, however, as ludicrous as the Brave New World's ideology of homogenizing its populace. So, despite his continuing interest in formal and informal pedagogies, Huxley presciently averred in 1933 that all systems of education are mere experiments, and that all we can do is sit back and wait to see how the newest experiments may unfold ('Discipline', 1933; *HCE3* 370–1), a statement he repeated in 1956 (see *HCE6* 203). Were he alive today, he would still be waiting to see how the experiment will turn out.

NOTES

1. J. Derbyshire, 'What Happened to Aldous Huxley?', *The New Criterion*, 21.6 (Feb. 2003): 13–22, at 18.
2. Derbyshire, 'What Happened', 22.
3. T. Horan, 'Revolutions from the Waist Downwards: Desire as Rebellion in Yevgeny Zamyatin's *We*, George Orwell's *1984*, and Aldous Huxley's *Brave New World*', *Extrapolation*, 48.2 (Summer 2007): 314–39, at 314.
4. See D.G. Izzo 'Introduction', in D.G. Izzo and K. Kirkpatrick (eds), *Huxley's 'Brave New World': Essays* (Jefferson, NC: McFarland, 2008), pp. 1–9, at p. 3.
5. H.P. Segal, *Utopias: A Brief History from Ancient Writings to Virtual Communities* (Oxford: Wiley-Blackwell, 2012), p. 10.
6. H. Ozmon, *Utopias and Education* (Minneapolis, MN: Burgess, 1969), pp. ix–x.

7. M.A. Peters and J. Freeman-Moir, 'Introducing Edutopias: Concept, Genealogy, Futures', in M.A. Peters and J. Freeman-Moir (eds), *Edutopias: New Utopian Thinking in Education* (Rotterdam: Sense, 2006), pp. 1–19, at pp. 1–3.
8. N. Frye, 'Varieties of Literary Utopias', *Daedalus*, 94.2 (Spring 1965): 323–47, at 335–6.
9. G. Massó, *Education in Utopias* (New York: AMS Press, 1972), p. 20.
10. M. Olsson, 'Totalitarianism and the "Repressed" Utopia of the Present: Moving beyond Hayek, Popper and Foucault', in Peters and Freeman-Moir (eds), *Edutopias*, pp. 99–124, at p. 100.
11. J. Meckier, 'Prepping for *Brave New World*: Aldous Huxley's Essays of the 1920s', *Utopian Studies*, 12.2 (2001): 234–45, at 245.
12. J. Meckier, 'A Neglected Huxley "Preface": His Earliest Synopsis of *Brave New World*', *Twentieth-Century Literature*, 25.1 (1979): 1–20, at 2–3.
13. Thompson in Ozmon, *Utopias and Education*, p. 110.
14. C. Rosenhan, '"The Knowledge Economy": Aldous Huxley's Critiques of Universal Education', in B. Nugel, U. Rasch, and G. Wagner (eds), *Aldous Huxley, Man of Letters: Thinker, Critic and Artist*, Proceedings of the Third Aldous Huxley Symposium Riga 2004. (Berlin: Lit Verlag, 2007), pp. 93–111.
15. H. Silver, *The Concept of Popular Education: A Study of Ideas and Social Movements in the Early Nineteenth Century* (London: Methuen, 1965), p. 102.
16. In *Brave New World Revisited* (1958) Huxley later imagined such an education in the grip of a totalitarian doctrine (see *BNWR* 127–39).
17. Meckier, 'A Neglected Huxley "Preface"', 10 and 16.
18. J. Dewey, 'Education' (1911), in P. Monroe (ed.), *A Cyclopedia of Education*, Vol. II (New York: Macmillan, 1911), pp. 398–401, at p. 389. Dewey in 'Nationalizing Education' (1916), in *The Essential Dewey—Vol. 1: Pragmatism, Education, Democracy*, ed. L.A. Hickman and T.M. Alexander (Bloomington, IN: Indiana University Press, 1998), pp. 265–9, at p. 268 asserts how exploiting education for such ends undermines its democratic claim and helps 'refeudalize' the system.
19. Silver, *The Concept of Popular Education*, p. 26.
20. See R.T. Fisher, *Classical Utopian Theories of Education* (New York: Bookman, 1963), pp. 17–18.
21. W. Godwin, *The Enquirer: Reflections on Education, Manners, and Literature* (London: G. G. and J. Robinson, 1797), p. 48.
22. See T. Lewis, 'The Architecture of Potentiality: Weak Utopianism and Educational Space in the Work of Giorgio Agamben', *Utopian Studies*, 23.2 (2012): 355–73, at 357.

23. Elsewhere Huxley argues that state education makes us believe 'dogmatically that only one thing can be true or right at one time' ('Some American Contradictions', 1929; *HCE3* 213).
24. Silver, *The Concept of Popular Education*, p. 45.
25. See, for example, H. Macleod, 'What Role Can Educational Multimedia Play in Narrowing the Digital Divide?', *The International Journal of Education and Development using Information and Communication Technology*, 1.4 (2005): 42–53.
26. K. Fenn, H.C. Nusbaum, and D. Margoliash, 'Consolidation During Sleep of Perceptual Learning of Spoken Language', *Nature*, 425 (2003): 614–6.
27. B.H. Fox and J.S. Robbin, in 'The Retention of Material Presented during Sleep', *Journal of Experimental Psychology*, 43.1 (1952): 75–9, for example, conclude that 'learning can occur during sleep', though J.L. Andreassi, in *Psychophysiology: Human Behaviour and Psychological Response*, 4th rev. ed. (Abingdon: Psychology Press, 2013), pp. 75–7, notes its impractical side, as hypnopaedia results in loss of restful sleep.
28. D.W. Surry, and J.D. Farquhar, 'Diffusion Theory and Instructional Technology', *Journal of Instructional Science and Technology*, 2.1 (1997): n.p. Available at http://www.southalabama.edu/coe/bset/surry/papers/dtit/dtit.htm (accessed 11 Oct. 2015). Huxley thought that the spoken word of a sound recording historically has a greater impact than the written word ('Censorship and Spoken Literature', 1955; *HCE5* 323–4). His support for an oral culture grew out of his interest in mysticism, which was steeped in the oral tradition ('Can We Be Well-Educated?', 1956; *HCE6* 205). In 'The Outlook for American Culture: Some Reflections in a Machine Age' (1927) Huxley describes how machinery 'has set up a tendency towards the realization of fuller life' (*HCE3* 187).
29. For 'neuromyths', see U. Goswami, 'Neuroscience and Education', *British Journal of Educational Psychology*, 74.1 (2004): 1–14. An announcement in 2007 by the Organisation for Economic Co-operation and Development (OECD) maintains that the 'future of education and the future of neuroscience are linked' (see Z. Stein, et al., 'Ethical Issues in Educational Neuroscience: Raising Children in a Brave New World', in J. Illes and B. Sahakian (eds) *The Oxford Handbook of Neuroethics* (Oxford: Oxford University Press, 2011), pp. 803–22).
30. Current references to pedagogical conditioning appear mostly in literature investigating the nexus of computers and learning. See, for example, H. Atsusi and M. Kebritchi, 'Examining the Pedagogical Foundations of Modern Educational Computer Games', *Computers & Education*, 51 (2008): 1729–43, and G. Conole, et al., 'Mapping Pedagogy and Tools for Effective Learning Design', *Computers & Education*, 43 (2004): 17–33.
31. Peters and Freeman-Moir, 'Introducing Edutopias', p. 18.

32. A. Carey-Webb, 'National and Colonial Education in Shakespeare's *The Tempest*', *Early Modern Literary Studies*, 5.1 (1999): 1–39, at 1; and A.F. Leach, *The Schools of Medieval England* (London: Methuen, 1915), p. 277.

33. Carey-Webb, 'National and Colonial Education', 16. See W. Shakespeare, *The Tempest*, ed. V.M. Vaughan and A.T. Vaughan (London: Arden, 1999).

34. See A. Aldridge, *The Scientific World View in Dystopia* (Ann Arbor, MI: UMI Research Press, 1984), pp. 50, 53, and 57.

35. See, for example, 'Literature and Examinations' (1936; *HCE4* 62). As the humanities were taught according to scientific standards, 'the scientific student of literature is one of the most comical figures of our day' ('Education', 1927; *HCE2* 215).

36. Hence Huxley's 1931 essay 'Foreheads Villainous Low' (*HCE3* 246–50).

37. Godwin, *The Enquirer*, p. 25.

38. G. Jaeger, 'The Palanese Way: Engaged Enlightenment in Aldous Huxley's *Island*', in C.C. Barfoot (ed.), *Aldous Huxley between East and West* (Amsterdam: Rodopi, 2001), pp. 113–30, at pp. 128–9.

39. E. Verne, 'Literacy and Industrialisation: The Dispossession of Speech' (1976), in H.J. Graff (ed.), *Literacy and Social Development in the West: A Reader* (Cambridge: Cambridge University Press, 1981), pp. 286–303, at p. 289.

40. Massó, *Education in Utopias*, p. 132 and p. 135.

41. More's *Utopia* and Campanella's *The City of the Sun* (1602) are examples in which citizens are shown spending most of their days in 'pleasant learning' (Fisher, *Classical Utopian Theories of Education*, p. 59 and p. 78).

42. Segal, *Utopias: A Brief History*, p. 26 and p. 96.

43. B. Buchanan, 'Oedipus in Dystopia: Freud and Lawrence in Aldous Huxley's *Brave New World*', *Journal of Modern Literature*, 25.3–4 (Summer 2002): 75–89, at 78.

44. P. Smethurst, '"O brave new world that has no poets in it": Shakespeare and Scientific Utopia in *Brave New World*', in Izzo and Kirkpatrick (eds), *Huxley's 'Brave New World'*, pp. 96–106, at p. 101.

45. J. Meckier, *Aldous Huxley, from Poet to Mystic* (Zurich: LIT Verlag, 2011), p. 240.

46. R.S. Baker, *Brave New World: History, Science, and Dystopia* (Boston: Twayne, 1990), p. 119.

47. S.A. Witters, 'Words Have to Mean Something More: Folkloric Reading in *Brave New World*', in Izzo and Kirkpatrick (eds), *Huxley's 'Brave New World'*, pp. 73–87, p. 84.

48. D.W. Sisk, *Transformations of Language in Modern Dystopias* (Westport, CT: Greenwood Press, 1997), p. 12.

49. Witters, 'Words Have to Mean Something More', p. 84.

50. Horan, 'Revolutions from the Waist Downwards'. Huxley, for example, wrote about the self-sufficiency and separateness of the Western alphabet, which conditions thought processes ('Adonis and the Alphabet', 1956; *HCE5* 235–9).
51. Huxley claims that 'all propaganda directed against an opposing group has but one aim: to substitute diabolical abstractions for concrete persons' ('Words and Behaviour', 1936; *HCE4* 57–8).
52. See N. Chomsky, *Language and Politics* (Montreal: Black Rose, 1988) and G. Orwell, 'The Prevention of Literature' (1946), in *The Collected Essays, Journalism and Letters—Volume 4: In Front of Your Nose 1945–1950*, ed. S. Orwell and I. Angus (London: Penguin, 1970), pp. 81–95.
53. M. Varricchio, 'Power of Images/Images of Power in *Brave New World* and *Nineteen Eighty-Four*', *Utopian Studies*, 10.1 (1999): 98–114, at 100.
54. S. Peller, in 'Laboring for a *Brave New World*: Our Ford and the Epsilons', in Izzo and Kirkpatrick (eds), *Huxley's 'Brave New World'*, pp. 62–72, at p. 63, notes that the *Brave New World* is driven towards the conformity and banality of mass culture.
55. N. Postman, *Amusing Ourselves to Death: Public Discourse in the Age of Show Business* (London: Methuen, 1985), p. 113.
56. The Dalton Plan encourages children with individual talents, abilities, and aptitudes to control their own learning process in an environment geared towards mutual support and cooperation.
57. D. Parsons, 'Dartington: A Principal Source of Inspiration Behind Aldous Huxley's *Island*', *The Journal of General Education*, 39.1 (1987): 10–25, at 13. See also M. Young, *The Elmhirsts of Dartington: The Creation of a Utopian Community* (Abingdon: Routledge and Kegan Paul, 1982).
58. E. Spiller, 'Shakespeare and the Making of Early Modern Science: Resituating Prospero's Art', *South Central Review*, 26.1–2 (Winter–Spring 2009): 24–41, at 27 and 29.
59. A. Arciero, 'Some Kind of *Brave New World*: Humans, Society, and Nature in the Dystopian Interpretations of Huxley and Orwell', in Izzo and Kirkpatrick (eds), *Huxley's 'Brave New World'*, pp. 46–61, at p. 47.
60. C. Snyder, '"When the Indian was in vogue": D.H. Lawrence, Aldous Huxley, and Ethnological Tourism in the Southwest', *Modern Fiction Studies*, 53.4 (Winter 2007): 662–96, at 682.
61. K. Mannheim, *Ideology and Utopia: An Introduction to the Sociology of Knowledge* (1929), trans. L. Wirth and E. Shils (New York: Harcourt, Brace & World, 1936), p. 9.
62. H. Schneiderman, 'Introduction', in A. Huxley, *Ends and Means: An Inquiry into the Nature of Ideals* (1937; New Brunswick: Transaction, 2012): pp. vii–xxvi.
63. Massó, *Education in Utopias*, p. 6.
64. D. Halpin, *Hope and Education: The Role of the Utopian Imagination* (London and New York: Routledge-Falmer, 2003), pp. 33–5.

CHAPTER 5

The Pleasures of Dystopia

Laura Frost

George Orwell's *Nineteen Eighty-Four* (1949), with its frightening surveillance culture, has been the most frequently invoked dystopic fiction in
the wake of Edward Snowden's revelations, racing to the top of Amazon's
bestseller list some 60 years after its initial publication date. However, as
much as the social policing elements of that novel seem uncannily predictive, Orwell was not particularly prescient about other aspects of the
future. He was especially amiss in his forecasting for technologies of pleasure. For his characters in Oceania, trudging to and from their joyless jobs
in party-issued overalls and rallying for their daily Two Minutes Hate,
non-procreative sexuality and intimacy are forbidden. In between bouts
of torture in Room 101, O'Brien tells Winston Smith about Big Brother's
plan for the future: "'The sex instinct will be eradicated. [...] We shall
abolish the orgasm.'"[1] While today sexual and reproductive rights are still
subject to politics everywhere, the austerity and sheer greyness of Orwell's
prognosis for pleasure, even to the most cynical critic of the culture industry, have not come to pass in most of the world.

Fredric Jameson asks 'Who will recount the pleasures of dystopia?' in 'Then You
Are Them' [review of Margaret Atwood, *The Year of the Flood* (2009)], *London
Review of Books*, 31.17 (10 Sep. 2009): 7–8.

L. Frost (✉)

© The Editor(s) (if applicable) and The Author(s) 2016   69
J. Greenberg, N. Waddell (eds.), Brave New World: *Contexts and
Legacies*, DOI 10.1057/978-1-137-44541-4_5

Of course, pleasure is not characteristically associated with dystopic texts, in which negation and repression are the more common notes. The generic ambitions of the dystopia, the attempt to depict a society gone awry, mean that images of degradation, pain, and oppression are the norm. By contrast, in *Brave New World* (1932), London in the Year A.F. 632 is a culture of genetic and psychological control that is paradoxically organized around pleasure. The Resident World Controller for Western Europe, Mustapha Mond, summarizes the routine: 'Seven and a half hours of mild, unexhausting labour, and then the *soma* ration and games and unrestricted copulation and the feelies', the cinema of pansensual stimulation (*BNW* 197). The theory is simple enough: ply people with drugs, orgy-porgy, easy sex, and mind-numbing entertainment, and they will have no thoughts of resistance. In this society where there is 'no leisure from pleasure' (*BNW* 47), compulsory hedonism is central to state control. Huxley's satiric vision feels not only generically innovative but also startlingly contemporary in this respect. Instead of Big Brother channelling libidinal energy into sadism, Huxley's characters flirt over Centrifugal Bumble-puppy, fornicate with abandon, and are kept politically pliant through obligatory fun.[2]

Brave New World has typically been read as 'the classic denunciation of mass culture in the interwar years', as leisure pursuits are manipulated to produce docile citizens.[3] The lengthy dialogues between John the Savage and Mustapha Mond clearly spell out the arrangement: for example, '"You've got to choose between happiness and what people used to call high art. We've sacrificed the high art. We have the feelies and the scent organ instead"' (*BNW* 194). Huxley voices the familiar modernist contrast between complex, challenging, and valuable high art, exemplified by contraband Shakespeare in *Brave New World*, and popular, passive, debased entertainments.[4]

Soma is Huxley's most well-known contribution to the fiction of vernacular pleasure. He presents its '[e]uphoric, narcotic, pleasantly hallucinant' (*BNW* 46) effects as a coma-like daze into which his characters drift on their '*soma* holiday'. *Soma* obliterates consciousness, which makes it the perfect opiate for the masses. But readers do not experience *soma*'s compelling properties from the inside but rather from an external point of view. The hospital-sanctioned overdose of John's mother at the end of the novel is the most explicitly described *soma* trip, and it is about as appealing as a roller coaster that has gone off its rails.

For Huxley, self-restraint is an obvious desideratum. One of his narrative challenges, then, was to render the triumph of the pleasure principle, the lifting of repression, not just unattractive but also dangerous. His own term for the novel—a 'negative utopia'—captures this contradiction.[5] Even though *Brave New World* is clearly a cautionary tale, Huxley's specific means of describing pleasure—and especially his treatment of erotic culture—is more complex. There is no doubt that Huxley disapproves of the impersonal, hollow, automatic nature of the sexual liaisons in *Brave New World*. That said, there are notable moments in the novel that produce funny or sensational reading effects that exist alongside Huxley's blatant critique. In his depictions of the free-love culture where 'everyone belongs to everyone else' (*BNW* 37) and children are schooled in erotic play, in the brave new woman Lenina Crowne, and in technologies of pleasure epitomized by the feelies, Huxley courts titillation alongside disapproval. Just as John the Savage is horrified by the attraction of this culture, Huxley makes a point of showing that attraction.

In creating desublimated practices of pleasure that are alarming but also imaginatively expansive, Huxley was influential and predictive. Although the amusements of *Brave New World* are cartoonish in their exaggeration of jazz-age novelties, and although they lack the corporate trademarks that are synonymous with leisure pursuits now (for example, sex-hormone chewing gum brought to you by Pfizer), what Huxley gets right is the ubiquity of capitalist leisure culture, the postmodern embrace of casual recreation (that is, 'hooking up' via Grindr or Tinder), and the technological ambition to constantly increase the reach and the extent of those pleasures. While Huxley ultimately takes erotic desublimation in a nightmarish direction in *Brave New World*, it was the core idea of several utopian sociopolitical schemes in the century, and would remain an enduring fantasy in fiction, film, and sexual subcultures up to our own time. Examining the legacy of *Brave New World*'s culture of pleasure, in fiction and film as well as in philosophy, psychology, and sociopolitical theory, to the virtual and augmented reality of the present, this essay will make the case that the novel's continuing resonance is the result of its many, often contradictory, registers. It is precisely Huxley's balance of fearsome and exciting elements that account for the novel's affinity with today's aspirational technologies—indeed, when we consider the sweep of leisure technologies from the 1930s to today, Huxley might be considered an unwitting 'early adopter' of cutting-edge technics—and ongoing conflicts about the value and meaning of different kinds of pleasure. Measuring Huxley's creative achievements by the distance between *Brave New World* and our own time yields results both impressive and sobering.

'Sex', Margaret Atwood notes, 'is often centre stage in utopias and dystopias—who can do what, with which set of genital organs, and with whom, being one of humanity's main preoccupations.'[6] Fiction writers have often made use of the idea that sex, a seemingly intimate and private zone of life, might be shaped by external, imposed social influences such as policing, surveillance, or an internalized panopticon effect. Dystopic sex is typically imagined as repressed, suppressed, or generally distorted or controlled, as in Katharine Burdekin's anti-fascist novel *Swastika Night* (1937), where women are reduced to breeding mares, or Atwood's *The Handmaid's Tale* (1985). In *Brave New World*, Huxley devotes a great deal of attention to the sexual life of his characters, from children's erotic play and episodes of orgy-porgy to men casually discussing what it is like to 'have' a particular woman, and women reminding one another to have more casual sex. However, the World State's prescribed sexual habits are radically different from most dystopias. In *Nineteen Eighty-Four*, for example, where Julia explains Big Brother's theory of sexual repression: '"When you make love you're using up energy; and afterwards you feel happy and don't give a damn for anything. They can't bear you to feel like that. They want you to be bursting with energy all the time. All this marching up and down and cheering and waving flags is simply sex gone sour. If you're happy inside yourself, why should you get excited about Big Brother and the Three-Year Plans and the Two Minutes Hate and all the rest of their bloody rot?"'[7]

In Huxley's novel, sexual taboos are eradicated in the service of a totalitarian-meets-utilitarian hedonic calculus. He claimed that *Brave New World* began as a parody of H.G. Wells's utopias and scientific romances.[8] The guileless nudism of *Men Like Gods* (1923), for example, and the free-love ideology associated with Wells himself become the extravagantly promiscuous credo of the Brave New World. Huxley observed, in his much-cited foreword to the 1946 edition of the novel, that '[a]s political and economic freedom diminishes, sexual freedom tends compensatingly to increase' (*BNW* xlix). By 'sexual freedom', Huxley really means obliga-tion or compulsion ('no leisure from pleasure'). 'Orgy-porgy, Ford and fun', the song goes in *Brave New World*, 'Kiss the girls and make them One. | Boys at one with girls at peace; | Orgy-porgy gives release' (*BNW* 73). Perfunctory sex is encouraged as a kind of hygienic discharge, while emotions and desires for intimacy are siphoned off by Violent Passion Surrogate (VPS) treatments.

Many readers of *Brave New World* have found its mechanistic and permissive sex one of the most repellent aspects of the novel. A *Times Literary Supplement* reviewer criticized the 'attention that [Huxley] gives to the abundant sex life of these denatured human beings'; Isaac Rosenfeld wrote that the 'real horror in *Brave New World* is sex, from the embryo bottle to the contraceptive belt.'[9] But is the sexual culture of the World State necessarily one of 'horror'? Certainly, it is impersonal, perfunctory, and perhaps dehumanizing, *if* one assumes monogamous, heterosexual, nuclear family structure is essential to civilization. However, the tenor of Huxley's treatment of sexual culture in *Brave New World* is substantially distinct from the other aforementioned dystopias (particularly from the violent sex of many feminist dystopias). While Huxley describes activities such as orgy-porgy as hollow and fatuous, they are also drawn with humor and, in some cases, more than a little prurience. For example, the considerable detail Huxley lavishes on the zippered lingerie, boots, form-fitting uniforms, and color co-ordinated Malthusian Belts of the women in *Brave New World* suggests his descriptions of women in Los Angeles during his 1926 trip there: 'exquisitely pretty flappers, dressed in bathing costumes so tight that every contour of the Mound of Venus and the Vale of Bliss was plainly visible' (*AHSL* 172). Huxley's censure is second only to his fascination with the parading bathing beauties. Modernist critiques of mass culture like Huxley's are forever shadowed by the stubborn fact that popular entertainments are, by nature, compelling, exciting, and amusing; they exert a very real, if uneasy, appeal. In *Brave New World*, we see this in John's rage at his susceptibility to pleasures that repulse him morally and ethically.

The feelies, the most intense vehicle of mass pleasure in *Brave New World*, and also the most technologically complex, are a prime example of debased yet imaginatively captivating entertainment. As a riff on the new cinematic experience of the 'talkies', Huxley extends the innovation of synchronized sound to all the senses.[10] The feelies are three-dimensional, scented, and tactile: metal knobs embedded in the audience's seats produce an 'almost intolerable galvanic pleasure' (*BNW* 146). The sensation is underscored by the inane plot of the feely Huxley describes in detail, *Three Weeks in a Helicopter*, in which an interracial couple ('a gigantic negro and a golden-haired young brachycephalic Beta-Plus female'; *BNW* 146) cavort on a bearskin rug. The man develops 'an exclusive and maniacal passion' for 'the Beta blonde' (*BNW* 146) and makes her his sex slave in a helicopter, from which she is rescued by, and becomes the 'mistress' of, 'three handsome young Alphas' (*BNW* 147).

Huxley portrays the feelies—and especially John's scandalized attitude toward them—as pornographic by design and in effect, as the audience emerges flushed and aroused. Despite the broad satire of the feelies' idiocy, Huxley dwells on their popularity, their allure, and their efficient mobilization of the body. He does the same with the 'uncommonly pretty' (*BNW* 13) and 'wonderfully pneumatic' (*BNW* 37) Lenina, who is closely related to the feelies. Her characteristics—sensual, female, modern, 'easy'—code her as an embodiment of mass culture. She is discussed by the men who have 'had' her, just as they discuss the merits of *Three Weeks in a Helicopter*. Huxley does not depict Lenina as being like the mechanistic Tiller Girls, for example, whom Siegfried Kracauer characterized as 'sexless bodies in bathing suits', but rather as magnetic in a debauched way.[11] The scene in the 'GIRLS' DRESSING-ROOM', for example, in which 'eighty vibro-vacuum massage machines were simultaneously kneading and sucking the firm and sunburnt flesh of eighty superb female specimens' (*BNW* 30) and Lenina emerges from her bath like some futurist Aphrodite, straddles the line between critique of conveyor-belt hygiene and soft-core fantasy, a scene of guilty pleasure that Huxley allows the reader to feel with his character (unlike the *soma* scenes, where readers are detached from the action). Even as Huxley emphasizes Lenina's artificiality, he effectively simulates John's arousal through funny but also charged scenes of fetishistic desire. When John discovers Lenina sleeping in bed, 'dressed in a pair of pink one-piece zippyjamas' (*BNW* 125), his romantic *Romeo and Juliet* sentiment quickly gives way to the desire to 'take hold of the zipper at her neck and give one long, strong pull ...' (*BNW* 126). Huxley's ellipsis invites the reader to conjure the body beneath those zippyjamas. One only has to compare Huxley's treatment of sex in his utopia, *Island* (1962)—tantric, all-fulfilling, and downright boring—to note that he inscribes erotic tension throughout *Brave New World* (for example, 'the last electric titillation' on Lenina's lips after *Three Weeks in a Helicopter* leaves 'fine shuddering roads of anxiety and pleasure across her skin'; *BNW* 147).

Huxley's is undoubtedly a reactionary view of mass culture and a defense of traditional, conservative sexual mores, but his descriptions of Lenina and the feelies are pronouncedly sensational. While some critics insist that these scenes are purely negative (Milton Birnbaum: 'The love-making scenes in [Huxley's] novels are always suffused with sardonic

revulsion'), Jocelyn Brooke's comment that 'Huxley's attitude to sex is
[…] at once sensualist and ascetic' seems more accurate.[12] John's rejection
of Lenina, the feelies, and other sensual pleasures is a puritanical hysteria
that Huxley criticizes as much as thoughtless consumption of the feelies,
soma, and orgy-porgy. 'Lenina's artificial charm and cellophane shame-
lessness', Theodor Adorno observed, 'produce by no means the unerotic
effect Huxley intended, but rather a highly seductive one, to which even
the infuriated cultural savage succumbs at the end of the novel' (*AHU*
15). John's hyper-vigilant rage against his attraction to Lenina and the
scenes of flagellation at the novel's end are excessive and go against his
own—and perhaps the reader's—desires. As June Deery observes: 'Huxley
has often confused his readers because not everything in *Brave New World*
is viewed as unpalatable.'[13]

The censorship history of *Brave New World* confirms this. In American
education, for example, the novel is both a staple of high-school English
classes and a fixture on banned book lists. Ever since it was published it has
been challenged because of its scenes of drug use and promiscuous sex.[14]
Generations of students have always known something many professional
critics seem to forget or have a hard time registering: that *Brave New
World* is full of sex, and some of it is distinctly salacious. Unlike dystopias
with an unremittingly negative tonal range, Huxley's novel generates volatile, less uniform effects, and is by turns provocative, playful, and alarming.
This dynamic serves to underscore the dangers of mass-culture pleasure:
it is threatening precisely because it is so compelling to so many people.
That *Brave New World* influenced subsequent imaginative culture is not
surprising; more curious, perhaps, is the synchronicity between Huxley's
novel and twentieth-century discourses of sexual revolution.

The hydraulic theory of libido that Huxley seems to promulgate in
Brave New World—the negative correlation between political and sexual
freedom—blends contemporary politics with Freudian repression and
sublimation inside a parodic fictional framework. At a time when some
public intellectuals and activists were questioning the inevitability of the
patriarchal family and monogamy, Huxley's novel imagines all social structures, including sexuality, as determined by the laws of production. He
puts the blame on Ford and Freud ('Our Freud had been the first to reveal
the appalling dangers of family life. The world was full of fathers—was
therefore full of misery; full of mothers—therefore of every kind of perversion from sadism to chastity; full of brothers, sisters, uncles, aunts—full of
madness and suicide'; *BNW* 33). The World State abolishes these stifling

familial bonds and, through the miracle of science, creates a world of bottled babies and free love. This is a strange extrapolation of Freud indeed. For Freud, restraint of instincts is the price of civilization, and sublimation leads to cultural achievement. The marked contrast between the Savage Reservation and the World State leaves no 'third alternative' (*BNW* xliii), as Huxley put it in his 1946 foreword to the novel. That is also the case for his treatment of pleasure and sexuality: as Adorno pointed out, Huxley 'fails to distinguish between the liberation of sexuality and its debasement' (*AHU* 103). But of course, there were (and are) many alternatives.

At the same moment at which Huxley was imagining totalitarian sexuality, the idiosyncratic theorist Wilhelm Reich was arguing just the opposite in correlating sexual liberation with political freedom. While the leading figures in psychoanalysis were focusing on transhistorical structures of personality and psychological development, Reich preached the power of sex and libido as a kind of 'bioenergy' (for example, in his 1927 work *The Function of the Orgasm*) and insisted that the 'unconscious itself is [...] socially determined.'[15] His *Sexual Revolution*—a phrase he coined—published the same year as Freud's *Civilization and its Discontents* (1930), made the case that 'antisocial impulses, which result from social repression of normal sexuality' have been mistakenly understood by psychoanalysts like Freud as 'biological facts' instead of the outcome of sociological-economic formations, whether authoritarian or capitalist.[16] Reich identified orgone energy as a life force that included but was not limited to orgasm.

Developing his ideas about 'sex economy' as he observed the rise of fascism in Germany, Reich argues in *The Mass Psychology of Fascism* (1933) that the authoritarian state leverages patriarchal family structure and 'dams up' libidinal energy as a means of social control. Fascist ideologues, he contends, make 'use of the dregs of sexual misery' and harness citizens' libidinal drives in order to serve the political and economic interests of the state:

> From the point of view of mass psychology, the effect of militarism is based essentially on a libidinous mechanism. The sexual effect of a uniform, the erotically provocative effect of rhythmically executed goose-stepping, the exhibitionistic nature of militaristic procedures, have been more practically comprehended by a salesgirl or an average secretary than by our most erudite politicians.[17]

Huxley's own *Point Counter Point* (1928) includes similar passages describing a British woman's erotic attraction to a magnetically brutish proto-fascist character. Reich's contention that '"fascism" is only the

organized political expression of the structure of the average man's character' and that '"fascism" is the basic emotional attitude of the suppressed
man of our authoritarian machine civilization and its mechanistic-mystical
conception of life' made it possible to extend his theory of politicized
libido beyond the context of fascist states to capitalist culture at large.[18]
Reich called for fellow revolutionaries to oppose 'pathological pleasure'
with their own 'positive sex-economy.'[19] His own early practical efforts to
promote this agenda included the creation of the Socialist Society for Sex-
Counseling and Sex-Research in Vienna, with the slogan 'Free Sexuality
Within an Egalitarian Society'.[20]

In the 1940s and following, both Reich and Huxley were on the minds
of many prominent social theorists and writers who were struggling to
understand the politics of culture. (Herbert Marcuse, Max Horkheimer,
Theodor Adorno, and Bertolt Brecht, among other intellectual luminar-
ies, all attended a 1942 conference on Huxley at the Institute for Social
Research in Los Angeles.)[21] 'Freudo-Marxist' writers such as Erich Fromm
(*Escape from Freedom*, 1941), Marcuse (*Eros and Civilization*, 1955; *One-
Dimensional Man*, 1964), and Norman O. Brown (*Life Against Death*,
1959) all took up Reich's call for the lifting of sexual repression in the
service of political freedom. However, they all had trouble explaining how
this might happen. Brown cryptically called for the 'resurrection of the
body' and Marcuse heralded the release of a repressed body, a 'resexualized' body with a 'polymorphous sexuality' that would 'make the human
body an instrument of pleasure rather than labor'.[22] Calling on the 'transformation of work into play'—insofar as play 'is entirely subject to the pleasure principle', while work serves functional ends—Marcuse announced:
'Today the fight for life, the fight for Eros, is the *political* fight.'[23]

As intriguing as these formulations may be, none lends itself to concrete
realization.[24] What would it be like to inhabit a 'resexualized' body in an
eroticized public sphere? A progressive eroticized workplace is difficult to
imagine, particularly as women still have not achieved equal pay for equal
work and are underrepresented in management, and as sexual harassment
and discrimination have only recently been legally codified. Huxley's version of a sexualized workplace in *Brave New World*—a workplace where
people cruise, make dates, and discuss one another's sexual performance,
and where bodies are perpetually available but never embroiled in passion-
ate relationships—is hardly liberating.

It was Reich who articulated one of the era's most concrete, if eccentric, models of visionary libidinal practice. When he moved to America,

Reich devised the 'orgone energy accumulator' box, which was supposed to increase biopower and 'orgastic potency', and cure physical and mental illness. The actual design of the box was remarkably low-tech: Reich's directions call for the construction of a large pine box (a 'collapsible cabinet') lined with layers of steel and glass wool.[25] While William Burroughs alleged that he had experienced a spontaneous orgasm while in his orgone box, Reich's descriptions of anticipated effects are more mundane, as users were instructed to do 'daily, regular sittings' in the box for limited periods of time as sensations of warmth flowed through them.

If we consider Reich's orgone box alongside Huxley's feelies—both vehicles for desublimation, but meant to be politically liberating in the first case and repressive in the second—the contrast is instructive. Reich's invention was crude from an engineering point of view, but as immense in its ambitions as Reich was earnest about the utopian potential for orgasm. Thanks to references in fiction such as Jack Kerouac's *On the Road* (1957) and coverage in *Time* magazine in January 1964 ('Wilhelm Reich may have been a prophet. For now it sometimes seems that all America is one big Orgone Box'), as well as the decidedly eccentric direction in which Reich's later life went, his invention has entered popular culture lore as a 'sex box', a joke, a ludicrous contraption, most notably parodied in the 'orgasmatron' in Woody Allen's futuristic 1973 comedy *Sleeper*.[26] By contrast, Huxley's feelies were so complex that they were not anywhere near achievable at the time he imagined them; yet they turn out to be startlingly close to today's cutting-edge technology, to which I will return in a moment.

In the 1960s and 1970s, several movements followed Reich's premise that 'sexual revolution' was a fundamental means of achieving sociopolitical liberation. The gay rights movement as well as many voices within feminism, including Audre Lorde ('Uses of the Erotic: The Erotic as Power', 1978), Erica Jong (*Fear of Flying*, 1973, with its sexual holy grail, the Zipless Fuck), and Nancy Friday (*My Secret Garden*, also 1973), made the case that erotic liberation and pleasure were key to political freedom; contemporary sexologists such as Masters and Johnson and health advocates like the collective behind *Our Bodies Ourselves* (1971) also emphasized the importance of sexual pleasure and expression. Even as a more skeptical note was sounded by some, such as Michel Foucault in his critique of the repressive hypothesis, to many, sexual revolution seemed, for a brief moment, to herald a new age of social rights and freedom.

Despite the clear ideological differences between Reich and Huxley, the contributions of the two were often merged in pop-culture fantasy of the

1960s and 1970s. As much as *Brave New World* draws on high-minded literary fiction such as *We* (1921), it also strikes many of the playful, campy, and bawdy notes that pulp fiction and B-movies amplify. From the swinging single culture and sexy sartorial getups to *Three Weeks in a Helicopter*'s 'sexophone' soundtrack, fetishistic rug, and episodic, polyamorous couplings, the stylistic tropes of *Brave New World* would be amplified in the golden age of American porn, the 1970s, which was driven by flouted taboos and the idea of sexual utopia. For example, everything about *Three Weeks in a Helicopter* (from the kisses to the interracial romp on the bearskin) that would not have been representable in mainstream cinema in 1932 thanks to the Hays Code, would be right in place in porn classics like *Behind the Green Door* (1972), the first mainstream X-rated film featuring interracial sex, and sexploitation films from the same era, such as *Shaft* (1971). Obviously, Huxley would have been horrified by this, or would at least have claimed to be.

Zany combinations of Reich and Huxley surface in the science-fiction fantasy of the 1960s and 1970s, for example, Robert A. Heinlein's *Stranger in a Strange Land* (1961), George H. Smith's *Those Sexy Saucer People* (1967), Gene Cross's *Nude in Orbit* (1968), Roger Vadim's *Barbarella: Queen of the Galaxy* (1968), Michael Benveniste's and Howard Ziehm's *Flesh Gordon* (1974), and Derek Ford's *The Girl from Starship Venus* (1975). (If the connection between sociopolitical theorists and fantasy pop culture seems far-fetched, we might well consider Jill Lepore's revelation that the cartoon character Wonder Woman was partially based on birth-control activist Margaret Sanger.[27]) Many of these films feature machines that manipulate libido for sociopolitical purposes. In the film *Flesh Gordon*, for example, the earth is menaced by a 'sex ray' that sends people into a libidinous frenzy. Vadim's *Barbarella*, which follows the interplanetary mission of a 'five-star, double-rated astronaticatrix', brings together a Reichian sex machine and Orwellian orgasm control with Huxleyan fashion and wit. *Barbarella* exploits several of the most dramatic technological and scientific developments in postwar culture: space exploration, nuclear anxiety, and reproductive technology. Amid gloriously low-budget landscapes and psychedelic special effects, Barbarella (Jane Fonda), wearing glamorously kinky leather, PVC, fur, and plastic outfits that rival Lenina Crowne's, braves snapping dolls, demented children, and a randy, hirsute trapper who propositions her. She explains that '"On earth, when our psychocardiograms are in harmony and we wish to make love [...] we take an exaltation transference pill"' and touch hands '"for one minute or until full rapport is achieved."' As for sex, Barbarella reports, "nobody's done that for centuries. Nobody except the very poor. [...] It was proven to be a distraction and a danger to maximum efficiency and it was pointless to continue when other supports for ego support and self-esteem were made available."' She gamely goes along with her less enlightened male companion, and she is surprised to find, as she concedes in a postcoital daze, that "'the old-fashioned ways are best of all."'

The film reaches its climax when Barbarella is captured by an evil scientist and imprisoned inside his Daliesque musical instrument called The Excessive Machine. The scientist plays the 'Sonata for the Execution of Various Young Women' and the keys caress Barbarella's body. She is told: "'You will die of pleasure."' As the music attains its cacophonous peak, her eyes roll back in her head. The machine starts to moan in sympathy and then smoke as flames rise. Barbarella collapses, sweating and spent, and the shuddering machine grinds to a halt. The scientist berates her: "'You've blown all its fuses, you've exhausted its power. It couldn't keep up with you. Incredible. What kind of girl are you? Have you no shame? ... Shame, shame on you!"'[28] Barbarella eventually escapes and saves Earth from destruction, and pleasure and love conquer all. Technology is trumped by Reichian 'bioenergy', as a machine designed to give a deathly excess of simulated pleasure is defeated by raw orgasmic strength, just as *soma*-like drug-induced ecstasy is overthrown by an old-fashioned roll in the hay.

In its own cartoonish manner, *Barbarella* expresses the utopic hedonism of its era and reflects the century's continuing preoccupation with the sociopolitical function of pleasure. The Excessive Machine scene underscores two major developments in the genealogy of pleasure during the late twentieth century: the impact of new reproductive technologies and feminism. As campy and 'objectifying' as the film was thought to be by some critics, its story of a woman's immense sexual appetite and power draws humor from its political moment, and the second wave of feminism. *Barbarella* launched a woman into space almost 20 years before the USA would do so.[29]

There is no hint of the women's movement in *Brave New World* but rather a flattening of gender differences: an assimilation of women to social practices of ectogenesis and reproductive control. No one would mistake *Brave New World* for a feminist novel (in an October 1916 letter to Ottoline Morrell, Huxley wrote: 'the more I try to understand psychology the more mysterious does it become for me ... particularly women, who seem to me ... most of them ... too utterly inexplicable'; *AHSL* 41, ellipses in original), but neither does Huxley emphasize gender oppression. In fact, as June Deery observes:

> It is possible to argue that in some areas, despite its being a dystopia, *Brave New World* offers women a better deal than the contemporary British society of the 1930s. There is no housework, no wifely subjugation, no need to balance children and a career. And if women do not appear to have the vote (which in Britain they had gained only six years earlier), then neither do the men, for all are equally disfranchised in his society.[30]

There are some subtle distinctions between men and women in *Brave New World*: few women seem to have been bred into the very highest class, men still run the organizations (there don't appear to be any female 'professors of feelies'), rule the state, and drive the helicopters. However, everyone is programmed to enjoy the same collective pleasures.

Despite substantial progress across the second half of the twentieth century, the idea of sexual revolution and erotic utopianism lost steam in the decades that followed. In mainstream culture, sexual adventurism became linked to deathliness and a distorted image of strong women. Particularly in the 1980s and early 1990s, with the AIDS epidemic and the backlash against feminism, the wave of femme fatale films such as *Basic Instinct* (1992) reflected not just a skepticism but also a fear of excessive or 'deviant' sexual pleasure. Money, not sex, was now the greatest aphrodisiac, and capitalism underwrote the new hedonism.[31] The historian of sexuality Dagmar Herzog has argued that the sexual revolution as envisioned by Reich and others was stalled in America by the religious right, as well as by 'the triple impact of Internet porn, sexual pharmacology, and the hypersexualization of popular culture and fashion', the contemporary versions of Huxley's feelies, *soma*, orgy-porgy, and zippicamiknicks.[32] However, if the era of utopic hedonism has passed, if the Reichian reverie of sexual revolution has faded, a related dream has persisted in technology, where the legacy of *Brave New World* is strongly felt.

Shortly after the publication of *Brave New World*, in a 1935 *Daily Express* article, Huxley imagines 'the retrospective gaze' of a journalist from 1960 looking back on the interwar period. He devotes considerable attention to prophecies about the cinema: 'As for the talkies, they took to color in the early forties and became stereoscopic about nine years later' ('The Next 25 Years'; *HCE3* 423–4). By the early 1950s, sound film was fully assimilated but mainstream commercial cinema did not take on any more sensual properties, other than becoming colorized (short-lived projects like Smell-O-Vision and AromaRoma notwithstanding), until the early 2000s, when 3-D 'stereoscopic' films became hugely popular. Yet commercial films are still incapable of delivering haptic effects, such as making audiences feel the hairs on a bearskin rug, or olfactory or gustatory sensations. The achievement of the feelies, the delivery of images that are 'dazzling and incomparably more solid-looking than they would have seemed in actual flesh and blood, far more real than reality' (*BNW* 146), remains elusive in cinema.

However, it is another story in the realm of contemporary technology that most closely resembles the feelies: virtual reality. While the term seems very postmodern, it dates from the same decade as *Brave New World*, from Artaud's modernist manifesto, *The Theater and its Double* (1938), where it was deployed in a more general sense, relating to dramatic spectacle rather than to the hi-tech, applied vision of Huxley's feelies. It took computer science many years to catch up: the digitally generated environments combining sight, sound, and the sensation of inhabiting 3-D space (known as 'presence') now associated with virtual reality were realized in the late 1980s and 1990s. Since then, simulations of touch, smell, and taste have been developed for limited, non-commercial use, but as yet no system offers all of these sensations simultaneously.[33] While the immersive wearable Google Glass flopped, there is a renewed competition to perfect virtual and augmented reality (VR and AR), with Microsoft, Google, Facebook, and other corporate giants aggressively investing in these areas. While VR development in the 1990s was primarily focused on leisure pursuits such as gaming, the field has expanded considerably in recent years to include telecommunications, medical imaging, journalism, and more.

Brave New World is a reference point in conversations about VR and AR far less than one would expect. Instead, cyberpunk authors such as William Gibson (*Neuromancer*) and Neal Stephenson (*Snow Crash*) are more likely to be invoked by VR/AR developers. In 2014, for example, the VR company Magic Leap hired Stephenson as a consultant/'chief futurist'.[34] Perhaps the feelies now seem unsophisticated beside architectures like cyberspace, the Internet, the metaverse, and the Matrix, but *Three Weeks in a Helicopter* actually points to several significant challenges for contemporary pleasure technologies. As VR developers attempt to solve technical issues such as the problem of 'latency' (the delay between the display of graphics and visual perception that makes many people motion sick) to produce a convincing sense of total immersion so that the images are 'realer than real', other concerns remain to be addressed.[35] For example, *Three Weeks in a Helicopter* and the other feely features mentioned in *Brave New World*—that is, 'the famous all-howling stereoscopic feely of the gorillas' wedding' (*BNW* 223) and *The Sperm Whale's Love-Life* (*BNW* 224)—reflect a key fact about emergent technology, including early cinema, video, the Internet, and VR: that it has consistently been propelled by and adopted for the purposes of recreational pleasure and pornography, particularly.[36] While the major multinational corporations currently investing in VR and AR are careful to restrict access to pornographic content using their platforms, and the public demos for products like HoloLens (Microsoft) and Oculus Rift (Facebook) are based on applications for gaming and SFW (Safe for Work) pursuits, parallel porn adaptations have flourished and there is no question that such applications will be massively lucrative.

'In conjunction with the freedom to daydream under the influence of dope and movies and the radio', Huxley wrote, sexual freedom 'will help to reconcile [...] subjects to the servitude which is their fate' (*BNW* xlix). He makes two assumptions here: one, that mass entertainment is inevitably hedonistic and narcotizing, and that it produces politically docile, apathetic citizens; and two, that pornographic pastimes like the feelies are necessarily socially damaging and morally corrosive. Both assumptions are questionable. In our own time, the same technologies that have enabled consumerism and government surveillance to blossom have also produced mechanisms of resistance such as the social media used in the Arab Spring, WikiLeaks, and citizen journalism.[37] Pornography has undergone its own transformation as it has moved away from 'the adult industry' into the hands of amateurs with digital cameras and webcams. The social implications of pornography's accessibility are not yet clear—certainly, they seem to be just as troubling as those of the collectively viewed, state-produced feelies—but the pornification of technology does not necessarily mean political indifference or capitulation to power any more than it inevitably means sexual revolution.

Huxley's conjecture that political oppression is facilitated by decadent pleasures and illusory sexual freedom has not been borne out by history, but other aspects of his vision of futuristic technology are salient. Despite the fact that *Brave New World* barely reflects the big story of the women's movement in the twentieth century, comparing Huxley's imagined world to the current one gives one pause. In 2013, 26 % of the computing workforce was women, and that number falls drastically when one considers the representation of women in the upper echelons of tech management.[38] Furthermore, 2014's so-called 'Gamergate', in which female journalists who criticized misogyny in video game culture were harassed and threatened, underscored the extent to which women are still not part of the decision-making process, the design, or even the audience of certain pleasure technologies.

Another, very Huxleyan, news story about the tech industry in 2014 was that both Apple and Facebook offered female employees the option to freeze their eggs as part of their benefits package. What seemed to some like a generous accommodation of women in the workforce struck others as more of the double standard, 'paying women to put off childbearing.'[39] As with the Malthusian protocol in *Brave New World* that anticipated the oral contraceptives of the 1960s, Huxley's inventions suggest how a 'benefit' or 'freedom' could have a repressive edge.

And what of pleasure, the elixir that makes life in the World State bearable? Today, women's pleasure is still 'the dark continent', underfunded and underresearched in comparison to men's.[40] Viagra monetized the male orgasm, but there is no equivalent for women; scientific studies of women's sexual response are few and far between.[41] Despite a proliferation of narratives about supposedly liberated women's lives and fantasies (chick lit, *Sex and the City*, *Fifty Shades of Grey*), 'VR porn for anything other than the heterosexual male does not exist, leaving women to roam glitchy sex simulator games if they want to get their VR freak on. No company has bothered to make their product compatible with sex toys for women, nor plans to do so any time soon.'[42] The female sex robots that have spiced up fiction since the birth of automata (and that continue unabated even in the bodiless, virtual fantasy of a man falling in love with an operating system in Spike Jonze's 2013 film *Her*) are rarely matched by similarly compelling male robots. Women's autonomy, power, and pleasure are a still-unfolding story of twenty-first-century culture, and Huxley offers no guidance on that front.

That said, as pleasures become increasingly mediated, increasingly digital, increasingly virtual, Huxley's basic questions about the value of different kinds of pleasure and about the correlation between politics and pleasure remain relevant. In becoming increasingly invested in experiences that are 'realer than real', do we abandon our commitment to the real itself? Are we settling for a 'negative utopia'? Even where *Brave New World* is outstripped by reality, Huxley created a fictional framework wide enough to accommodate subsequent decades' fears, excitements, intimacies, and hopes for the future of pleasure.

NOTES

1. G. Orwell, *Nineteen Eighty-Four* (1949), introd. T. Pynchon (London: Penguin, 2003), p. 306.
2. See G. Miller, 'Political Repression and Sexual Freedom in *Brave New World* and *1984*', in D.G. Izzo and K. Kirkpatrick (eds), *Huxley's 'Brave New World': Essays* (Jefferson, NC: McFarland, 2008), pp. 17–25, at p. 17; and T. Horan, 'Revolutions from the Waist Downwards: Desire as Rebellion in Yevgeny Zamyatin's *We*, George Orwell's *1984*, and Aldous Huxley's *Brave New World*', *Extrapolation*, 48.2 (Summer 2007): 314–39.
3. J. Carey, *The Intellectuals and the Masses: Pride and Prejudice among the Literary Intelligentsia, 1880–1939* (London: Faber and Faber, 1992), p. 86.
4. Huxley's 1923 essay 'Pleasures' (*HCE1* 354–7) is a classic articulation of this sentiment: 'Of all the various poisons which modern civilization, by a process of auto-intoxication, brews quietly up within its own bowels, few, it seems to me, are more deadly (while none appears more harmless) than that curious and appalling thing that is technically known as "pleasure." "Pleasure" (I place the word between inverted commas to show that I mean, not real pleasure, but the organized activities officially known by the same name) "pleasure"—what nightmare visions the word evokes! [...] The horrors of modern "pleasure" arise from the fact that every kind of organized distraction tends to become progressively more and more imbecile. [...] In place of the old pleasures demanding intelligence and personal initiative, we have vast organizations that provide us with ready-made distractions—distractions which demand from pleasure-seekers no personal participation and no intellectual effort of any sort' (*HCE1* 355–6).
5. A. Huxley, 'Utopias, Positive and Negative' (1963), ed. J. Sexton, *Aldous Huxley Annual*, 1 (2001), pp. 1–5.
6. M. Atwood, 'Everybody is Happy Now', *The Guardian* (16 Nov. 2007): n.p. Available at http://www.theguardian.com/books/2007/nov/17/classics.margaretatwood (accessed 11 Oct. 2015).
7. Orwell, *Nineteen Eighty-Four*, p. 153.
8. An 'American acquaintance' recalled that Huxley remarked he had 'been having a little fun pulling the leg of H.G. Wells', but then he 'got caught up in the excitement of his own ideas' (see S. Bedford, *Aldous Huxley: A Biography* (Chicago: Ivan R. Dee, 2002), p. 244).

9. Quoted in [Anon.], 'The Story Behind the Story', in *Aldous Huxley's 'Brave New World'* (Bloom's Guides), introd. H. Bloom and ed. A. Goodman (New York: Chelsea House, 2004), pp. 12–15, at p. 14; I. Rosenfeld, *Preserving the Hunger: An Isaac Rosenfeld Reader*, ed. M. Shechner (Detroit, MI: Wayne State University Press, 1988), p. 227.

10. See L. Frost, 'Huxley's Feelies: Engineered Pleasure in *Brave New World*', in *The Problem with Pleasure: Modernism and its Discontents* (New York: Columbia University Press, 2013), pp. 130–60.

11. S. Kracauer, 'The Mass Ornament' (1927), in *The Mass Ornament: Weimar Essays*, ed. and trans. Thomas Y. Levin (Cambridge, MA: Harvard University Press, 1995), pp. 75–86, at p. 76.

12. M. Birnbaum, *Aldous Huxley: A Quest for Values* (Brunswick, NJ: Transaction Publishers, 2006), p. 125; J. Brooke, 'Obituary' (12 Dec. 1963), in D. Watt (ed.), *Aldous Huxley: The Critical Heritage* (London and Boston: Routledge & Kegan Paul, 1975), pp. 462–5, at p. 464.

13. J. Deery, 'Technology and Gender in Aldous Huxley's Alternative(?) Worlds', *Extrapolation*, 33.3 (Fall 1992): 258–73, at 261.

14. See A. Flood, '*Brave New World* Among Top 10 Books Americans Most Want Banned', *The Guardian* (12 Apr. 2011): n.p. Available at http://www.theguardian.com/books/2011/apr/12/brave-new-world-challenged-books (accessed 11 Oct. 2015). See also the discussion of the novel's censorship in Birnbaum, *Aldous Huxley*.

15. W. Reich, 'Sexual Repression, Instinctual Renunciation, and Sex Reform', in J. Escoffier (ed.), *Sexual Revolution* (New York: Thunder's Mouth Press, 2003), pp. 578–98, at p. 586.

16. Reich, 'Sexual Repression', p. 585.

17. W. Reich, *The Mass Psychology of Fascism* (1933), trans. V.R. Carfagno (New York: Farrar, Straus and Giroux, 1970), pp. 202–3 and p. 52.

18. Reich, *The Mass Psychology of Fascism*, p. xiii.

19. Reich, *The Mass Psychology of Fascism*, p. xiii and p. 141.

20. C. Turner, '*Sex-Pol: Essays, 1929–1934* by Wilhelm Reich—Review', *The Guardian* (1 May 2013): n.p. Available at http://www.theguardian.com/books/2013/may/01/sex-pol-essays-reich-review (accessed 11 Oct. 2015).

21. H. Marcuse, *Herbert Marcuse: A Critical Reader*, ed. J. Abromeit and W.M. Cobb (London: Routledge, 2003), p. 53; L. Jäger, *Adorno: A Political Biography*, trans. S. Spencer (New Haven: Yale University Press, 2004), p. 111.

22. N.O. Brown, *Life Against Death: The Psychoanalytic Meaning of History* (1959; Middletown, CT: Wesleyan University Press, 1985), p. 307; H. Marcuse, *Eros and Civilization: A Philosophical Inquiry into Freud* (1955; Boston: Beacon Press, 1966), p. 201 and p. xv.

23. Marcuse, *Eros and Civilization*, p. xxv.

24. See J. Weeks, 'An "Untenable Illusion"? The Problematic Marriage of Freud and Marx', *Sitegeist: A Journal of Psychoanalysis and Philosophy*, 3 (Autumn 2009): 9–26.
25. Orgone Accumulator Building Plan from J. Greenfield, *Wilhelm Reich vs. the U.S.A.* (New York: W. W. Norton, 1974), pp. 368–70.
26. For the *Time* magazine reference, see C. Turner, *Adventures in the Orgasmatron: How the Sexual Revolution Came to America* (New York: Farrar, Straus and Giroux, 2011), p. 13.
27. See J. Lepore, *The Secret History of Wonder Woman* (New York: Knopf, 2014).
28. *Barbarella*, dir. R. Vadim (Dino de Laurentiis Cinematografica / Marianne Productions, 1968).
29. See L. Parks, 'Bringing *Barbarella* Down to Earth: Astronaut and Feminine Sexuality in the 1960s', in H. Radner and M. Luckett (eds), *Swinging Single: Representing Sexuality in the 1960s* (Minneapolis: University of Minnesota Press, 1999), pp. 253–75.
30. Deery, 'Technology and Gender', p. 260.
31. See, for example, L.R. Williams, *The Erotic Thriller in Contemporary Cinema* (Bloomington, IN: Indiana University Press, 2005) and S. Faludi, *Backlash: The Undeclared War Against American Women* (New York: Crown, 1991).
32. D. Herzog, *Sex in Crisis: The New Sexual Revolution and the Future of American Politics* (New York: Basic Books, 2008), p. xiii.
33. See J. Dorrier, 'Virtual Reality May Become the Next Great Media Platform— But Can It Fool All Five Senses?', *SingularityHUB* (28 Sep. 2014): n.p. Available at http://singularityhub.com/2014/09/28/virtual-reality-may-become-the-next-great-media-platform-but-can-it-fool-all-five-senses/ (accessed 11 Oct. 2015) and C.J. Haines, '5 Amazing Upcoming Virtual Reality Technologies (One For Each of Your Senses)', *Curiousmatic* (25 Mar. 2014): n.p. Available at http://curiousmatic.com/5-amazing-upcoming-virtual-reality-technologies-one-senses/ (accessed 11 Oct. 2015).
34. D. Alba, 'Sci-fi Author Neal Stephenson Joins Mystery Startup Magic Leap as "Chief Futurist"', *Wired* (16 Dec. 2014); n.p. Available at http://www.wired.com/2014/12/neal-stephenson-magic-leap/ (accessed 11 Oct. 2015).
35. K. Orland, 'How Fast Does "Virtual Reality" Have to Be to Look Like "Actual Reality"?', *Ars Technica* (3 Jan. 2013): n.p. Available at http://arstechnica.com/gaming/2013/01/how-fast-does-virtual-reality-have-to-be-to-look-like-actual-reality/ (accessed 11 Oct. 2015).
36. One should not overstate this case: military investments in early technology have certainly been far more significant and influential than those of the adult film industry.
37. E. Steel, 'Vice Uses Virtual Reality to Immerse Viewers in News', *The New York Times* (23 Jan. 2015): n.p. Available at http://www.nytimes.com/2015/01/23/business/media/vice-uses-virtual-reality-to-immerse-viewers-in-news.html?_r=0 (accessed 11 Oct. 2015).

38. See L. Gilpin, 'The State of Women in Technology: 15 Data Points You Should Know', *TechRepublic* (8 July 2014): n.p. Available at http://www.techrepublic.com/article/the-state-of-women-in-technology-15-data-points-you-should-know/ (accessed 11 Oct. 2015); and Women in Technology Education Foundation, 'WITEF Facts', *WITEF* (n.d.): n.p. Available at http://www.womenintechnology.org/witef/resources (accessed 11 Oct. 2015); and S. Sandberg, *Lean In: Women, Work, and the Will to Lead* (New York: Knopf, 2013).
39. C.C. Miller, 'Freezing Eggs as Part of Employee Benefits: Some Women See Darker Message', *The New York Times* (10 Oct. 2014): n.p. Available at http://www.nytimes.com/2014/10/15/upshot/egg-freezing-as-a-work-benefit-some-women-see-darker-message.html?_r=0&abt=0002&abg=1 (accessed 11 Oct. 2015).
40. D. Bergner, *What Do Women Want? Adventures in the Science of Desire* (New York: Ecco, 2013) explores the work of scientists focusing on female desire.
41. In August 2015, the US Food and Drug Administration (FDA) approved Addyi, a so-called 'female Viagra'. According to Reuters, 'women who took Addyi in a clinical study had an increase of about one sexually satisfying event per month compared with those taking a placebo. Advocates claim that increase is meaningful. Critics say the small benefit is outweighed by the drug's risks.' See T. Clarke and R. Pierson, 'FDA Approves "Female Viagra" with Strong Warning', Reuters (19 Aug. 2015). Available at http://www.reuters.com/article/2015/08/19/us-pink-viagra-fda-idUSKCN0QN2BH20150819 (accessed 11 Oct. 2015).
42. F. Eordogh, 'When Porn and Virtual Reality Collide (NSFW)' *Gizmodo* (20 Nov. 2014): n.p. Available at http://gizmodo.com/when-porn-and-virtual-reality-collide-nsfw-1660603261 (accessed 11 Oct. 2015).

CHAPTER 6

Huxley and Reproduction

Aaron Matz

The story opens in a familiar way. We are led into a realm both recognizable (central London) and alien (a hatchery and conditioning center, according to the sign above the entrance). It is not immediately clear how we got here. There is a guide to this nightmarish domain, as in the *Inferno*. Here, though, the role of Virgil is being played by a bureaucratic director talking about human ova and gametes.

The bravura opening of *Brave New World* (1932) acknowledges tradition, but the most famous thing about it—perhaps the most famous thing about the whole novel—is its glimpse into an imagined reproductive future. As generations of readers have learned, the novel has barely begun before Aldous Huxley reveals an imminent dystopia where humans are engineered in bottles and conditioned embryonically into classes in order to create a 'stabilize[d] [...] population' (*BNW* 5) that can ensure the stratified social order of the World State. Before 1932 no significant novelist had depicted so prominently the human manipulation of procreation. Here was a novel that did so eminently, in its first pages—and then went even further, revealing that by the year A.F. 632 (AD 2540) procreation would be officially severed from sex, sex leading to procreation would be

A. Matz (✉)
Department of English, Scripps College, Claremont, CA, USA

© The Editor(s) (if applicable) and The Author(s) 2016
J. Greenberg, N. Waddell (eds.), Brave New World: *Contexts and Legacies*, DOI 10.1057/978-1-137-44541-4_6

considered immoral and disgusting, and non-procreative sex would be not only permitted but strenuously championed by the state.

These well-known facts about the book are all true. Yet they have perhaps created in the popular imagination a misrepresentation or simplification of Huxley's attitude toward reproduction: that we are to understand interference into human procreation as itself the great dystopian peril. Or that the value of Huxley's book lies chiefly in the way it anticipates cloning. Huxley was certainly an opponent of the totalitarian procreative regime he imagined for the World State; and *Brave New World* is indeed prescient, sometimes eerily so, of contemporary advances in reproductive technologies like *in vitro* fertilization and cloning. But it is more accurate to say that the 1932 book was part of a much larger kaleidoscopic view of procreation that only the totality of Huxley's work can provide, and that his moral thinking concerning the creation of new life was rather more vexed. He satirized the control of populations, but he fretted throughout his life about overpopulation. He was not as strident an advocate of eugenics as Shaw or Wells, but he never came out against it, and indeed often he was inclined to see its merits. His generally liberal and tolerant attitude on most matters of sexuality never quite stifled a revulsion toward fecundity. His novels very frequently betray a kind of dread at the idea of producing children.

One hazard of dystopias is that they can give the false impression that some opposite course of future action is to be preferred. Indeed, is it even possible to posit an opposite to Huxley's prophecy of our reproductive fate in *Brave New World*? Certainly the idea of governed birth control is presented as a nightmare—and the novel's vast influence on later writers has made this seem like the biggest nightmare of the book—but over the course of his career Huxley devoted much more energy to advocating for birth control, indeed for insisting on its centrality to any possibility of what we now might call a sustainable ecology or politics. Quite often it seems that Huxley saw the creation of people as an ethical quandary in its own right, whatever the method. In this respect the opening scene of *Brave New World* doesn't merely sound an alarm about engineering babies in bottles. It initiates us into a much larger investigation into procreative morality that occupied Huxley from his first novel (*Crome Yellow*, 1921) to his last (*Island*, 1962).

Of all the ironies about reproduction in *Brave New World*, all the ways in which it seems so ill-fitting with Huxley's larger attitude on the subject, the most obvious may also be the most significant. The World State's pre-natal control of human populations certainly appears to be an easy satire on eugenics. The conceit is brilliant—eggs fertilized in receptacles, allowing five classes of people to be created from them, sometimes in great quantities—even if the terminology that Huxley devised ('Bokanovsky's Process', 'Podsnap's Technique') is cruder and more ridiculous than even he probably intended. The Director of Hatcheries and Conditioning, who so dominates the opening chapter with his cold rationalism and supreme confidence, is a useful vessel for the satirist's scorn. He is exactly the kind of figure we might have expected for this role: the self-assured eugenist, who explains everything calmly and meticulously.

But in 'A Note on Eugenics', published only five years before *Brave New World* in the 1927 essay collection *Proper Studies*, Huxley summarizes the standard eugenist views (the division between 'inferior' and 'superior' types, the alarming preservation of 'defective individuals' in greater numbers than ever before, the more than ordinary fertility rates of that population; see *HCE2* 281) without disputing them. Huxley then notes how eugenics advocates have responded to this situation—plots have ranged from 'modest proposals' (*HCE2* 281) of sterilization to the 'wildest schemes for making stallions of men of genius and forbidding ordinary human beings to have any children at all'—but then backs away: 'None of these schemes requires discussion here. In the present essay I am not concerned to argue for or against eugenic reform' (*HCE2* 282).

We could be forgiven for thinking that Huxley is being merely modest in his ambitions. In truth his 'Note on Eugenics' suggests that when he declines to take up the case of debating eugenics it is because he cannot resist much of that ideology's appeal. Huxley voices a peculiar kind of ambivalence on the topic. He does not quite defend eugenics on ethical grounds; this particular essay is free of some of his contemporaries' more racist and noxious attitudes.[1] Huxley floats a specific argument: a society descended mainly from successful, highly gifted, or superior people would result in a state of perpetual conflict, of 'chronic civil war' (*HCE2* 284). A world made exclusively of desirable people would be overwhelmed by their clashing will and ambition. In a sentence that could be easily lifted from *Brave New World* (since this is exactly what Mustapha Mond explains to John, and the very lesson the World State had learned from its Cyprus experiment many years earlier), Huxley claims: 'States function as smoothly as they do, because the greater part of the population is not very intelligent, dreads responsibility, and desires nothing better than to be told what to do' (*HCE2* 284). Huxley thereby has it both ways: he avoids making a moral or ethical argument for eugenics in order to make a sort of political argument against it. And in doing so he sets forth the basic design for his famous novel, in which a manipulation of prenatal life allows precisely that smooth functioning (and where the drug *soma* takes care of the rest).

Indeed 'A Note on Eugenics' can tell us a lot about *Brave New World*, a book that upon a slack reading can seem like a warning about eugenics but which ends up revealing a more resigned attitude. It is in the 1927 essay that Huxley seems to have first used the specific term 'breed babies in bottles' (*HCE2* 283), though the same idea had appeared six years earlier in *Crome Yellow*. Huxley was always interested in the double sense of the term 'breeding'; his dystopian novel, like his essay on eugenics, suggests that he was not averse to considering the biological kind of breeding as a plausible method of enforcing the kind having to do with class.[2] And indeed by the following decade, in essays like 'Science and Civilisation' (1932) and 'What is Happening to Our Population?' (1934), Huxley's advocacy of eugenics became less ambivalent and more conventional: in the first essay his main reservation is only that eugenics 'are not yet practical politics' (*HCE3* 153); and in the second, where he comes out unambiguously for compulsory sterilization of '[i]diots and imbeciles' (*HCE3* 401), he sounds little different from H.G. Wells.[3]

'Eugenics' can seem to us now like a specter haunting mostly the late nineteenth century and the first half of the twentieth. Certainly Nazism has a lot to do with its decline in prestige among intellectuals after 1945. 'Overpopulation', however, has been for those same kinds of intellectuals a menace no less since the war than before it—indeed you could say that it is precisely the energy of argument and worry that fueled the eugenics debates between 1880 and 1945 that was shifted, rerouted, onto the slightly different rhetorical and ideological terrain of the overpopulation discourse that is still with us. In many respects it is overpopulation, not eugenics, that underlies much of Huxley's attitude toward procreation, not only in *Brave New World* but throughout his larger body of work.

His essay 'The Double Crisis', published in the collection *Themes and Variations* in 1950, is a fine indication of this slippage from one way of thinking about population to another. The two crises of Huxley's title refer to what he calls a political or economic crisis (rooted mostly in mid-century totalitarianism) and secondly a 'demographic and ecological' one (*HCE5* 124). It is revealing that by the time of this essay Huxley is still dividing sectors of the population, but earlier allusions to idiots and imbeciles have been modified euphemistically to 'the least intelligent persons' (*HCE5* 128), and there is no more talk of sterilization.

Indeed Huxley's interest seems no longer to lie especially in the question of fit and unfit populations. He is focused instead on resources: on the less polarizing question of whether 'the planet possesses abundant resources to feed, clothe, house and provide amenities for its existing population and for any immediately foreseeable increase in that population' (*HCE5* 125).

Certainly this kind of concern casts Huxley's attitude toward reproduction in a warmer light than did his essays of two decades earlier. It would be unfair, though, to say that Huxley's career traced such an easy shift to a more palatable kind of population worry: in truth his apprehension had always been rooted in a complex interplay of demographic, environmental, and ethical factors. In the postwar writings this is more explicit. Overpopulation turns out to be probably the main concern of the 1958 *Brave New World Revisited*: it is the subject of its second chapter, and it casts a shadow upon all the rest of Huxley's bugbears, like propaganda, hypnopaedia, chemical persuasion—the kinds of threats we would more immediately recognize from *Brave New World* itself. The coming era, according to Huxley, 'will not be the Space Age; it will be the age of Overpopulation' (*BNWR* 10). The view from 1958 is not, in fact, free of eugenist prejudice—Huxley is still distressed by the 'biologically poorer quality' (*BNWR* 20) of the overpopulating masses—but his concerns lie more deeply with the threat of totalitarianism and perpetual war, along with the kinds of shortages and ruin that would give rise to them: soil erosion, the squandering of mineral capital, global overcrowding.

The anxieties of *Brave New World Revisited* can seem like postwar modifications of Huxley's prewar prejudices. Yet he had been thinking about population and reproduction in these terms—not only as a threat from 'inferior' peoples but as a planetary catastrophe in the making—for most of his life as a writer. His finest novel, *Point Counter Point* (1928), is remarkable for its prescience in what we might call ecological apprehension. In one comic scene early in the novel, the right-wing character Everard Webley corners the intellectually ambitious but in most other ways ingenuous figure Lord Edward. Webley wants Lord Edward to support the British Freemen, and when 'politics' fails as a tactic of persuasion he tries 'progress' instead:

> Lord Edward started at the word. It touched a trigger, it released a flood of energy. [...] 'Progress! You politicians are always talking about it. As though it were going to last. Indefinitely. More motors, more babies, more food, more advertising, more money, more everything, for ever. [...] What do you propose to do about phosphorus, for example?' (*PCP* 78)

When Webley, impatient, protests that phosphorus has nothing to do with him or his political aims, he receives this reply:

> 'Then it ought to', Lord Edward answered sternly. 'That's the trouble with you politicians. You don't even think of the important things. Talking about progress and votes and Bolshevism and every year allowing a million tons of phosphorus pentoxide to run away into the sea. [...] You think we're being progressive because we're living on our capital. Phosphates, coal, petroleum, nitre—squander them all. That's your policy.' (*PCP* 79)

Webley finally asks if he wants a revolution or not. But this is the only answer Lord Edward can supply: '"Will it reduce the population and check production?"' (*PCP* 80).

Huxley rarely misses an opportunity to mock Lord Edward: his 'childish habits' (*PCP* 26) are, like Walter Bidlake's indecisiveness and Maurice Spandrell's political naïveté, one of the recurring satiric targets of *Point Counter Point*. But in assigning him this horror of phosphorus loss Huxley is allowing Lord Edward a certain prognostication. We cannot help thinking of the process of 'phosphorous recovery' that Henry will explain to Lenina four years later in *Brave New World*—it is collected from burning bodies at the crematorium and used for fertilizer—and yet Lord Edward is less sinister, and less preposterous, in his obsession. For this imaginary person of 1928 is not foolish when, later in the novel, he returns to the same theme, this time in conversation to his assistant, the would-be Marxist revolutionary Illidge: '"Take coal, for example. Man's using a hundred and ten times as much as he used in 1800. But population's only two and a half times what it was. With other animals ... Surely quite different. Consumption's proportionate to numbers"' (*PCP* 180). Illidge responds that all animals can be expected to take more than they need, though he mostly agrees with Lord Edward about the human squandering of natural resources. '"Chilean nitre, Mexican oil, Tunisian phosphates [...]. One can imagine the comments of the lunar astronomers. 'These creatures have a remarkable and perhaps unique tropism toward fossilized carrion'"' (*PCP* 181).[4]

A tropism toward fossilized carrion: it is difficult to think of a better, a more damning and precise, diagnosis of our present quandary and crisis in the face of global warming. Of course Lord Edward does not manage to predict exactly our contemporary reality. Later in the novel, when he is trying to calculate the precise quantity of P_2O_5 dispersed into the sea, we feel Huxley's ridicule ('He had never been able to multiply correctly'; *PCP* 548) more than his identification. Lord Edward is single-minded to the point of fanaticism, and in this dialogical novel of counterpoint, where monomania is always ironized, that trait is never one to admire. But it would be foolish not to register *Point Counter Point*'s very real worry about environmental degradation and the overpopulation of the planet that underlies it. Lord Edward is no less obsessed with the world population than with the squandering of resources like phosphorus: it is after all 'more babies' that will push such damage beyond repair. His anxiety, meanwhile, spills across much of the rest of the novel. In a different scene it is Philip Quarles (modeled mostly on Huxley) who says to Mark Rampion (based on D.H. Lawrence) that the political impossibility of progress is rooted in overpopulation: "'Industrialism made possible the doubling of the world's population in a hundred years'" (*PCP* 416). Rampion, at the end of a Lawrentian screed about the atrophy of all the vitality of human life, claims that the interlocking problems of industrialism, population, and war will only be solved by the most comprehensive reduction of mankind: "'When humanity's destroyed, obviously there'll be no problem'" (*PCP* 417).

The brilliance of *Point Counter Point* often lies in its ambiguous relation to its satirized object; it is subtler than *Brave New World*. Everyone in this novel is frequently ludicrous, sometimes dangerously so, but this does not mean that the threats they identify, or their regular disquiet, are always themselves to be dismissed. The book's contrapuntal method allows these threats and anxieties to reverberate internally, never fully to emerge as authorial doctrine but never to dissipate either. Lord Edward's dread is both ironized and quite serious. Indeed Huxley's assumption of this essentially environmental fear compounded by overpopulation would require little adaptation when rendered 30 years later in *Brave New World Revisited*. Overpopulation, like its cousin eugenics, was a concern that first registered in Huxley's early books and, in some form, persisted throughout his career. Unlike eugenics, though, it conveys a more capacious aspect of Huxley's constant return to reproductive subjects and dilemmas. Unlike eugenics, which seeks to impose its procreative morality selectively, on specific kinds of people deemed unworthy of genetic perpetuation, overpopulation—in Huxley's rendering at least—was a peril on a planetary scale. *Point Counter Point*, an earlier book than *Brave New World*, was in its way a more mature and prognostic one.

If we are to applaud Huxley for his humane concern about the reproductive future of humanity, we should do so less for his warnings about babies in bottles, and more for his imagination of this other dystopian vision: a world of depleted resources, caused in some portion by overpopulation. This is again his theme in the essay 'Tomorrow and Tomorrow and Tomorrow', published in the 1956 collection of the same name (in the UK the book's title was *Adonis and the Alphabet*). Early in the essay Huxley essentially reprises the conversation between Lord Edward and Illidge, now in his own voice: 'Man is a wild species, breeding at random and always propagating his kind to the limit of available food supplies' (*HCE5* 314). This, according to Huxley, points to the ironic and devastating fact that 'we are living in a Golden Age, the most gilded Golden Age of human history [...]. At an ever-accelerating rate we are now squandering the capital of metallic ores and fossil fuels accumulated in the earth's crust during hundreds of millions of years. How long can this spending spree go on?' (*HCE5* 314). It is one of the more interesting twists of the Huxleyan imagination that the only solution to this familiar problem is precisely the scheme that had been one apparent subject of satire in *Brave New World*. For it is only birth control that holds forth the promise of slowing this spree. Huxley is not sanguine about this promise. The leaders of sovereign states cannot after all agree on other policies like economics, disarmament, or civil liberties. 'Is it likely, is it even conceivable, that they will agree on a common policy in relation to the much more ticklish matter of birth control?' (*HCE5* 315) Huxley wonders. In his view it is almost unimaginable, perhaps only possible under 'totalitarian methods' (*HCE5* 315)—presumably something resembling the World State of *Brave New World*.

Huxley's pessimism about the possibility of universal but non-coercive birth control does not mean he ever relinquished it as a principle or ideal, even as a *sine qua non* for the survival of the species. His morally dubious attraction in his early career to large-scale sterilization gave way, in later years, to a more moderate conviction that only contraception might save us from the interlocking evils of political repression, ecological degradation, and war. In 1936 he had written the foreword to *Birth-Control Methods*, by the Australian doctor Norman Haire; in a letter that year to Haire, Huxley put the case succinctly: 'the important thing is that there shouldn't be too many involuntary babies' (*AHSL* 316). (His letters find him frequently returning to the subject: 20 years later he joked to Max Eastman that '[s]omeone ought to persuade the U.N. to adopt a new motto: Copulation without Population: or alternatively, *E pluribus nihil*'; *AHSL* 462).

Aldous Huxley is the great evangelist, the great oracle, of contraception in English literature. As a writer of the middle five decades of the twentieth century especially, Huxley occupies an important position, coincident with the expansion (in availability and acceptability) of birth control in Western societies. This marks a crucial distinction from earlier novelists—from Thomas Hardy, for instance, in whose novels characters seem doomed to procreate because they possess sexual desire but not contraception.[5] In Huxley birth control has moved from the implied background of the fiction (as in the late Victorian novel, where it may be absent but in which it is precisely such absence that is so significant) to the very explicit foreground. In *Brave New World* contraception is loudly, even ridiculously, paraded: the 'Malthusian belt' with its 'regulation supply of contraceptives' (*BNW* 43) that women like Lenina wear, to say nothing of the 'freemartins', the 70 % of females who are made sterile at birth. Again it is revealing that a mostly satirized target in the 1932 book becomes rather more sympathetically imagined in Huxley's later work. For the relation in *Brave New World* between sexual fulfillment and birth control, between state-endorsed promiscuity and state-enforced population control, cannot endure in Huxley's writing without extensive revision.

In 'Appendix', the final essay of the 1956 collection *Tomorrow and Tomorrow and Tomorrow*, Huxley arrives at a kind of resolution to this lifelong concern, the problem of human sexuality in a world of overpopulation. He writes admiringly of the Oneida Community, especially John Humphrey Noyes's emphasis on male continence or *coitus reservatus*, one of the central tenets and practices at Oneida. By this time Huxley had also become friendly with his fellow Angeleno Swami Prabhavananda, whose teachings in Vedanta included instruction in Tantra. In 'Appendix', Huxley fuses these two sources—Oneida and Tantra—and, via a brief tour of sexual continence in literature, from Petronius to Ben Jonson to the D.H. Lawrence of *The Plumed Serpent* (1926), emerges with a hearty endorsement of the tantric method. Huxley directs his animus at the Catholic Church, which continues to ban actual contraception while only permitting the rhythm method (useless, according to Huxley) and continence (which the Church ostensibly tolerates but doesn't even bother to teach).

'Appendix' might be a minor curiosity among Huxley's many essays were it not for *Island*, his final novel, published in 1962. It is in *Island* where Huxley proposes a kind of culmination or synthesis of his long inquiry into these interconnected themes: procreation, overpopulation, resource depletion, sexual activity, and now Tantra. Fittingly, *Island* begins with petroleum. Its ambivalent and even desultory protagonist, Will Farnaby, has arrived at the forbidden island of Pala. He has been sent by the industrialist Lord Aldehyde, who wants the kingdom's huge oil reserves for his Southeast Asia Petroleum Company. Fossil fuels—a distinct but distant concern in *Point Counter Point*, later a consistent source of anxiety across Huxley's mid-century non-fiction—have in *Island* become the very premise of the action. The novel traces Farnaby's gradual education in the practices and attitudes of the impossibly humane and peaceful island of Pala, even while it is on the cusp of falling to nefarious influences, domestic and foreign, that will spell the end of the paradise.

Critics have long cited Huxley's remark about *Island* (then a work-in-progress) in his *Paris Review* interview: this late book was 'a kind of reverse *Brave New World*.'[6] Many things about *Island* make this true: its sacred drug *moksha* is a happy correction to the earlier book's *soma*, which dulled the masses; its decentralized politics (with no army) is the very opposite of that of the World State. The procreative utopia that Huxley imagines for Pala is no less significant for its rewriting or reversal of the babies in bottles of *Brave New World*. This utopia is based on the very ideology (or methodology) that Huxley had described in 'Appendix'. Early in the book Farnaby is asked whether he knows about *maithuna* or Tantra. Since 'Will had to admit that he had only the haziest notion' (*I* 80), we are supplied with a typical multi-page Huxleyan excursus about the Mahayana Buddhist heritage of the island and especially the 'yoga of love' (*I* 82) that provides the basis of Palanese sexuality.

Maithuna is what the Oneida Community called 'male continence' and the Catholic Church *coitus reservatus*. It is what we would now usually call tantric sex; for his part, Farnaby concludes that it's 'just birth control without contraceptives' (*I* 83). At last Huxley has imagined a perfect kind of procreative scenario: sex is copious; espoused but not enforced; the source of even greater pleasure than an Englishman might have thought possible; and—crucially—only procreative when it is supposed to be. On this last point the Palanese man explaining all this to Farnaby clarifies that *maithuna* is not Pala's only tactic for preventing unwanted populations. Sometimes married people want to have babies, he clarifies:

> 'And those who don't want to have babies, but who might like to have a little change from *maithuna*—what do *they* do?'
>
> 'Contraceptives', said Ranga laconically.
>
> 'And are the contraceptives available?'

'Available! They're distributed by the government. Free, gratis, and for nothing—except, of course, that they have to be paid for out of taxes.'

'The postman,' Radha added, 'delivers a thirty-night supply at the beginning of each month.'

'And the babies don't arrive?'

'Only those we want. Nobody has more than three, and most people stop at two.'

'With the result,' said Ranga, reverting, with the statistics, to his pedantic manner, 'that our population is increasing at less than a third of one percent per annum.' (*I* 86)

We might accuse Huxley too of being pedantic, were it not for the admirably absolute paradise that by dint of being imagined might absolve him of that or any fault. *Island*'s world of tantric sex and free contraception, delivered conveniently by post, is actually utopian—utopian in a way that perhaps nothing in Butler or Swift or More is. It is birth control that underlies the entire logic and functioning of this ideal society. Later in the novel a different character, speaking to Farnaby, makes this axiomatically clear: 'Electricity minus heavy industry plus birth control equals democracy and plenty' (*I* 163); and—rewriting Corinthians to the point of blasphemy—adding an inverse aphorism to make the same point in negative terms: 'Ignorance, militarism and breeding, these three—and the greatest of these is breeding' (*I* 164). In emphasizing the utopian promise of contraception (and other methods of birth control) Huxley is bringing to light something that had long lurked within literary speculations about possible perfect worlds, like *Gulliver's Travels* (1726): the question of controlling populations. The main difference is that Huxley lived in an era of actual contraception. And so he encourages us to understand that a serious utopia can exist right in front of us: it entails the promise of sexual fulfillment—achieved through a tantric awareness of a sexuality that is '"diffused through the whole organism"' (*I* 83)—without the worry of having unwanted children.

'Birth control', Huxley had written a few years earlier in *Brave New World Revisited*, 'depends on the co-operation of an entire people' (*BNWR* 8). *Island* makes this explicit: contraception is as much a matter of social co-ordination as of individual choice or liberty. The island of Pala is similarly invested in a kind of socialized postnatal care of children too. All Palanese belong to a 'MAC': a mutual adoption club, each consisting of around twenty couples of all ages, from blood relations to 'deputy' relations, for the collective rearing of children (*I* 98–9). This family structure is '[n]ot exclusive, like your families' (*I* 98), the highly sympathetic character Susila tells Farnaby. The Palanese version is again reminiscent of earlier utopias, like *The Republic* (Book V) and, in different ways, books I and IV of *Gulliver's Travels*, but with a warm kibbutz-like atmosphere in place of the strictness of those earlier models. The anti-'exclusivity' of Pala's MACs also recalls Hardy's *Jude the Obscure* (1895), in which the title figure criticizes the '"mean exclusiveness"' of the '"excessive regard of parents for their own children."'[7] As in Huxley, a utopian idea of raising children contains the suggestion that we must relinquish the restricted or privileged nuclear family in favor of this communitarian principle.[8]

The logic for Huxley, as for Hardy, is clear: we should be skeptical of having children, but if we go ahead and have them anyway, we should break our habits of assuming that we must rear them on our own. It is similar to Philip Larkin's logic in 'This Be the Verse' (1971): our mum and dad fuck us up, and so therefore we shouldn't have kids ourselves (or at least raise them). It was an idea that had lifelong resonance for Huxley. In his first novel *Crome Yellow*, it is the cold skeptic figure Mr Scogan, in the same passage in which he provides the germ for the eventual babies-in-bottles idea of *Brave New World*—'In vast state incubators, rows upon rows of gravid bottles will supply the world with the population it requires'—who predicts that as a result '[t]he family system will disappear' (*CY* 23). Fifteen years later, in Huxley's 1936 novel *Eyeless in Gaza*, Mary Amberley expresses the same sentiment in a similarly excessive way: '"I've often thought of founding a league for the abolition of families [...]. Parents ought never to be allowed to come near their children"' (*EG* 144). When Anthony reminds her that Plato thought so too, Mary clarifies: '"but he wanted children to be bullied by the state [...]. I don't want them to be bullied by anyone"' (*EG* 145).[9]

Mary's moderation of her initial severe avowal is just as revealing as the avowal itself. Huxley's fiction and essays raise just often enough the idea of communal care for children—and, with the exception of *Island*, they tend to depict parents as so consistently inept—that we should take seriously any proposal that claims to dismantle the family structure for reasons of humaneness. In this respect the 'mutual adoption clubs' of *Island* represent one more way in which Huxley's final novel 'reverses' *Brave New World*. The MACs effectively replace or correct the many rites concerning procreation and children in Huxley's more famous dystopia. The management of procreation or its consequences is still imagined on a comprehensive scale, but postnatal cooperation is substituted for prenatal conditioning.

Brave New World is in fact typical of dystopian fiction for its idea of a nightmarishly massive regulation of procreation and fertility: in *Nineteen Eighty-Four* (1949) Oceania's aim is for a future in which "'[p]rocreation will be an annual formality like the renewal of a ration card'"; and in Huxley's own *Ape and Essence* (1948), only 'two weeks of actual mating' (*AE* 102) are officially permitted in the post-apocalyptic California survivor society.[10] By his last novel, on the other hand, Huxley has kept the idea of an enormous and uniform scale but transformed utterly the practice. As the end of *Island* makes clear, with Pala on the brink of conquest, this utopia—tantric sex and contraception for everybody, and excellent childcare for the children who do come into existence—is too good to last.

For all *Island*'s explicit attention to Huxley's familiar reproductive themes, the book also registers a more subtle and finally more interesting ambivalence about the creation of new life. This is an ambivalence rooted as much in authorial sensibility, in what seems to have been for Huxley a personal and idiosyncratic predisposition, as in any ideological or political position about eugenics, overpopulation, or contraception. Farnaby, Huxley's morally flawed protagonist, is a widower; the marriage had been childless. Late in the novel, when he sees a woman nursing a baby—the image is of a burst bubble of milk and belching—Huxley allows this little insight: 'He was not much interested in babies and had always been thankful for those repeated miscarriages which had frustrated all Molly's hopes and longings for a child' (*I* 212). There is a minor comedy in this premise—that all the talk in Pala about contraception and population has been directed at someone not much interested in children in the first place. But Farnaby's brief moment of contemplation conveys something more serious too, for this aspect of his personality points to a larger Huxleyan tendency. It is a tendency we find in *Point Counter Point*, which even begins with a similar idea. As the story opens, Marjorie Carling is three months pregnant: she feels sick and exhausted, but she hopes that the baby will bring her closer to Walter Bidlake, her lover and the father of the child. For his part, Walter—in love with another woman—is shackled by the situation: "'Why on earth did she ever allow it to come into existence?'" (*PCP* 5).[11]

On one level this opening scene exists to lay bare certain necessary things about Walter: his cowardice, his male aloofness and insensitivity, his unfaithfulness. On another level this exposition provides an intimate domestic window on what will become, in *Point Counter Point*, a theme mostly addressed in macrocosmic terms: the world's overpopulation and its menacing effect on phosphorous and fossil fuels. A novel that features various characters going on at great length about populations begins with one character facing the rather more pressing crisis of his own imminent child.

In spite of his ironic detachment from all these figures, there is a portion of Huxleyan identification in Walter Bidlake's horror of creating new life, and in Will Farnaby's relief that his marriage did not produce any children. What lies at the root of that feeling is something elemental in Huxley's sensibility and imagination. It underlies all the sociological treatises and dystopian prophecies about eugenics, galloping populations, resource depletion, and the role of the state in intervening in such things. But this feeling is individual and eccentric before it is political. It is perhaps above all metaphysical and aesthetic. Indeed we would be misreading *Island* if we did not recognize the authorial sympathy for the Buddhist foundations of birth control in Pala:

> They were good Buddhists, and every good Buddhist knows that begetting is merely postponed assassination. Do your best to get off the Wheel of Birth and Death, and for heaven's sake don't go about putting superfluous victims onto the Wheel. For a good Buddhist, birth control makes metaphysical sense. (*I* 91)

I call this both 'metaphysical' and 'aesthetic' because for Huxley these two categories were never far apart. The ascetic or abstinent wish to stay off the wheel is one aspect of the Huxleyan uneasiness or squeamishness before the untidiness of fecund reality. We need think only of the scene in the last chapter of *Island* where Farnaby watches with a kind of fascinated horror as two praying mantises copulate; in the midst of the action the female devours the head of the male. Despite his attraction to sexual subjects Huxley could never quite contain his revulsion for mating (in this respect the scene reveals a palpable anxiety about female sexuality in particular: the same is true of *Brave New World*). The general sexual paradise of *Island* represents a certain kind of wish fulfillment, to be sure, but the praying mantises—and indeed the half-repellent, half-prurient sexuality of *Brave New World*—come closer to Huxley's authentic sensibility. And of course this was a matter not just of sexuality in the broadest sense but of human procreation especially. It was his frequent aversion toward the individual act of procreation—the sex act and the moment of conception—that motivated Huxley's more theoretical opinions about human populations.

One recurring image in Huxley's books captures this tendency with impressive economy. In *Brave New World* first, where the Director of Hatcheries and Conditioning explains the modern fertilizing process:

> (and he now took them to watch the operation) this receptacle was immersed in a warm bouillon containing free-swimming spermatozoa—at a minimum concentration of one hundred thousand per cubic centimetre, he insisted; and how, after ten minutes, the container was lifted out of the liquor and its contents re-examined; how, if any of the eggs remained unfertilized, it was again immersed, and if necessary, yet again; how the fertilized ova went back to the incubators[.] (*BNW* 3)

Later in the novel we are back with the Director in the Centre:

> Under the microscopes, their long tails furiously lashing, spermatozoa were burrowing head first into the eggs; and, fertilized, the eggs were expanding[.] (*BNW* 127)

Lest we think this is an image that only *Brave New World* could generate, here is a scene from *Eyeless in Gaza*: the protagonist Anthony Beavis has been reading Lawrence's *The Man Who Died*, and the sequence where Christ first comes back to life makes him think that other emblems of 'life irrepressibly living itself out' are actually more 'vividly impressive':

> He remembered that film he had seen of the fertilization of a rabbit's ovum. Spermatozoa, a span long on the screen, ferociously struggling towards their goal—the moon-like sphere of the egg. Countless, aimed from every side, their *flagella* in frantic vibration. And now the foremost had reached their objective, were burrowing into it, thrusting through the outer wall of living matter[.] (*EG* 233)

'Life under the microscope', Anthony concludes, 'seemed far more vehement and irrepressible than in the larger world' (*EG* 234). This seems true in *Ape and Essence*, too. The second part of that novel consists of a dystopian script by the screenwriter William Tallis, featuring a grotesque character called the Arch-Vicar:

> 'Copulation resulted in population—with a vengeance!'
> Once again the Arch-Vicar utters his shrill laugh.

> Dissolve to a shot through a powerful microscope of spermatozoa franti-
> cally struggling to reach their Final End, the vast moonlike ovum in the top
> left-hand corner of the slide. [...] Cut to an aerial view of London in 1800.
> Then back to the Darwinian race for survival and self-perpetuation. Then
> to a view of London in 1900—and again to the spermatozoa—and again to
> London, as the German airmen saw it in 1940. (*AE* 91)

A similar Darwinian logic also defines the series of verses that Huxley
called the 'Philosopher's Songs' (first published in the collection *Leda* in
1920). Here is the opening of the fifth poem:

> A MILLION million spermatozoa,
> All of them alive:
> Out of their cataclysm but one poor Noah
> Dare hope to survive.[12]

The spermatozoa of Huxley's imagination are perfect emblems for his liter-
ary-sexual sensibility: they are always swarming, of course, always ferocious
and irrepressible, innumerable to the point of being infinite. They are,
invariably, minatory. They represent not merely the specter of new life but
the threat of overwhelming life, a kind of unbearable fecundity. In this way
you could say they are laboratory images of the very procreative anxiety
that disturbs Will Farnaby, Walter Bidlake, and other Huxley characters. A
kind of moral hesitation about the wisdom of reproduction takes a perverse
aesthetic form, highly stylized in its pictorial effect: millions of spermatozoa, at once human-like (they swim, they struggle) and utterly impersonal.

There is perhaps something juvenile in this recurrent image. It brings to
mind Lawrence's disparagement that Huxley's novels were written by 'a sort
of precocious adolescent.'[13] Huxley's fiction does often suffer from a puerility
in representation—a frequent failure to imagine adults behaving like adults,
for instance—despite the great sophistication of their intellectual play. Still,
the spermatozoa that return throughout his writings might also stand for
an aesthetic distaste for fecundity, for richness of life, that is not necessarily
adolescent. They embody the danger of unrestrained energy, and they reflect
an anxiety—about a world hurtling out of control—that is always especially
acute for writers like Huxley who cherish order and even austerity.[14]

Any study of population or procreation in *Brave New World* that does
not consider this essential point, the way in which the dystopian novel actually transmits an ordinary disinclination on the part of its author, will fail to
understand that novel and that author. The scenes that dramatize the general

abhorrence of fertility—Mustapha Mond's speech in Chapter III about the formerly 'viviparous' (*BNW* 4) methods of procreation and Lenina's disgust, on the Reservation in Chapter VII, when she learns how Linda actually gave birth to John—are ridiculous in their way. But as so often with Huxley, the satire reveals a kind of sneaking sympathy. We cannot help suspecting that Huxley was himself repelled and even horrified by dirt, by messy human processes, and perhaps by biological reproduction. That enduring line from *Brave New World*—'babies in lovely clean bottles—everything so clean, and no nasty smells, no dirt at all' (*BNW* 110)—can be at once a frightening picture of dystopia and a reluctant imagination of paradise.

Similarly, the 'Malthusian blues' that the jazz band plays at the Westminster Abbey Cabaret, with its opening couplet 'Bottle of mine, it's you I've always wanted! | Bottle of mine, why was I ever decanted?' (*BNW* 66), can be both a clever, silly adaptation of a familiar Delta blues conceit and, in its way, a reminder of Huxley's abiding ambivalence about reproduction. The Malthusian blues registers a kind of existential melancholy that in *Brave New World* can often get obscured by the glittering high-concept satire. (We are 'vainly begot', as the Fulke Greville epigraph to *Point Counter Point* reminds us.) As in other contemporaneous satires, like Waugh's *Vile Bodies* (1930) and *Black Mischief* (1932), a protracted satiric fantasy involving population or birth control ends up yielding a rather more desolate sense of procreative doubt. And as with the later writers so indebted to Huxley's example—like Margaret Atwood and especially Michel Houellebecq—the rendering of a looming world is invigorated by an outrageous speculation about future procreative methods while also being tempered by an unmistakable despair about humanity's prospects. It is a testament to Huxley's frequently clairvoyant imagination that he could anticipate so much of our contemporary procreative-skeptical literature, the dominant mode of which is still to dramatize various reproductive dilemmas—whether to have children, how many, and by what methods—with a Huxleyan combination of jesting and dread.

NOTES

1. On eugenics and early twentieth-century writers, see especially D. Childs, *Modernism and Eugenics: Woolf, Eliot, Yeats, and the Culture of Degeneration* (Cambridge: Cambridge University Press, 2001). For a rather more agitated and polemical discussion of the same topic, see J. Carey, *The Intellectuals and the Masses: Pride and Prejudice among the Literary Intelligentsia, 1880–1939* (London: Faber and Faber, 1992).

2. On 'breeding' in the satiric eighteenth-century literature that had a considerable influence on Huxley, see J. Davidson, *Breeding: A Partial History of the Eighteenth Century* (New York: Columbia University Press, 2009).

3. Both essays are collected in A. Huxley, *Between the Wars*, ed. D. Bradshaw (Chicago: Ivan R. Dee, 1994), which was published in the UK by Faber as *The Hidden Huxley: Contempt and Compassion for the Masses*. See also D. Bradshaw, 'Huxley's Slump: Planning, Eugenics and the "Ultimate Need" of Stability', in J. Batchelor (ed.), *The Art of Literary Biography* (Oxford: Clarendon Press, 1995): pp. 151–71 and J. Woiak, 'Designing a Brave New World: Eugenics, Politics, and Fiction', *The Public Historian*, 29.3 (Summer 2007): 105–29. It is in large part thanks to Bradshaw's editorial and critical work in the 1990s that this more capacious view of Huxley and eugenics has become possible.

4. On phosphorus in both books, see J. Meckier, *Aldous Huxley: Satire and Structure* (London: Chatto & Windus, 1969), p. 22.

5. On contraception (or its absence) in Hardy, see A. Matz, 'Hardy and the Vanity of Procreation', *Victorian Studies*, 57.1 (Autumn 2014): 7–32.

6. G. Wickes and R. Frazer, 'Aldous Huxley', in *Writers at Work: The 'Paris Review' Interviews, Second Series* (New York: Viking, 1965), pp. 193–214, at p. 198. These same critics haven't noted, however, that this kind of 'reverse' relationship of a late utopia to an earlier dystopia is characteristic of a very similar pair of books: Samuel Butler's *Erewhon* (1872) and *Erewhon Revisited* (1901). As with Huxley's two books, Butler's mark a major diminution of quality—of satiric bite in particular—from first to second. The analog of Huxley to Butler would be less interesting if Butler's satire were not itself interested in procreative morality (in its 'Birth Formulae' and 'World of the Unborn' chapters)—or indeed if *Island* did not allude explicitly to *Erewhon* in the first place (see *I* 18 and 50).

7. T. Hardy, *Jude the Obscure* (1895), ed. D. Taylor (London: Penguin, 1998), p. 275.

8. See Matz, 'Hardy and the Vanity of Procreation', 24.

9. The announced humaneness of the MACs—they exist to counteract the 'parental jailers' (*I* 100) of Western societies—reflects again how much Huxley was influenced by Butler, in particular the theme of parental ineptitude and cruelty that dominates both *Erewhon* and *The Way of All Flesh* (1903).

10. G. Orwell, *Nineteen Eighty-Four* (1949), introd. T. Pynchon (London: Penguin, 2003), p. 306. See also the appendix to Orwell's novel (p. 349), where procreative sex (*goodsex*: 'for the sole purpose of begetting children') is split from sex for pleasure (*sexcrime*) in a way reminiscent of *Brave New World*, but with one crucial difference: the state's repression of sexual activity is substituted for Huxley's World State's endorsement of it.

11. See also Coleman's aside about women, children, and reproduction ('[d]elightful and horrifying') in A. Huxley, *Antic Hay* (1923; London: Penguin, 1948), p. 54.
12. A. Huxley, *Leda* (New York: George H. Doran, 1920), p. 33.
13. See D.H. Lawrence, *The Letters of D.H. Lawrence—Volume VII: November 1928–February 1930*, ed. K. Sagar and J.T. Boulton (Cambridge: Cambridge University Press, 1993), p. 164; see also pp. 169–70. In saying this Lawrence seems partly to have been referring to the death of the young Phil Quarles in *Point Counter Point*.
14. A final example from Huxley's writings is worth citing. In his essay 'Hyperion to a Satyr' (1956), collected in *Tomorrow and Tomorrow and Tomorrow*, he begins with an anecdote about walking on the beach in Los Angeles with Thomas Mann in 1939. The scene is bucolic—Huxley and Mann talk about Shakespeare—until they notice that the sand 'was covered with small whitish objects, like dead caterpillars' (*HCE5* 325). They realize that they are looking at innumerable condoms ('emblems of modern love', 'Malthusian flotsam and unspeakable jetsam'; *HCE5* 326) discharged in 'orgiastic profusion' (*HCE5* 326) from the Los Angeles sewer system. The essay is mostly about the history of dirt and sewage management, from antiquity to modernity, but the opening image especially recalls the spermatozoa of Huxley's fiction and verse.

CHAPTER 7

What Huxley Got Wrong

Jonathan Greenberg

Speaking of the future in a 1942 letter to his brother Julian, Aldous Huxley asserted, 'the one thing that can certainly be said is that we are totally incapable of foreseeing it accurately' (*AHL* 483). The future, Huxley concedes, is unknowable, a time without substance, what Vladimir Nabokov called 'a quack at the court of Chronos.'[1] Yet it is a surprise to hear this concession come from Huxley of all people, whose fame rests largely on his penchant for sociopolitical prognostication. What, we might ask, would it mean to take Huxley at his word about the future's unknowability? In this essay I suggest that to do so entails questioning our reflexive critical assessment of Huxley as visionary or social prophet. Huxley, like all writers, was bound by his time, and historical hindsight should attend not only to the ways in which his prognostications have been realized, but also to the ways in which they have not. In so dispensing with our notion of the author as a vatic figure, endowed with a far-seeing wisdom rooted in moral bravery, we need not diminish the value of *Brave New World* (1932) or of Huxley's work in general. Instead we can recognize Huxley as a keen if flawed critic of his own present, one whose blindnesses as well as insights can help us to recognize how tentative any analysis of the present must be, whether in 1932 or 2016.

J. Greenberg (✉)
Department of English, Montclair State University, Montclair, NJ, USA

© The Editor(s) (if applicable) and The Author(s) 2016
J. Greenberg, N. Waddell (eds.), Brave New World: *Contexts and Legacies*, DOI 10.1057/978-1-137-44541-4_7

Fredric Jameson is surely not the first to observe how quickly imagined futures, especially utopian ones, become dated. Any 'particular Utopian future', he notes, 'turn[s] out to have been merely the future of one moment of what is now our own past.'[2] Take the cartoon series *The Jetsons*. The show chronicles a future middle-class American family living in 2062, but it was produced in 1962. Nothing, not *Mad Men*, not Audrey Hepburn in *Breakfast at Tiffany's*, not the Zapruder film, summons the early 1960s better than *The Jetsons*. The harmonies and instrumentation of the theme song, the references to the Beatles and beauty pageants, the 'Space Age' design reminiscent of Disney's Tomorrowland, the utter avoidance of non-white characters—these tell us far more about our past than our future. Especially visible from today's vantage is the portrait of the mid-century American family: an infantile, shopaholic mother who doesn't work; a beleaguered father who slaves away for one of two identical corporations; a boy-crazy daughter driven wild by rock 'n' roll; a whiz-kid son whose facility with gadgets embodies a post-Sputnik ideal of American know-how; even an aproned housekeeper, albeit an android one, to help with the household chores. Clearly William Hanna and Joseph Barbera had not yet read *The Feminine Mystique*.

As with Hanna-Barbera, so with Huxley. If we could strip away the pieties about *Brave New World*'s prescience, we might notice not only its keen prediction of test-tube babies and Prozac-like *soma* but also its failures of foresight. In Huxley's future, for example, information storage depends upon gigantic card catalogues—'"Eighty-eight cubic metres of card-index," said Mr. Foster with relish' (*BNW* 7)—and communications technologies are comically dated, as we see when a terrified Deputy Sub-Bursar, faced with a mob of rioting low-caste workers, begins frantically 'looking up a number in the telephone book' (*BNW* 186). Of course, to point out the anachronism of the card catalogue and the phonebook may seem like taking potshots, since these details appear incidental to Huxley's social critique, but they help to make the point: posterity may have no use for what we today regard as the innovations that will change the world, and in the banal details of a near-future novel we can see most clearly its ties to the moment of its origin. Peter Firchow pointed out years ago that '[t]he present is what matters most in *Brave New World*', adding: 'Huxley only uses the lens of future time (as preceding satirists had often resorted to geographical or past remoteness) in order to discover better the latent diseases of the here and now.'[3] Yet Huxley's 'here and now' is now our past, and his vision of the future shows us, however unwittingly, the distance between his present and our own.[4]

GENDER, RACE, DISABILITY

What, then, did Huxley get wrong in *Brave New World*? One limitation to Huxley's vision is the role that he assigns to women in his novel. The society is rigidly patriarchal, far more than today's, and the most surprising aspect of the opening scene is likely to be not the mass-production of embryos but the masculinist bias of the educational system. The students to whom the Director of Hatcheries lectures are described as 'boys' (*BNW* 2)—white boys, moreover, 'pink and callow' (*BNW* 2); evidently the process of opening education to women has, somewhere between AD 1932 and A.F. 632, been reversed. As June Deery notes, every character identified as an Alpha and every figure of power or status—the Director, the World Controller, the Arch-Community-Songster—is male, while women are invariably shown in roles such as nurses, teachers, and factory workers.[5] Lenina and Fanny are never identified by caste, but Lenina is described as a 'nurse' (*BNW* 13) and shown performing the routine work of a technician characteristic of a Beta. Deery notes further anomalies too. A men's changing room is reserved for Alphas, while the women's room is merely designated for 'Girls' (*BNW* 30), with no caste specified. The woman in the novel with the highest professional status, the Eton Headmistress, is called 'Miss Keate'—a title that not only subordinates her to the male Provost, Dr Gaffney, but also presents 'an anachronistic form of address in a society where there is no marriage.'[6] Deery is surely on target in her surmise that this anachronism, like Huxley's representation of women in general, stems not from any satirical attack on patriarchal norms but from blind spots in Huxley's view of the world.

A patriarchal power structure similarly governs sexual behavior in the Brave New World. Huxley did imagine a sexual revolution, one in which the increasing sexual freedom of his own era was taken to an extreme. Yet this revolution is not accompanied by any achievement in women's rights. He gives no sign that the feminist movement has changed patterns of social behavior, despite the accomplishments of feminism during his own lifetime. Although sexual repression appears to be largely eradicated, men retain most if not all of the sexual agency. (Lenina's attempted seduction of John, a key exception, I discuss below.) Sexual freedom in Huxley's future thus means making women more sexually available to men, rather than a greater degree of equality between the sexes, in sex or any other realm of life. Charlotte Haldane teased Huxley about his invention of the Malthusian belt, observing that 'no young lady six hundred years in the future would wear so primitive a garment as a Malthusian belt stuffed with contraceptives when a periodic injection of suitable hormones would afford her ample protection', and Huxley seems not to have noticed that he has, in a world replete with biotechnological and pharmacological innovation, burdened women with the entire responsibility of contraception.[7] Finally, the dating and sexual rituals of Huxley's future retain a patriarchal structure. It is men who desire 'to have' women and ask them out, while women merely accept or refuse. Men even retain social prerogatives such as piloting the helicopters. It is true that Bernard expresses unhappiness with the prevailing objectification of women as 'meat' (*BNW* 39), but his criticism stems less from moral conviction than from envy of more sexually successful rivals. Indeed, once Bernard gains fame through his association with John, he starts to pile up his own conquests, forgetting his distaste for viewing women as objects. In short, Huxley's revulsion, and his satire, extend only to the promiscuity of the Brave New Worlders, not to the power imbalance that accompanies this promiscuity. Indeed Huxley himself displays something of Bernard's hypocrisy. His lurid (if, by today's standards, tame) introduction of a nearly naked Lenina in a locker room amid 'a deafening chaos of arms and bosoms and underclothing', along with his images of machines 'kneading and sucking the firm and sunburnt flesh of eighty superb female specimens' (*BNW* 30), appears today as a provocation that conceals its voyeuristic excitement under a pose of blasé worldliness.

As the novel's most prominent female character, Lenina offers an opportunity for Huxley to critique the patriarchal norms of the Brave New World, and she initially resists her society's normalization of promiscuity, confessing to Fanny that she has slept with no one but Henry for four months (*BNW* 34). But she never questions patriarchy *per se*, and she abandons her advocacy of emotional attachment in a way that suggests a contradiction in Huxley's vision. When Lenina falls in love with John, she is overcome with emotion, lamenting that she has too much 'V.P.' (*BNW* 163–4), or violent passion. Driven by this passion, and encouraged by Fanny, she tries to seduce John. But John subscribes to a Victorian standard of sexual morality, and links love to marriage. At this point Lenina becomes 'genuinely shocked', and she exclaims: '"What a horrible idea!"'

(*BNW* 168). She instantaneously transforms into a spokeswoman for the free-loving values of the Brave New World, rejecting both the idea of marriage and John's entire ethos of masochistic denial, answering his sound bites from Shakespeare with hypnopaedic slogans and lines from popular songs. She abandons her role as an advocate of monogamy and emotional commitment as John emerges as a more articulate champion of traditional sexual codes. As in the opening shower scene, Lenina here reverts to the woman's fundamental role in Huxley's imagined future: not a dissident who questions the state-imposed ban on love, but rather a sexual object who promotes her own objectification.[8]

If the feminist movement escaped Huxley's prophetic vision, so did the fight for racial equality. Just as women remain 'girls' in the novel, so the few non-white characters are low-caste service workers like those whom Bernard and Lenina encounter in New Mexico: 'an Epsilon-plus negro porter' (*BNW* 87) and 'an octoroon in Gamma-green uniform' (*BNW* 90). Without exception Huxley places Africans among the lower castes and frequently links them to physical deformity. The Delta-minus valets who retrieve Bernard's helicopter are 'small, black, and hideous' (*BNW* 55); a group of 'almost noseless black brachycephalic Deltas' (*BNW* 138) press steel on an assembly line; foundry workers are 'heat-conditioned Epsilon Senegalese' (*BNW* 138). South Asians and East Asians seem to have fared better (if one can judge ethnicity from surnames): the narrator mentions a scientist named Kawaguchi (*BNW* 39) and Lenina has dated a Jean-Jacques Habibullah (*BNW* 75).[9] In contrast, no African, Latino, or Native American names are represented among the elites of the World State. Most significantly, Huxley imagines race in a eugenic context. The Director of Hatcheries articulates stunningly outdated views as he laments the inability of Europeans to breed at the rate of Africans or Asians:

> 'But of course they've done much better', he rattled on, 'in some of the tropical Centres. Singapore has often produced over sixteen thousand five hundred; and Mombasa has actually touched the seventeen thousand mark. But then they have unfair advantages. You should see the way a negro ovary responds to pituitary! It's quite astonishing, when you're used to working with European material. Still', he added, with a laugh (but the light of combat was in his eyes and the lift of his chin was challenging), 'still, we mean to beat them if we can.' (*BNW* 6)

These absurd notions about African fertility are not held up for satiric critique; only the pomposity of the Director's tone is mocked. Instead, such crude ideas actually serve as the basis for a research program that, in Huxley's imagination, proves scientifically workable. The Director even references a 'Pilkington' who, working in Mombasa, 'had produced individuals who were sexually mature at four and full grown at six and a half' (*BNW* 12). Six hundred years in the future, Englishmen still run the show in Kenya.

Furthermore, although stability is the watchword of the World State, the Director is nonetheless motivated by 'combat' and 'challenge' in his efforts to breed Europeans. This suggestion of a Darwinian fertility competition among Asian, African, and European races for primacy on Earth echoes the fears of racial swamping expressed by white supremacist authors like Lothrop Stoddard, and anticipates the crackpot theories of William Herbert Sheldon, the American eugenist whose work Huxley approvingly cites in *Brave New World Revisited* (1958).[10] Thus although some of his public statements link Huxley with a liberal, 'reformist' strain of eugenics, the evidence of *Brave New World* more uncomfortably suggests that his beliefs were bound up with fears of what Theodore Roosevelt and others notoriously called race suicide.[11] Huxley's scientific training apparently was of little use in helping him discern the fallacies of eugenic pseudoscience. If anything, his confidence in the authority of scientific discourse may have made him more susceptible to such fallacious thinking, allowing him to cloak his own class and racial biases in the language of objective truth.

Native Americans fare no better than Africans 600 years from now, excluded from the greater society and preserved as representatives of old, 'savage' ways. Here, however, Huxley does lay in satiric scorn, as when an Eton schoolteacher describes 'a savage reservation' as 'a place which, owing to unfavourable climate or geological conditions, or poverty of natural resources, has not been worth the expense of civilizing' (*BNW* 141). As Carey Snyder has shown, Bernard's and Lenina's trip to the Reservation satirizes a kind of ethno-tourism, popular at the time, which reduces a foreign culture to one more variety of entertainment or spectacle.[12] Yet even though Huxley signals compassion for the squalid conditions forced upon Native Americans, he still makes his dissident outsider the child of two white English parents. John the Savage, Huxley's most articulate spokesman for the old order, must be a true blue Englishman by birth.[13] For all Huxley's satiric edge, he goes soft in the knees when he introduces John: 'The dress of the young man who now stepped out on to the terrace was Indian, but his plaited hair was straw-coloured, his eyes a pale blue, and his skin a white skin, bronzed' (*BNW* 100). John takes his place in a long series of white men gone native that runs from Edgar Rice Burroughs's *Tarzan of the Apes* (1914) through James Cameron's *Avatar* (2009).

Both African-American and Native American culture, moreover, are linked with what Snyder calls 'stereotypes of savagery' common to the era.[14] The community song-turned-orgy that Bernard attends is represented as something like the Christian revivalist meetings that Huxley's friend H.L. Mencken gleefully mocked. The orgiastic behavior is clearly coded as regressive and 'black'. It proceeds to the sound of 'the soft indefatigable beating of drums' (*BNW* 69), which builds to a 'fever of tom-tomming' (*BNW* 72), over which '[t]enderly [a] deep Voice croon[s] and coo[s]', like 'some enormous negro dove [...] hovering benevolently over the now prone or supine dancers' (*BNW* 73). Native Americans are likewise associated with this surrender to bodily instinct, and Lenina connects the 'steady remorseless persistence of the drums' at the snake dance with the rhythmic drumbeats of '"a lower-caste Community Sing"' (*BNW* 97). This 'primitive' behaviour among the Brave New Worlders is a sign of their debasement, their refusal of higher, hard-earned satisfactions, while the same behavior among Native Americans serves to signal the unredeemed (albeit authentic) barbarism of their practices.

Even Bernard Marx reveals racialist stereotyping that was prevalent in 1932 but that now strikes us as historically blinkered. As Adorno notes, Bernard is 'a caricature of a Jew', a 'radical Jewish intellectual' whose critical insights into the flaws of his society are undercut by 'vulgar snobbism' and 'reprehensible moral cowardice' (*AHU* 106). Of course Jews (or religious minorities of any kind) don't exist in the Brave New World, where the only religion is a worship of Henry Ford fused to vestiges of Christian ritual, but Bernard is coded as an insecure, neurotic, weak-willed, and self-serving malcontent, lacking the strength of character possessed by John and Helmholtz. Bernard's failures of nerve, first when his friends stage their rebellion at the hospice, and again when they are brought before Mustapha Mond, are disturbingly derived from his 'inferior', non-Aryan body type: 'Bernard's physique was hardly better than the average Gamma. He stood eight centimeters short of the standard Alpha height and was slender in proportion' (*BNW* 55). As was common in pre-Nazi racial pseudoscience, physical and moral traits are linked, and Huxley ascribes the strongest moral character to John with his straw-colored hair, pale blue eyes, and suntanned white skin.

The representation of both gender and race, then, fits a larger pattern of what John Carey has disparaged as Huxley's elitism. One much-discussed facet of this elitism is his belief in eugenics (just seen in his treatment of Africans).[15] Huxley's essays from this period return time and again to the themes of genetic decline; a 1934 piece, 'What Is Happening to Our Population?', thunders against the rising numbers of 'idiots' and 'imbeciles' in England. It attributes their spread to unchecked breeding among the 'social problem group', predicts that 'in a century or two' as much as 'a quarter of the population of these islands will consist of half-wits', and prescribes forced sterilization as a solution (*HCE3* 401–3). In hindsight, *Brave New World*'s attention to the intelligence and the head shapes of its lower castes reveals to the contemporary reader the radical transformation that views of disability have undergone since Huxley's time. Details like the 'pug-faced' eight-year-old 'twins' (*BNW* 178) in Linda's hospice who stare 'with the frightened and stupid curiosity of animals' (*BNW* 177), or the description of Deltas as 'less than human monsters' (*BNW* 187) startle us because educated sentiment about disability has become markedly more sensitive and humane since 1932. Huxley, however, regards the 'feeble-minded' masses as an enemy, and the rebellion of John and Helmholtz takes the form not of a revolt against their overlord Mond (whom they hold in high regard) but rather of an act of violence against the masses themselves, one that culminates in John 'punch[ing] the indistinguishable faces of his assailants' (*BNW* 187). The mentally impaired, represented as a swarm of ugliness and stupidity, are John's true antagonists. Meanwhile, according to Mond, whose views Huxley seems to be entertaining seriously if not fully condoning, '"[t]he optimum population [...] is modelled on the iceberg—eight-ninths below the water line, one-ninth above"' (*BNW* 197). Mond endorses social stability achieved not only by 'eugenics' but by what Huxley elsewhere calls 'dysgenics' (*BNWR* 19), the deliberate 'breeding' of human beings of 'biologically poorer quality' (*BNWR* 20).

The point here is not to smugly hold up Huxley's objectionable views for censure. It is rather to help us see that in many ways he was not a successful visionary at all, that his 'predictions' often failed to register or foresee significant social changes, especially in the freedom and respect accorded to women, racial minorities, and the physically or mentally impaired. Why did Huxley fail to anticipate these changes? To a degree he was a product of his time, and this is no trivial point; every prognosticator will be limited by the horizons of his historical moment. Still, contemporaneous satires and dystopias—Charlotte Haldane's *Man's World* (1926), George Schuyler's *Black No More* (1931), Nathanael West's *A Cool Million* (1934)—prove more sensitive to these questions, some of them suggesting that the future will bring changes in the ways we think about categories like race and gender. Joanne Woiak suggests that '[Huxley's] fascination with classifying and ranking people—especially according to inborn mental abilities—shaped his skepticism about democracy', but perhaps something close to the converse is also true: that Huxley's deep skepticism about democracy prevented him from crediting those social movements that would flourish in some of the greatest accomplishments of liberalism in the century after *Brave New World*—the expansion of rights, respect, and opportunity to an ever-greater swathe of humanity.[16] The demands of his genre may have played a role here too: suggesting that things are slowly getting better rarely makes for powerful satire.

Huxley's worldview, furthermore, is shaped by his class upbringing, including his formal education. Adorno scores cheap but funny points in describing John the Savage. He calls him 'the type of shy, aesthetic youth, tied to his mother and inhibited, who prefers to enjoy his satisfaction in the lyrical transfiguration of the beloved', then adds: 'This type, incidentally, is bred at Oxford and Cambridge no less than are Epsilons in test tubes' (*AHU* 105). With such a jibe in mind, the reader might see the dialogue with Mustapha Mond not as a clash between two grand philosophical visions, but instead as a petty drama in which three impertinent undergraduates are called into the office of an Oxford don before being 'sent down'. The subsequent scene, in which Bernard and Helmholtz bid farewell to John before their exile, illustrates *Brave New World*'s underlying values:

'We've come to say good-bye', [Helmholtz] went on in another tone. 'We're off to-morrow morning.'

'Yes, we're off to-morrow', said Bernard on whose face the Savage remarked a new expression of determined resignation. 'And by the way, John', he continued, leaning forward in his chair and laying a hand on the Savage's knee, 'I want to say how sorry I am about everything that happened yesterday.' He blushed. 'How ashamed', he went on, in spite of the unsteadiness of his voice, 'how really ...'

The Savage cut him short and, taking his hand, affectionately pressed it.

'Helmholtz was wonderful to me', Bernard resumed, after a little pause. 'If it hadn't been for him, I should ...'

'Now, now,' Helmholtz protested.

> There was a silence. In spite of their sadness—because of it, even; for their sadness was the symptom of their love for one another—the three young men were happy. (*BNW* 214)

This moment of homosocial bonding articulates Huxley's true utopia: a small group of the elect—white, male, Alpha-plus—standing aloof from society, pressing their hands together, rubbing each other's knees. They are happy to suffer for their beliefs, and happy to share their suffering with similarly noble young men.

CULTURE, POWER, TIME

Huxley's misplaced confidence in eugenic pseudoscience and his class-bound mistrust of democracy thus combined to prevent him from envisioning those social changes that from today's vantage stand out as positive achievements of liberalism. Similar limitations may have led to similar failures of foresight in *Brave New World*'s representation of popular culture and technology. Huxley's imagination of the 'feelies', for example, represents little technological or social change from the 'talkies' aside from the introduction of color film and the amusing addition of perfumes spritzed through the air.[17] But the social rituals surrounding cinema-going, the introductory music, and even the titles ('AN ALL-SUPER-SINGING, SYNTHETIC-TALKING, COLOURED, STEREOSCOPIC FEELY'; *BNW* 145) belong firmly to the early thirties. No revolution in computing, communications, and digital technology has occurred, as we note when Bernard waits impatiently for three minutes to complete a transatlantic phone call (*BNW* 89). Movies and TV are not available in the handheld modes of today, nor has the entertainment market yet fragmented from a homogeneous whole into dozens of demographic niches. (Huxley was more attuned to developments in biology than in physics and engineering.) Similarly, the music of *Brave New World* is the product of the Jazz Age, having developed little in 600 years; R & B, rock, punk, new wave, rap, and hip-hop are nowhere on Huxley's horizon.

Huxley may have neglected to imagine developments in the form and content of popular culture because of his disdain for it. In this novel as in several of his others, popular entertainment appears as merely a mass opiate.[18] In Laura Frost's words, Huxley considered mass-cultural consumption as 'intoxication, addiction, deluded reverie, and gluttony', and found it generally 'symptomatic of cultural degeneration.'[19] He links this (ostensibly) regressive nature of mass culture to race. We have seen how African-American music accompanies the compulsory orgies; we should also note, following Frost, that the feely *Three Weeks in a Helicopter*, with its story of a 'golden-haired' Beta-plus woman abducted by a 'gigantic negro' (of no specified caste), draws on a tradition in early cinema of sensationalizing anxieties of miscegenation.[20] Although John Carey's view that such a phobic view of mass culture is characteristic of modernism as a whole is surely wrong, Huxley still fails to foresee the artistic potential of lowbrow and middlebrow culture.

Indeed, the very forms Huxley disparages as mindless distractions— big band jazz and classic Hollywood cinema—are now generally regarded with nostalgia and reverence. Mocking Huxley's dire predictions, film and popular music have, it virtually goes without saying, proved powerful vehicles for trenchant social criticism and lasting aesthetic achievement. Even the most disparaged forms of mass culture have found champions among the intellectual class.

Even a fellow mandarin such as Adorno (whose own view of jazz as fascistic has aged poorly) finds Huxley's opposition between high and mass culture reductive, noting that 'Huxley rather flatly equates [the mind] with the products of traditional culture, exemplified by Shakespeare' (*AHU* 102). Adorno was always on guard lest his and Horkheimer's criticism of the culture industry be appropriated by a traditionalist rearguard, and he uses *Brave New World* to distinguish his position from the conservative one it superficially resembles: 'We criticize mass culture not because it gives men too much or makes their life too secure—that we may leave to Lutheran theology—but rather because it contributes to a condition in which men get too little and what they get is bad' (*AHU* 109). In Adorno's analysis, Huxley's attack on mass culture fails for the same reason that his attack on free love fails: by condemning material satisfaction as such, Huxley relegates the good strictly to the spiritual realm, positing a 'crude alternative of objective meaning and subjective happiness, conceived as mutually exclusive' (*AHU* 112).

Ironically, the most enduring legacy of *Brave New World* may well be its influence on the very popular culture its author scorned. Huxley cannot be said to have created dystopian fiction, but he was an enormously influential practitioner, and the subgenre of novel that he elevated to public prominence has proved enormously hospitable to mass-market fiction and popular entertainment. Huxley enjoys a robust afterlife in dystopian

Hollywood blockbusters like *The Matrix* (1999) and *The Hunger Games* (2012–15), and beyond them in uncounted narratives in television, film, adolescent fiction, and even video games. If we are in fact dumbing ourselves down with popular culture, we are doing it with works derived in some measure from Huxley's own imaginative achievement.

But perhaps the most significant way in which Huxley remains a product of his time is in his vision of how power operates in *Brave New World*. His economic view of the World State posits a culture of disposability: '[e]nding is better than mending' (*BNW* 44), '[t]he more stitches, the less riches' (*BNW* 44). But although this rampant consumerism is indeed very much with us today, Huxley imagined that such consumerism would need to be *compulsory*, forced upon the populace through governmental policy and behavioral training. In *Brave New World*, the World State has been brought into existence by 'the great Economic Collapse' (*BNW* 41), an obvious echo of the Depression; planned obsolescence—which began in the 1930s as a policy prescription to stimulate a moribund economy—has become the law of the land because it is considered economically essential.[21] After the Collapse, an unnamed voice tells us, '[e]very man, woman and child [was] compelled to consume so much a year. In the interests of industry' (*BNW* 42). Huxley thus correctly anticipates a burgeoning consumer market for sporting goods, but in the Brave New World, implausibly, all new games must be approved by the Controllers, and none gains approval unless it requires the purchase of absurd amounts of equipment (*BNW* 25–6). Today, in marked contrast, consumption has exploded not because of social engineering or coerced behavior but because of *de*centralized markets. As Richard Posner notes, Huxley, writing from 'the depths of a world depression', assumed that economic engineering and central planning would always be needed to correct the failures of the market: 'Capitalism was believed to have failed, for lack of sufficient coordination or rationalization, resulting in excessive, destructive competition.'[22] During the Depression and before the collapse of Communism, top-down economic engineering appeared to Huxley as the inevitable endpoint for a capitalist economy.

As with economics, so with psychology. Huxley was in some ways a critic of behaviorism, believing that the human mind has natural drives, and this skepticism emerges in the occasional moments of the novel where conditioning seems to fail. Nonetheless, his Brave New World is governed by the then-popular faith in behaviorist tenets, through which a cabal of World Controllers easily manipulates the minds of millions. The flashiest of Huxley's behaviorist innovations is hypnopaedia, which is shown to have effected profound changes in the thought and behavior of the populace. Yet although this idea has thrived in science fiction and the popular imagination (partly due to Huxley's influence), it has of course never been realized. Still, Huxley took it seriously enough to devote a chapter to it in *Brave New World Revisited*—even though the very scholarship he cites actually casts doubt upon its effectiveness (*BNWR* 115–18). A new idea in the 1920s, hypnopaedia may have captured Huxley's imagination for its novelty and shock value, but it retains at best metaphorical value as a way of representing the unthinking ways that people absorb ideas. Today not only hypnopaedia but behaviorism as a whole is viewed warily by psychologists, who no longer credit grand Skinnerian pronouncements about the infinite malleability of the human mind. As Steven Pinker has declared, '[s]trict behaviorism is pretty much dead in psychology.'[23] Pinker links behaviorism to a Lockean model of the mind as a 'blank slate' that (he argues) has underwritten top-down, utopian schemes ranging from Stalin's genocidal re-engineering of society to Oscar Niemeyer's Brasilia, a failed effort at urban planning.[24]

Nonetheless, the rise of behaviorism, as David Seed has shown, allowed old tropes from Gothic fiction to gain credibility within new narratives of state-sponsored mind control. *Brave New World* is only the most influential of many novels of the inter-war era that envision all-powerful governments using 'scientific' techniques to alter individual consciousness on a mass scale and to cultivate a docile populace.[25] (The imagined governments of utopian and dystopian fiction and the actual totalitarian governments of Europe may have drawn upon a common belief in the feasibility of such large-scale indoctrination.) During the early years of the Cold War, such mind-control narratives initially served an anti-Communist ideology that contrasted Western freedom of thought to totalitarian 'brainwashing', but Huxley and others on the left turned such accounts inside-out, arguing that Western governments and corporations were just as manipulative as their adversaries, and just as invested in the insidious alignment of individual thoughts and desires with the needs of the state.[26] By the time Huxley published *Brave New World Revisited* in 1958, he could confidently endorse popular pseudoscience about 'subliminal messaging', drawing on Vance Packard's best-selling *The Hidden Persuaders* to blithely equate the work of Madison Avenue admen with that of Joseph Goebbels (*BNWR* 51–9).[27] Yet even as Huxley was promulgating such notions, the science behind brainwashing, subliminal messaging, and hypnopaedia was being debunked.[28]

In subscribing to an economic model based on central planning, and a psychological model of a populace easily subject to manipulation by elites, Huxley inscribed in *Brave New World* the opposition between the intellectuals and the masses that Carey lambasts. Indeed, it may be that Huxley's very propensity for playing the prophet, his tendency to make sententious predictions about the future of the human race, derives from this hierarchical view. It made perfect sense to him that an intellectual's role should be to impart his wisdom to the masses. Of course, Huxley was balanced enough in his thought to foresee the problems of utopian master plans and the failures of the elites who made those plans. Yet he ultimately envisioned any resistance to the World State as itself an affair of the elite (Helmholtz, John, Bernard). The conflict in *Brave New World* is the rebellion of one elite against another.

The conception of power that underlies this view is fundamentally a classical model of what Foucault called sovereignty, a model in which, to use a much-quoted line, 'we still have not cut off the head of the king.'[29] The economic and psychological engineering that saturates the Brave New World demonstrates the sovereign model well enough, but we see it also in the behind-the-scenes glimpses of Mustapha Mond and his library of forbidden books. High culture and radical ideas have not been forgotten by an indifferent public; they have been actively repressed by its overlords. And of course, when Helmholtz and John stage their revolt at the hospice, the police are called in (*BNW* 188). Even if the work of subduing the mob is done gently with *soma* vapor and soothing rhetoric, it is still backed by force.

The novel's representation of sexuality similarly illustrates the utopia's dependence on centralized state power. Huxley's vision of sexuality, of course, appears not as one of Stalinist repression but instead as one of permissiveness. Yet when Fanny tells Lenina to sleep with more men, she invokes a sovereign, patriarchal authority: '"You know how strongly the DHC objects to anything intense or long-drawn. Four months of Henry Foster, without having another man—why, he'd be furious if he knew"' (*BNW* 34–5). The orgies are mandatory ('Alternate Thursdays were Bernard's Solidarity Service days'; *BNW* 67) and are run by a humorless 'President of the Group', whose strict insistence on punctuality doesn't feel very orgy-friendly (*BNW* 69). This is not a world in which people attend orgies because they enjoy them; Huxley's pleasures are engineered and thus can hardly count as pleasures at all. (In Adorno's formulation, Huxley 'denies [pleasure] by granting it' (*AHU* 106).) Similarly, the

Director demands properly 'infantile' behavior from Bernard: 'If ever I hear again of any lapse from a proper standard of infantile decorum, I shall ask for your transference to a Sub-Centre—preferably to Iceland' (*BNW* 85). The state may not murder or torture its citizens, but it relies on compulsory exile as an ultimate means of enforcing its norms.

Thus although Huxley would later make a point of opposing the permissive system of his dystopia to the repressive one of Orwell's *Nineteen Eighty-Four* (*BNWR* 4–6), Bülent Diken points out that '*Brave New World* cannot be structurally separated from, but contains within itself its own, *1984* [*sic*].'[30] Huxley's future is Orwellian in that it requires total state control. In contrast, Diken maintains, in today's world of diffused power, 'there is no Big Other [or Big Brother] which commands us to obey' because 'the system is us.'[31] In other words, those features of Huxley's dystopia that have been realized today have emerged without the compulsions of a hegemonic cabal. We have a world of 'disciplinary' power in which, as Foucault would have it, the liberatory narrative of Enlightenment is simultaneously a narrative of control.[32] Huxley cannot conceive of such a Foucauldian model in which power circulates multidirectionally; for him power still flows from the will of the sovereign. With his World Controllers, he thus comes very close to envisioning a paranoid conspiracy theory ironically akin to those disseminated by one of the central targets of his satire, Henry Ford, the promoter and publisher of *The Protocols of the Elders of Zion*.

This centralized, even conspiratorial understanding of power accompanies the elevation of stability to an end in itself, as enshrined in the motto of the World State, 'COMMUNITY, IDENTITY, STABILITY' (*BNW* 1). It eliminates from the design of the Brave New World what economists call unintended consequences or externalities.[33] Of course, the author must make some concessions to instability merely to create a narrative. Without chance or accident no Bernard Marx or Helmholtz Watson would be born to question the Brave New World, and without the unforeseen consequences of the Director of Hatcheries' youthful escapades, there would be no John the Savage to disrupt its hard-won stasis. Still, stability is the norm, and stability demands the gratification of all desire, a world that permits no 'interval of time between desire and its consummation' (*BNW* 37). Huxley's vision requires, then, not only the eradication of sexual or Oedipal antagonism (no mothers or fathers, no sexual rivalry), but also something like the eradication of temporality itself. In a study of modernist fiction, Martin Hägglund links 'the constitutive difference of desire'—the difference between the desiring subject and the desired object—'to the condition of time.' In language reminiscent of Mustapha Mond, Hägglund writes: 'Without a temporal delay there would be no desire, since there would be no time to reach out toward or to aspire to anything whatsoever.'[34] In eliminating such 'temporal delay', *Brave New World* gives us a perpetual present, one in which history is bunk, in which no one fears death, in which human '[c]haracters remain constant throughout a whole lifetime' (*BNW* 47). It is a future that lacks any idea of its own future. Like a *soma* trip, it is out of time altogether because it is so stable that no change can occur within it.

Of course instability, desire, time, and chance cannot be so easily eradicated. Huxley discerned and diagnosed many trends in his own day that would persist or accelerate over the next 80 years, but the methods through which he imagines utopia to be achieved and maintained themselves offer too easy a gratification. Between blueprint and utopia exists no interval or delay; the utopian planners of the Brave New World encounter no resistance to their desires. The most significant omission, therefore, from Huxley's view of the future may not be any specific political development such as the civil rights movement or any technological innovation such as the iPhone, but rather what H.G. Wells identified as the 'kinetic' (*MU* 5) nature of the modern world itself. What *Brave New World* overlooks is the very possibility of overlooking.

NOTES

1. V. Nabokov, *Ada, or Ardor: A Family Chronicle* (New York: McGraw-Hill, 1969), pp. 596–7.
2. F. Jameson, *Archaeologies of the Future: The Desire Called Utopia and Other Science Fictions* (New York: Verso, 2005), p. 286.
3. P. Firchow, *Aldous Huxley, Satirist and Novelist* (Minneapolis: University of Minnesota Press, 1972), p. 119.
4. Jameson argues for the value of fictional futures in helping us 'to defamiliarize and restructure our experience of our own *present*' by providing a '"method" for apprehending the present as history' (Jameson, *Archaeologies*, p. 288).
5. J. Deery, 'Technology and Gender in Aldous Huxley's Alternative(?) Worlds', *Extrapolation*, 33.3 (Fall 1992): 258–73, at 263.
6. Deery, 'Technology and Gender', p. 262.
7. C. Haldane, 'Dr. Huxley and Mr. Arnold' (23 Apr. 1932), in D. Watt (ed.), *Aldous Huxley: The Critical Heritage* (London and Boston: Routledge & Kegan Paul, 1975): pp. 207–9, at p. 208.

8. In an early critique of the novel, Theodor Adorno objected to Huxley's representation of sexuality as 'failing to distinguish between the liberation of sexuality and its debasement', and numbered his fellow Southern Californian émigré among 'those who are less concerned with the dehumanization of the industrial age than with the decline of its morals.' Huxley's revulsion from sexual freedom signals that his 'consciousness is preformed by the very Puritanism he abjures' (*AHU* 103–6).

9. Habibullah probably refers to Muhammad Habibullah (1869–1948), a prominent Indian politician.

10. Huxley quotes Sheldon's claim that '[o]ur best stock tends to be outbred by stock that is inferior to it in every respect' (*BNWR* 20), and, with no further evidence, categorically declares that 'IQ's and physical vigor are on the decline' (*BNWR* 21) [*sic*]. On Sheldon, see R.M. Griffith, *Born Again Bodies: Flesh and Spirit in American Christianity* (Berkeley: University of California Press, 2004), pp. 131–40 and R. Rosenbaum, 'The Great Ivy League Nude Posture Photo Scandal', *The New York Times Sunday Magazine* (15 Jan. 1995): 55–6.

11. J. Woiak, 'Designing a Brave New World: Eugenics, Politics, and Fiction', *The Public Historian*, 29.3 (Summer 2007): 105–29, at 109. On Roosevelt, see D.K. English, *Unnatural Selections: Eugenics in American Modernism and the Harlem Renaissance* (Chapel Hill: University of North Carolina Press, 2004), p. 11.

12. C. Snyder, '"When the Indian was in vogue": D.H. Lawrence, Aldous Huxley, and Ethnological Tourism in the Southwest', *Modern Fiction Studies*, 53.4 (Winter 2007): 662–96.

13. As John Carey scoffs, '[t]hat a savage who had grown up on an Indian reservation among practitioners of fertility cults should emerge, as John does, with the inhibitions and cultural preferences of a late nineteenth-century public schoolboy could not be called a realistic development' (J. Carey, *The Intellectuals and the Masses: Pride and Prejudice among the Literary Intelligentsia, 1880–1939* (London: Faber and Faber, 1992), p. 89).

14. Snyder, '"When the Indian was in vogue"', p. 686.

15. See especially *HH* and Woiak, 'Designing a Brave New World'.

16. Woiak, 'Designing a Brave New World', p. 113.

17. Laura Frost gives him credit for his attention to the 'bodily, visceral experiences' of cinemagoing (L. Frost, 'Huxley's Feelies: Engineered Pleasure in *Brave New World*', in *The Problem with Pleasure: Modernism and its Discontents* (New York: Columbia University Press, 2013), pp. 130–60, at p. 131).

18. See also V. Clark, *Aldous Huxley and Film* (Metuchen, NJ: Scarecrow Press, 1987).

19. Frost, *The Problem with Pleasure*, p. 132 and p. 134.

20. Frost, *The Problem with Pleasure*, p. 459.
21. On the origins of planned obsolescence, see G. Slade, *Made to Break: Technology and Obsolescence in America* (Cambridge, MA: Harvard University Press, 2006), pp. 57–81.
22. R.A. Posner, 'Orwell versus Huxley: Economics, Technology, Privacy, and Satire', *Philosophy and Literature*, 24.1 (Apr. 2000): 1–33, at 5 and 11.
23. S. Pinker, *The Blank Slate: The Modern Denial of Human Nature* (London: Allen Lane, 2002), p. 21.
24. Pinker, *Blank Slate*, p. 170.
25. D. Seed, *Brainwashing: The Fictions of Mind Control* (Kent, OH: Kent State University Press, 2004), esp. pp. xix–viv.
26. Seed, *Brainwashing, passim*. See also M.W. Dunne, *A Cold War State of Mind: Brainwashing and Postwar American Society* (Amherst, MA: University of Massachusetts Press, 2013).
27. Packard's ideas about mind control were shaped by *Nineteen Eighty-Four* (1949), which in turn was influenced by *Brave New World*, making Huxley's citation of Packard (*BNW* 64) a circular reference. See Seed, *Brainwashing*, p. 73.
28. D. Greenberg, *Republic of Spin: An Inside History of the American Presidency* (New York: W.W. Norton, 2016), chapter 34.
29. M. Foucault, *The History of Sexuality—Volume I: An Introduction*, trans. R. Hurley (1976; New York: Vintage, 1978), pp. 88–9. On the concept of sovereignty, see Foucault, *Discipline and Punish: The Birth of the Prison*, trans. A. Sheridan (1975; London: Penguin, 1991), pp. 47–50. See also B. Diken, 'Huxley's *Brave New World*—and Ours', *Journal for Cultural Research*, 15.2 (2011): 153–72, at 156–7.
30. Diken, 'Huxley's *Brave New World*', p. 157.
31. Diken, 'Huxley's *Brave New World*', p. 163.
32. Diken also describes Huxley's misunderstanding in terms of Zygmunt Bauman's distinction between 'solid' and 'liquid' modernities. Huxley imagined a solid modernity whereas society has developed into a liquid one (Diken, 'Huxley's *Brave New World*', p. 167).
33. Posner, 'Orwell versus Huxley', 10.
34. M. Hägglund, *Dying for Time: Proust, Woolf, Nabokov* (Cambridge, MA: Harvard University Press, 2012), p. 3.

CHAPTER 8

Brave New World and Vanity Fair: A 'Draught that Will Make You [...] Lighthearted and Gay'

Carey Snyder

From 1926 to 1928, Aldous Huxley had a feature page in *Vanity Fair*, the stylish American magazine that served upwardly mobile readers as a guidebook to modern art and culture. Although Jerome Meckier noted in 2000 that Huxley's essays should be 'required reading' for students of *Brave New World* (1932), scholars have given scant attention to the novel's periodical context.[1] Yet Huxley's *Vanity Fair* essays—which envision pleasure as an 'appalling' toxin and the comfort of modern society as enfeebling—clearly prefigure his dystopia's critique of a culture of vapid consumerism, ease, and amusement.[2] There is considerable irony in Huxley penning his screed against modern society within the glossy pages of an American magazine that largely promotes the values he satirizes, for *Vanity Fair* styles itself as a 'draught that will make you [...] lighthearted and gay', presenting a fashionable new world of wealth and leisure, full of labor-saving technologies, thrilling diversions, and the trendiest art and ideas.[3] However, by examining Huxley's *Vanity Fair* essays in their original periodical context, we recover not only a greater appreciation of the

C. Snyder (✉)
Department of English, Ohio University, Athens, OH, USA

© The Editor(s) (if applicable) and The Author(s) 2016
J. Greenberg, N. Waddell (eds.), Brave New World: *Contexts and Legacies*, DOI 10.1057/978-1-137-44541-4_8

127

satirical vision that shaped *Brave New World*, but also a more nuanced view of this deceptively light publication.

From 1921 to 1923, Huxley worked as a staff writer for Condé Nast Publications, which included, along with *Vanity Fair*, *Vogue* and *House and Garden*. He characterized his writing for the latter as 'the most fantastic hackwork' imaginable, though 'happily well paid', a sentiment echoed by biographer Nicholas Murray's characterization of this stint as 'dreary diurnal office work' (*MAH* 127) that crowded out Huxley's creative and intellectual writing. Though a contract with Chatto & Windus liberated Huxley from this full-time career in journalism, he continued to produce essays prolifically throughout the decade leading up to *Brave New World*, including 53 pieces for *Vanity Fair* between 1926 and 1930.[4] More than ephemeral essays 'turned out to order' (*MAH* 173), as Murray styles them, these writings launch an implicit assault on the mainstream ethos of Jazz Age America and on modernity in general that in turn would invigorate Huxley's best-known work.[5]

Taking a job with Condé Nast meant swallowing his reservations about publishing in more popular venues, a decision Huxley repeatedly justifies in his letters of the period, rationalizing that highbrow magazines like the *Nation* and the *Statesman* 'besides being hard work [...] pay so atrociously' (*AHL* 216)[6] and that the only lucrative 'papers are those with pictures' (*AHL* 191).[7] The latter certainly includes the graphically sumptuous *Vanity Fair*, replete with illustrations, photographs, and abundant advertisements. Though in February 1922 Huxley slighted the publication as 'not inordinately high i' the brow' (quoted in *HH* 17),[8] his ongoing relationship with *Vanity Fair* throughout the 1920s hints that its value to him exceeded the opportunity for mere 'hackwork'.

Huxley's concern about prostituting himself to a paper 'with pictures', however well paying, emerges from an anxiety shared with other modernists about the growing gulf between intellectuals and mass society, as reflected in a December 1922 letter to H.L. Mencken, in which Huxley laments: 'In twenty years time [*sic*] a man of science or a serious artist will need an interpreter in order to talk to a cinema proprietor or a member of his audience' (quoted in *HH* 19). In his *Vanity Fair* essays, Huxley lays the blame for this trend on the popular press, the cinema, and other modern distractions that sap creativity and render consumers mindless and passive—a state fully and nightmarishly realized by the average citizens of *Brave New World*. Huxley's perhaps facetiously snobbish characterization of *Vanity Fair* as not 'inordinately' highbrow begs the question of where he positioned the magazine in the cultural economy: its large-folio, glossy photo-laden, advertisement-strewn format may have suggested an uncomfortable kinship with the popular publications Huxley derides. However, the playful tone of his disparagement hints at an acknowledgement of the magazine's more slippery and interesting status as neither 'high' nor 'low', but rather middlebrow—poised between mass-circulation weeklies like *The Saturday Evening Post* and more erudite, staid publications like *The Athenaeum* (for which Huxley was an assistant editor, 1919–1920).[9]

Along with *The Smart Set* and later *The New Yorker*, *Vanity Fair* was classified as a 'smart magazine', a marketing niche that George Douglas describes as 'intelligent, thought-provoking, lighthearted, but still substantial'.[10] While affecting an appeal to the frankly affluent who could afford to purchase the luxury automobiles, jewelry, and high-end clothing advertised in its pages, like other smart magazines *Vanity Fair* was in fact more broadly marketed to 'aspirant' readers of the middle class longing for the 'education in sophistication' that the magazine overtly set out to deliver.[11] This pedagogical function was characteristic of middlebrow publications and institutions (like the book-of-the-month club), which sought to explicate high culture for upwardly mobile readers.[12] Its heavily visual component, combined with its frequently glib tone, may have suggested frivolity, but, as Douglas suggests, *Vanity Fair* was 'infused with a seriousness [...] that belied its allegedly frivolous exterior'.[13] Its contents amounted to a smorgasbord of reviews and features covering the cultural spectrum: theater and film, opera and jazz, the Charleston and the ballet, literature, sports, motorcars, and politics. Serious columns, on politics and world affairs, the arts, and current ideas, counterbalance the lighthearted tone the magazine affects.

The editor Frank Crowninshield—modern art patron and publicist for the Armory Show, which introduced Cubism, Fauvism, and Futurism to the American public—turned *Vanity Fair* into a major vehicle for promoting visual and literary modernism, overcoming Condé Nast's objections that this art was too avant-garde for their readership. The May 1923 issue, to take a representative sample, included a review of Jean Cocteau's *Antigone*; Max Jacob discussing Picasso; Dorothy Richardson on talent and genius; Edmund Wilson reviewing works by Sherwood Anderson and Hilaire Belloc; and poetry by Djuna Barnes, G.K. Chesterton, and Edna St. Vincent Millay; along with Huxley's essay, 'Pleasures' (which lambasts the 'auto-intoxicating' tendencies of modern society). Other issues featured works by and essays on Man Ray, Matisse, Van Gogh, Gauguin,

Gertrude Stein, James Joyce, Tristan Tzara, and D.H. Lawrence, among many others. As this cross-section of contents suggests, the magazine could serve as a crash course on modernism. *Vanity Fair* countered the popular perception of the movement's inaccessibility by packaging these selections as ready-consumables—'Literary Hors d'Oeuvres', in the catchphrase of a regular section title, rather than the main course. Yet as Catherine Keyser has argued, the apparent lightness of the fare was often deceptive, as with the seemingly flippant satirical sketches by Dorothy Parker and Anita Loos, which, Keyser persuades, were actually character- ized by razor-sharp irony and wit.[14] While playfully eschewing the image of a highbrow publication, *Vanity Fair* nevertheless promoted both the difficult pleasures of modernism and surprisingly barbed social satire, including Huxley's own.

In a March 1914 editorial, shortly after taking the helm, Crowninshield set the tone for the new *Vanity Fair*, vowing that it would celebrate the nation's 'devotion to pleasure, to happiness, to dancing, to sport, [...] to all forms of cheerfulness'.[15] Though the editorial highlights the maga- zine's intent to inform as well as to entertain—underscoring its aim to chronicle 'the progress and promise of American life' as well as to spot- light the nation's latest amusements—Crowninshield's rhetoric empha- sizes the latter, helping to produce a jubilant, youthful image for *Vanity Fair* in implicit contrast to the serious tone of more conservative periodi- cals.[16] A decade later, in the context of this still-pervasive editorial mis- sion, Huxley's is a dissonant voice in its emphatic rejection of the modern 'devotion to pleasure', and its querying of the very idea of cultural prog- ress.[17] The magazine continued to project a relentlessly cheerful self-image into the 1920s, marketing itself to Prohibition-era America as a legal joy- 'cocktail' that would 'plunge' the reader 'into new pleasures'—an 'exhila- rating concoction' of trendy art, culture, and ideas, readily available for consumption (Feb. 1926).

The February 1926 cover depicting a dance floor crammed with flap- pers and debonair men (by the artist Anne Harriet Sefton, known as 'Fish') epitomizes the magazine's jubilant tone (Fig. 8.1). In this sketch of the Roaring Twenties of popular repute, young moderns amorously clutch each other as they swing and dip with romantic abandon; several couples openly kiss; and one man ogles another's partner. This is the lav- ish, gleeful, free-loving society that Huxley rails against in such *Vanity Fair* essays as 'Fashions in Love' and 'Recreation', as he formulates his satirical themes for *Brave New World*.

Fig. 8.1 Jazz Age Revellers: February 1926 cover illustration by A.H. Fish

Its humor notwithstanding, *Vanity Fair* was also marketed as a guide-book for aspiring sophisticates: a 'resumé and forecast of conversation at the clubs, [or] in smart cafés'; a must-read for those who 'want to keep up with the procession' (vol. 25.5 (Jan. 1926): 115). The promoters bluntly prom-ise that the magazine will make the reader a 'social asset', for 'the more one knows about [...] currents of thought, about the arts, the greater one's suc-cess in business' (vol. 25.6 (Feb. 1926): 119). The implication that cultural capital is a commodity that can 'be bought like a toaster or the latest Model T' would have been repellent to Huxley, whose essays protest the com-modification of cultural products and proclaim the value of arduous mental and creative effort.[18] Equally repellent to the author of *Brave New World*—with its troubling forecast of the death of individuality—would have been the persistent bandwagon appeal of these ads that undergirded the whole editorial mission of the magazine, which aimed to *produce* the distinctive audience to which it was ostensibly marketed. Somewhat ironically, then, Huxley's *Vanity Fair* essays underscore the vital importance of individuality in the face of pressures to conform, as in 'Silence is Golden' (1929), where Huxley rejoices in having overcome a chronic youthful fear of missing the last 'bus' to 'the ever-receding goals of Modernity and Sophistication' (*HCE2* 19).[19] *Vanity Fair* certainly fashions itself as that bus, conveying readers to these reassuringly attainable destinations.

While not unique in its satire of Jazz Age folly, Huxley's voice is still incongruous with the magazine's emphasis on humor, luxury, and con-sumption—as reinforced by the copious advertisements, which outweigh the magazine's other contents by volume.[20] By the *fin de siècle*, ads, rather than newsstand sales and subscription revenues, paid for magazines, and this new prominence helped shape a culture of consumption, in which *Vanity Fair* enthusiastically participated. Driven by the technological innovations that culminated in Henry Ford's system of mass production, national brand advertising responded to the increased supply of consumer goods, seeming to open new 'vistas of free choice and self-improvement' and to outline 'personal and class identities for readers to step into through purchases'.[21] Condé Nast excelled at attracting lucrative advertis-ers, having pioneered the concept of the 'class publication' that targeted a select, affluent readership appealing to the manufacturers and retailers of luxury goods and services; in 1915, *Vanity Fair* could boast 'more lines of advertising than any other magazine.'[22] Accordingly, the visually rich, frequently large-format ads played no small part in crafting *Vanity Fair*'s sophisticated, jubilant, modern image.

The ads reflect the culture of ease, pleasure, and consumption that Huxley criticizes, both in his *Vanity Fair* essays, and in *Brave New World*. Travel ads promise almost utopian idleness and pleasure, often in tropical locations: Mediterranean cruises provide opportunities for 'Luxurious Loafing' and 'Delightful Diversion' (vols 20.3 (May 1923): 21; 25.5 (Jan. 1926): 24); 'Hawaii laughs at winter' (vol. 25.5 (Jan. 1926): 26); 'Troubles have a way of disappearing' in Florida's Coral Gables (vol. 25.5 (Jan. 1926): 14); and Miami is 'Pleasure's winter capital', a 'haven of rest and recuperation', where 'useful lives', having earned a 'respite from the grind', are renewed 'through the magic of warming rays' (29.5 (Jan. 1928): 36). In much the same way, citizens of the New World are revitalized by *soma* 'holidays' and, in theory, by ethnographic and adventure tourism to destinations like the Southwestern Savage Reservation or the North Pole, though Lenina's experiences suggest that such excursions are less than revitalizing.

Sharing the pages with such ads, Huxley's essays ironically rail against the new culture of ease and comfort, historicizing these modern fetishes and lamenting the erosion of ambition, intellect, and imagination they supposedly induce. In 'The New Comfort' (Apr. 1927), Huxley stresses the novelty of modern conveniences like the padded chair, central heating, and the hot bath, which 300 years ago were 'unknown to the greatest kings' (*HCE2* 285).[23] While Huxley admits the benefit of some modern comforts—such as 'rapid and easy transport' that can enlarge the mind by 'enlarging the world', and 'labor-saving devices' 'that 'economize time and energy which may be devoted to mental labor' (*HCE2* 292)—he fears that modern society regards comfort as an end in itself, such that the world risks becoming 'one vast feather-bed, with man's body dozing on top of it and his mind underneath, like Desdemona, smothered' (*HCE2* 292). A similar point is made in 'On Making Things Too Easy' (Jan. 1926), which *Vanity Fair* gives the blunt caption: 'How Modern Inventions and Distractions May Assist in Inducing Mental Decay'.[24] Rather than celebrating the potential artistic agency imparted by the personal camera or the greater access to musical variety proffered by the gramophone, Huxley views these new technologies as part of a move to standardize entertainment and to erode creativity.

Huxley's anti-advertisements for modern technologies run in ironic counterpoint to ads for motorcars, Victrolas, Kodaks, personal movie cameras, and exercise contraptions that will make you 'slimmer and trimmer in a new, easy way', even doing 'the work of exercising for you' (Apr. 1928: 33). These ads enthusiastically celebrate the inventions of the Machine Age, bearing out Roland Marchand's claim that in the 1920s American advertisers positioned themselves as 'apostles of modernity [...] herald[ing] a new society transforming itself at breathless speed'.[25] The ads and articles blur together in the copious copy celebrating the new car culture sweeping America: a May 1923 article announces that 'Ford, Durant, and General Motors Will Be the Year's Storm Centers of Production' (78), while ads for luxury cars like Cadillac, Rolls Royce, and Pierce-Arrow abound. An ad for the Ford motor company serves as propaganda for the new commercial airline industry, described as 'busily turning out new planes to meet the steadily increasing demand'; the consumer is cautioned not to let 'sensational failures in the air blind [him/her] to the steady progress of non-sensational commercial flying. The prairie trails marked by the wrecks of Covered Wagons were soon enough obliterated by farm tractors and disk harrows!' (119). The rhetoric eerily ignores the toll of human lives that the motor of progress apparently demands, much as citizens of Huxley's New World are conditioned to regard the individual's death as irrelevant to the supposed greater good of the social machine (as Henry Foster remarks blithely of the practice of recovering phosphorus from incinerated corpses: '"Fine to think we can go on being socially useful even after we're dead"'; *BNW* 63). An ad for a self-winding watch, which similarly reads like an ode to progress, exalts the modern era as an 'Age of Wonders': 'Man flies round the world, stays aloft for days and travels faster than sound. His ships and motor cars surpass themselves; he sings across a continent and his pictures speak' (Dec. 1928: 22). Ads like this market modernity itself as much as the individual brand or product. A dissonant voice in the chorus, Huxley attacks Machine Age values in his *Vanity Fair* essays, ultimately translating such idolatry into his dystopian vision of the Ford-worshipping New World that adopts the Model T as its most revered symbol.

To Huxley, the cost of living in an increasingly mechanized and standardized society far outweighs the benefits of labor-saving devices and even an improved standard of living. He elaborates on this trend's devastating effects on humanity in 'This Community Business' (Dec. 1929), arguing that society has been transformed into a soul-killing machine:

> Production and yet more production—that is the fundamental law of the machine's being. The necessary corollary to this law is consumption.

[...] The machine murders fantasy and suppresses personal idiosyncrasies. Its slaves must work in the way (the, for most modern workers, senseless, monotonous, and imbecile way) which it finds suitable to its mechanical needs; they must consume the standardized objects it has created. (*HCE3* 223)[26]

These ideas find their expression in *Brave New World* in advertising jingles and endlessly repeated hynopaediac phrases that condition citizens to be rabid consumers: 'In the nurseries, the Elementary Class Consciousness lesson was over, the voices were adapting future demand to future industrial supply. "I do love flying", they whispered. "I do love flying, I do love having new clothes, I do love ..."' (*BNW* 41). The conditioning goes beyond turning the masses into placid consumers: it aims at 'making people like their unescapable social destiny' as cogs in the production-consumption machine (*BNW* 12).

In extending a feature page to Huxley, *Vanity Fair* made a calculated appeal to the smart set—banking that the sophisticated reader could critically scrutinize her joy cocktail and drink it too. The magazine positions Huxley as a 'lone individualist' critiquing mainstream values; a cultural outsider who examines American culture with 'devastating acumen'.[27] Reinforcing this impression, the April 1927 issue features a full-page celebrity photograph of the author, formally attired, gazing out with the disarming directness and sobriety displayed in his monthly column. Writing in the Roaring Twenties in an American magazine, then, from the start, Huxley adopts the role of killjoy—a role not as anomalous as it first seems in the context of *Vanity Fair*'s devotion to sophisticated rather than simple pleasures—denouncing the era's culture of amusement and comfort.

In his 1946 foreword to *Brave New World*, Huxley writes that the totalitarian states of the future will succeed by mastering 'the problem of happiness'—'the problem of making people love their servitude' (*BNW* xlviii)—a problem that is solved in the New World through mass entertainment, sexual promiscuity, and plentiful *soma*. In his aforementioned 'Pleasures' (May 1923), Huxley condemns what he figures as the 'horrors of modern "pleasure"' (*HCE1* 355) such as these—his scare quotes signaling the inauthenticity of the modern version, in contrast to what he figures to be the legitimate pleasures of more enlightened eras.[28] Huxley maintains that historically, even for the masses, civilized pleasures like watching *Othello* or singing a madrigal required mental effort to enjoy, whereas now, in 'place of the old pleasures demanding intelligence and personal initiative, we have vast organizations that provide us with ready-made distractions—distractions which demand from pleasure-seekers no personal participation and no intellectual effort of any sort' (*HCE1* 356). Huxley's frequent pejorative, 'ready-made' (evocative at once of mass-produced fashion and of Dada artists' repurposing of commercial objects as art)[29] bespeaks elitist anxiety about the rise of mass culture, and anticipates Max Horkheimer and Theodor Adorno's theory of the culture industry—the idea that movies, radio programs, and magazines are churned out like any other factory product, rendering consumers docile and content.[30] Under Huxley's umbrella of dubious modern pleasures falls the press, which, he asserts, exists only '[n]ominally [...] to impart information', 'its real function [being] to provide, like the cinema, a distraction which shall occupy the mind without demanding [...] the fatigue of a single thought' (*HCE1* 356). Leisure, like work, requires 'no mental effort, no individuality, no initiative' but is 'mechanically stereotyped' (*HCE1* 356). Rather than an exhilarating cocktail, Huxley treats the amusements celebrated in the magazine's pages as the most deadly of postwar 'poisons'. (As Laura Frost notes, this suspicion of 'somatic, accessible pleasures' is a hallmark of modernist writing, which frequently depicts such allures as vacuous and dangerous.[31]) This dichotomy of supposedly authentic pleasures versus spurious ones is replayed in *Brave New World* in Huxley's contrasting of the implicitly worthy, difficult pleasures of Shakespeare with the formulaic cinematic 'feelies' that epitomize the mind-numbing appeal of mass culture.

Huxley continues this assault on what he dubs the 1920s' 'Good Time' culture in 'Recreations' (July 1927): 'all over the world, in thousands upon thousands of hotels and cabarets, casinos and restaurants and night clubs, an exactly similar Good Time is being supplied, ready made and standardized, by those whose business it is to sell it' (*HCE2* 86).[32] A by-product of new technologies of transportation and communication, the standardization of leisure activities repels Huxley. He further laments the commodification of sport (in a magazine that faithfully covers sporting events and advertises the latest athletic fashions and equipment), expressing nostalgia for the days when 'amateur athletics were still amateurish' (*HCE2* 86) and likening the rise of spectator sports to the gladiatorial shows of ancient Rome. Like Roman spectacle, according to Huxley, Good Time culture quells potential discontent among the masses. It is easy to see the extension of these ideas in the giddy, drugged citizens of *Brave New World*.

In lambasting Good Timers, Huxley challenges readers not only to reflect critically on their potentially mindless mass-produced pleasures, but also to resist the emotional manipulations of the modern advertisements that pervade mass-circulation magazines like the one under discussion. In 'The Psychology of Suggestion' (*Vanity Fair*, Aug. 1925), Huxley remarks on the apparently limitless suggestibility of human beings, who can be persuaded to 'believe or feel anything' and 'to act in the most manifestly irrational and preposterous ways' (*HCE1* 391).[33] Capitalizing on this weakness for suggestion is not only political propaganda but also the 'flourishing, exuberant' (*HCE1* 392) modern advertising industry, which, Huxley observes, succeeds in manufacturing desires for products 'that are not naturally in universal demand' through 'endless repetition' (*HCE1* 393) and emotional appeals to the 'primary herd instinct which is in all of us—to our fear of public opinion, our snobbishness, or our sense of shame' (*HCE1* 394). Anticipating Raymond Williams's observation that modern advertising functions as a kind of magic, offering 'charms and expedients' to address problems for which modern society has no answer—like 'death, loneliness, frustration, the need for identity and respect'—Huxley notes that ads appeal to our 'wistful but hopeless desire' (*HCE1* 394) to be ever young, beautiful, part of elegant society.[34] The implication is that advertisers inadvertently seduce readers with an impossibly flawless, happy, hygienic, (brave new) world, while disavowing the side of existence that doesn't accord with this utopian fantasy. Huxley's analysis of advertising's power to create an illusory world concurs with Williams's assessment that advertising 'operates to preserve the consumption ideal from the criticism inexorably made of it by experience'.[35] Economic disparity, pollution, disease, old age, and death—all abjected from Huxley's New World—form part of that experiential realm that threatens to pierce advertisers' alluring bubble of an ideal existence for purchase. *Brave New World* dramatizes this piercing of consumer culture's utopian bubble, as when John's mother is dragged before the Director and horrified onlookers: anathema to the culture of youth and beauty, the naturally aged woman is as disconcerting a spectacle in the New World as she would be if she walked onto the pages of *Vanity Fair*.

Huxley's indictment of modern hedonism gained force and focus during his trip to America: as recorded in his travelogue *Jesting Pilate* (1926), for Huxley Los Angeles epitomized the noxious pursuit of pleasure that he would satirize in *Brave New World*.[36] With its enormous portions of food, overflowing cocktails, and unfettered amorous embraces, to Huxley, 'Joy

City' (as he dubbed Los Angeles) was a land of Rabelaisian excess where even the giant Pantagruel 'would have soon died of fatigue and boredom' (*HCE2* 553). In his contemporaneous *Harper's* essay, 'The Outlook for American Culture: Some Reflections in a Machine Age' (Aug. 1927), Huxley blasts consumer society in a passage that could serve as a gloss on *Brave New World*: 'Given food, drink, the company of their fellows, sexual enjoyment, and plenty of noisy distractions from without, they are happy. They enjoy bodily, but hate mental, exercise. They cannot bear to be alone, or to think' (*HCE3* 187).[37] In a word, Huxley indicts modern society for being overly *somatic*—all body and no mind. Given enough prosperity and leisure, Huxley claims, the bulk of humanity will descend to an animal level, abandoning intellectual and creative pursuits.

The restive masses are rendered docile not just by bread and circuses (food and 'noisy distractions') in Huxley's view, but also by a trend toward promiscuity. Huxley's 'Fashions in Love' (*Vanity Fair*, Dec. 1928) objects that modern lovemaking, freed from old social and moral restraints, has become banal.[38] Historically, religious restraints intensified passion by pressuring emotion to run in channels deemed acceptable (monogamous, heterosexual). But in the twentieth century, psychoanalysis stripped sex of its taboo ('all the forms of sexual behavior previously regarded as wicked, perverse, unnatural' have been shown to be 'statistically normal'; *HCE2* 345), thus modern romance has become overly pragmatic: accustomed to talk 'freely and more or less scientifically about sexual matters, the young no longer regard love with that feeling of rather guilty excitement and thrilling shame' (*HCE2* 345). Further, 'the practice of birth-control has robbed amorous indulgence' of its associations with sinfulness 'by robbing it of its socially disastrous effects' (*HCE2* 345) such that sex has become 'a perfectly normal, almost commonplace, activity', like 'dancing or tennis, a sport, a recreation, a pastime' (*HCE2* 346). Huxley's raillery against these other modern pastimes gives an indication of his contempt for the promiscuity trend. 'Rob' is a curious verb to use for the alleviation of the 'disastrous' social stigma that has historically surrounded unchaste women, as is the adjective 'thrilling' to depict the shame that cloaked sexual acts. Lest Huxley begin to sound nostalgic for the good old days of shame, ostracism, and unwanted pregnancies (a nostalgia that it is hard to imagine a female author expressing), he hastens to acknowledge the defects of the old model—namely, 'it inflicted unnecessary and undeserved suffering on the many [...] whose congenital and acquired modes of love-making did not conform to the fashionable Christian-romantic pattern' (*HCE2* 346).

Huxley turns to D.H. Lawrence's 'new mythology of nature' (*HCE2* 347) for a solution—one that restrains promiscuity through an act of will, rather than through external moral sanctions.

Brave New World synthesizes the *Vanity Fair* essays' thoroughgoing critique of modern society into scathing satire. Both reflecting and perpetuating the infantile pleasures of the New World are the popular media that have engulfed the entire cultural sphere: The Bible, the *Odyssey*, and *King Lear* have been replaced by the futuristic equivalents of popular cinema (feelies), jazz (played on sexophones), and tabloid journalism (like *The Delta Mirror*, modeled on the *Daily Mirror* and written 'in words exclusively of one syllable'; *BNW* 56). When not working, citizens are expected to be consuming—whether shopping, playing Centrifugal Bumble-puppy, or taking a *soma* holiday. One detects Huxley's contempt for Jazz Age joviality in the quip that the New World affords 'no leisure from pleasure' (*BNW* 47).

Huxley's protagonists Bernard Marx, Helmholtz Watson, and John all reject the New World's insipid distractions, preferring, like Huxley himself, painful individualism to mindless pleasure with the herd. Coded as a Romantic individualist, Bernard is labeled an enemy to society for preferring walks in the Lake District to Electro-magnetic Golf (*BNW* 77). The would-be poet Helmholtz, too, is flagged as a social menace, when he tires of churning out moral propaganda and endeavors to 'engineer' (*BNW* 157) rhymes that convey his sense of isolation and futility. Reminiscent of Huxley's attempt to free himself from journalism's daily grind for an artistic career, Helmholtz's attempt at verse represents the rejection of commercial culture for the supposed aesthetic purity of poetry. These dissidents' ultimate exile attests to the intransigence of the World State's regime.

Most dramatically, John rejects the New World's foolish amusements, clinging to Shakespeare as the paradigm for desecrated high culture ("*Othello*'s better than those feelies. [...] they don't mean anything. [...] they're told by an idiot"'; *BNW* 194). The World Controller Mustapha Mond explains that social stability depends upon a prevailing mediocrity, if not mass idiocy; and lowbrow entertainment, as much as *soma*, helps maintain a quiescent population. According to Mond, mass production has necessitated the societal shift from a pursuit of 'truth and beauty'—the supposed goals of science and high art—to that of 'comfort and happiness' (*BNW* 201), which Huxley takes to be the facile goals of modern society, as his *Vanity Fair* essays make clear.

John's attempt to incite a social uprising by urging Deltas to refuse their *soma* rations realizes Huxley's thought experiment in 'Recreations'—

'One day, perhaps, there will be a revolt. People will suddenly turn to their neighbors and say, "But why are we boring ourselves in this dull, insipid, and expensive fashion?"' (*HCE2* 88)—except that the Deltas are impervious to John's wake-up call. Like Huxley, John rejects the new comfort and happiness as ends in themselves, claiming the right to suffer, in order to be in touch with the full range of human experiences: '"I don't want comfort. I want God, I want poetry, I want real danger, I want freedom, I want goodness. I want sin"' (*BNW* 211). John's self-imposed exile to a Surrey lighthouse represents a dramatic repudiation of modernity—a return to the natural world, spiritual practices, and non-alienated labor associated with the Savage Reservation. It also represents a rejection of the role of consumer that the New World has foisted upon him: as he tells Helmholtz, '"I *ate* civilization. [...] It poisoned me; I was defiled"' (*BNW* 213, emphasis added). Raymond Williams highlights the oddity of the popular usage of the word 'consumer' to describe 'the ordinary member of modern capitalist society': '"consumption" is a very strange description of our ordinary use of goods and services. [...] [Yet] it is as consumers that the majority of people are seen. We are the market, which the system of industrial production has organized. We are the channels along which the product flows and disappears'.[39] John's ritual self-purification with purgative mustard rejects the dehumanizing production-consumption loop, recasting consumer culture as defilement, while subverting the discourse of 'civilization' as hygienically superior to 'savage' life. Like Huxley, John deems this culture of false pleasure 'poisonous'.

At first glance, Lenina Crowne epitomizes the modern values that *Brave New World* satirizes. An unquestioning consumer, she sports trendy fashions (for '[e]nding is better than mending'; *BNW* 42) and enjoys the requisite sports—responding in bafflement to Bernard's quip that Electro-magnetic Golf is 'a waste of time' (*BNW* 76) with '"what's time for?"' (*BNW* 77). Delighted by the wholly artificial, Club-Med-like atmosphere of the Santa Fe hotel, with '[l]iquid air, television, vibro-vacuum massage, radio, boiling caffeine solution, hot contraceptives, and eight different kinds of scent', Lenina reiterates a modern platitude that the whole work ironizes: '"progress *is* lovely, isn't it?"' (*BNW* 86). 'Lovely' (*BNW* 147) is also her unreflective word for the feelies that John regards as horrifying in their all-encompassing physicality, echoing Huxley's damning view of the supposedly cheap thrills of modern cinema. Apparently content with bottled existence, like most New World citizens, she freely consumes mass culture and commodities alike, staving off potential unpleasantness with liberal doses of *soma*.

Lenina is clearly modeled on the American flappers whose faces Huxley describes in *Jesting Pilate* as 'curiously uniform, unindividual, and blank' and whose scantily-clad bodies promise 'pneumatic bliss', but 'not much else' (*HCE2* 551). The adjective 'pneumatic', borrowed from T. S. Eliot to portray a full-bosomed woman, is echoed in Henry Foster's description of Lenina (*BNW* 37; see also 80), with the implication, as in Huxley's travelogue, that she likewise promises such bliss 'but not much else'.[40] Recurring in period advertisements for automobile tires, 'pneumatic' is an aptly dehumanizing descriptor in this Fordian context, conjuring an image of an inanimate, air-filled, synthetic object. It is also a gendered term, suggesting that even though 'everyone belongs to everyone else', in the New World, the male gaze still prevails. The phrase angers Bernard by suggesting that men view Lenina as 'so much meat' (*BNW* 45) (another product to consume), but Lenina accepts this purely physical interest in her body as normative. Displaying new and evidently threatening female sexual agency, Lenina faithfully practices her 'Malthusian [birth control] drill[s]' (*BNW* 67) and has had dozens of lovers.

Yet, despite Lenina's association with mindless consumerism and easy pleasure, her conformity is incomplete, and the very frequency with which she imbibes *soma* hints at submerged discontentment with New World norms. Lenina's scandalously protracted (four-month) relationship with Henry Foster prompts Fanny to chide her—'"you *ought* to be a little more promiscuous"' (*BNW* 36)—a concern that Lenina's developing interest in the misfit Bernard Marx does little to alleviate. Although she is annoyed by Bernard's abnormality, her subsequent attraction to the Savage suggests a pattern of involvement with outcasts that again hints at Lenina's unconscious resistance to her social programming.

By pitting modern promiscuity against the officially obsolete social practice of monogamous romance, *Brave New World* stages a conflict between the old and new 'Fashions in Love' analysed in Huxley's *Vanity Fair* essay of that title. In the novel, Huxley comically extends the essay's observation that Freudian psychology has stripped modern love of its taboo, with a description of a pair of seven-year olds engaged in a 'rudimentary sexual game' that prompts the Director to remark, to the great amusement of his tour group, 'erotic play between children [used to be] regarded as abnormal' (*BNW* 27). Sexual mores in the novel realize Huxley's misgivings about current trends: birth control in the form of the 'Malthusian belt' (*BNW* 43) is a fashion statement and sex has become another form of recreation—devoid of guilt, shame, or even intense desire, since it is freely attainable and therefore, to Huxley, degraded.

John is the defender of old fashioned monogamy, as practiced on the Savage Reservation, and romance, as enshrined in Shakespeare's tragedies. Romantic passion, Huxley declares in the *Vanity Fair* essay, was a product of religious restraint: the New World has neutered passion by closing the gap 'between desire and its consummation' (*BNW* 37). Schooled by the Bard in the outmoded conventions of romance, John seeks to widen that gap, to endlessly defer consummation. His longing to 'nobly' undergo some baseness to prove himself worthy of Lenina is unintelligible in a world of readily gratified desires, as is his attempt to transform her into the virginal paradigm of Shakespearean romance. When he quotes Prospero's patriarchal warning to Ferdinand to quell his own lust for Lenina—'If thou dost break her virgin knot before all sanctimonious ceremonies may with full and holy rite'—Lenina exclaims: '"For Ford's sake John, talk sense"' (*BNW* 168). Taking his cue from Shakespeare, John adheres to a sexual code that is obsolete. She counters with her own 'poetry': '"Hug me till you drug me, honey. […] kiss me till I'm in a coma"' (*BNW* 170). Huxley thus pits modernity's supposedly facile aesthetic and sexual pleasures against what are posited as the difficult and rewarding challenges of traditional romance and high art.

When his attempt to construct Lenina in the virginal mold of Juliet or Miranda fails, John has recourse to the archetypal counterpart of these figures: the whore. The old, shame-based model of romance that Huxley comes close to nostalgically celebrating in his *Vanity Fair* essay relies upon a virgin–whore dichotomy that polices female sexuality. When John violently turns on Lenina and, in a scene foreshadowing the ending, shouts '"Whore! Impudent strumpet!"' (*BNW* 170), he places her in the only cognitive category available to him: he cannot conceive of sexual assertiveness in a woman as normal, or morally acceptable. The Brave New fashions in love are anathema to the patriarchal mores of traditional romance. Like Huxley, John is troubled by the excessive easiness of modern sexual encounters (read: excessive 'easiness' of modern women), which blur disturbingly for John with the softcore pornographic pleasures of the feelies: Lenina's arms are so 'deliciously soft, so warm and electric that inevitably he [finds] himself thinking of the embraces in *Three Weeks in a Helicopter*. Ooh! ooh! the stereoscopic blonde and aah! the more than real blackamoor. Horror, horror, horror' (*BNW* 168). The feely's bathetic rendition of *Othello*'s tortured romance enacts mass culture's supposed degradation of both art and love: the 'horror' for John (as for Huxley) is that these cheap pleasures are not earned.

John exchanges the New World's easy pleasures for elective suffering in the form of purging and self-flagellation, but though he takes refuge in a recreated premodern world, the novel suggests that he cannot escape modernity. The mass-media machine springs to action, profaning his private rituals by transforming John into the 'Sensation in Surrey' (*BNW* 221), a formulaic tabloid news item. Periodicals across the cultural spectrum, from the *Fordian Science Monitor* to the *New York Times*, participate in this clearly lucrative production of news-as-entertainment, realizing Huxley's criticism of the modern press. Huxley satirizes the sensational journalist's predatory approach to human suffering by enlisting 'the Feely Corporation's most expert big game photographer' to film John's 'frantic and distorted face' (*BNW* 223)—footage that is incorporated, with dark irony, into a widely successful feely (*BNW* 224). John's struggle to free himself from trashy consumer culture ends with his becoming its raw material, refashioned into a consumable product.

In *Vanity Fair* Huxley condemned the tendency among minds 'atrophied by lack of use' to require 'the grossest stimulants of an ever-increasing violence and crudity' ('Pleasures'; *HCE1* 357), akin to Roman gladiator fights. In *Brave New World*, the mindless crowd that throngs John in Surrey dramatizes this crude craving for violent stimulation, as they goad the Savage in unison to do 'the whipping stunt' (*BNW* 226), becoming unwitting accessories to murder. Their nightmarishly uniform chant evokes not only the rising spectacle of fascism but also, in Huxley's analysis, that of mass tourism and mass entertainment.[41]

Lenina's notable distance from the crowd marks her awakening to individuality. As Frost perceptively observes, her characteristics—'sensual, female, modern, available to everyone—code her as an embodiment of mass culture', but here she is distinguished from that maligned sphere: 'on that peach-bright, doll-beautiful face of hers appeared a strangely incongruous expression of yearning distress' (*BNW* 227).[42] Though still flawlessly standardized in her doll-like beauty, Lenina is humanized by her agonized emotional response, expressive of unrequited desire and genuine unhappiness (punctuated by two tears rolling down her cheeks), both anathema to mass culture as Huxley sees it.

Again taking his cue from the Bard, John casts Lenina as Desdemona to his Othello in this final scene, crying 'Strumpet!' (*BNW* 227) as he brutally lashes her. On the one hand, the ludicrous misconstruction of Lenina as a blushing virgin can be read as an ironic means of conveying the supposed degradation of love in the New World. On the other hand, the intertext accords her death the dignity of tragedy. Like Desdemona, Lenina is an innocent here, a 'goodly book' inscribed by (antiquated) male narratives. The violent denouement recalls Huxley's assessment in 'Fashions in Love' that old sexual mores 'inflicted unnecessary and undeserved suffering' (*HCE2* 346) on those who didn't conform to the monogamous ideal. While condemning modern promiscuity, the novel stops short of unquestioningly valorizing patriarchal romantic paradigms.

In the 1946 'Foreword', Huxley famously faulted his novel for offering the Savage only two flawed alternatives: 'an insane life in Utopia, or the life of a primitive in an Indian village, a life more human in some respects, but in others hardly less queer and abnormal' (*BNW* xlii). For Huxley, the antidote to modernity's problems was neither to be found in a technology-dominated future nor in a Lawrentian return to the primitive.[43] While a third, 'sane' alternative is not developed in *Brave New World*, Huxley's *Vanity Fair* essays hint at the possibility for salutary change. A cynical reading might posit Huxley as the readily commodified highbrow, whose absorption into celebrity culture is epitomized by *Vanity Fair*'s inclusion of the author's glossy studio photograph: his satire of consumer culture is not just overwhelmed by the magazine's consumption milieu in this reading, for the celebrity author's satire is part of the sophisticated 'cocktail' that the magazine sells. I want to suggest that Huxley himself was less cynical than this: as Robert S. Baker notes, Huxley's journalism 'was informed by a genuine impetus to engage his contemporaries in a critical dialogue' (*HCE2* xi), and his sustained relationship with *Vanity Fair* presumes faith in a readership receptive to his thoroughgoing satire of modern life. His contributions confirm that the magazine remained open to criticizing the cheery culture of consumption, relaxed sexual mores, and popular entertainment that it simultaneously celebrated. That it was likely profitable for it to do so does not negate Huxley's message.

NOTES

1. See J. Meckier, 'Prepping for *Brave New World*: Aldus Huxley's Essays of the 1920s', *Utopian Studies*, 12.2 (2001): 234–45. While Meckier traces significant thematic links between several of Huxley's essays and his dystopia, he is not interested in the periodical context per se.
2. Huxley asserts that of all modern vices, few are 'more deadly (while none appears more harmless) than that curious and appalling thing that is technically known as 'pleasure''' ('Pleasures', *Vanity Fair*, 1923; *HCE1* 355).

He derides modern comfort in another essay, writing: 'The road has become wonderfully smooth; but the travellers, made flabby by the effortlessness of their journey, lack the strength to push on to remoter goals' ('On Making Things Too Easy', *Vanity Fair*, 1926; *HCE2* 55).

3. Advertisement for the magazine in the February 1926 issue of *Vanity Fair* (p. 119).

4. This three-a-year contract presented its own pressures, though Huxley preferred the rewards of creative writing to his 'strenuous journalistic career' (Huxley quoted in *MAH* 122). Given that one of these books was typically a collection of essays, there was a dual economic incentive for Huxley to continue contributing to periodicals.

5. While Jazz Age America can be read as an implicit target of Huxley's satire within its periodical context, it becomes an explicit target in his 1926 travelogue *Jesting Pilate* and in his 1927 *Harper's* essay, 'The Outlook for American Culture'. However England, where Huxley was living at the time when not globetrotting, does not escape his ridicule.

6. Letter to Robert Nichols (2 July 1923); quoted by Bradshaw in *HH* 17.

7. Letter to Naomi Mitchison (1 Nov. 1920).

8. Letter to H.L. Mencken (5 Feb. 1922).

9. For scholarship on *Vanity Fair* as middlebrow, see F. Hammill, *Sophistication: A Literary and Cultural History* (Liverpool: Liverpool University Press, 2010); C. Keyser, *Playing Smart: New York Women Writers and Modern Magazine Culture* (New Brunswick: Rutgers University Press, 2010); and D. Tracy, 'Investing in "Modernism": Smart Magazines, Parody, and Middlebrow Professional Judgment', *The Journal of Modern Periodical Studies*, 1.1 (2010): 38–63. As Tracy explains, '"[m]iddlebrow culture" includes the increasing number of apparatuses for learning "high culture"—the literary and other artistic productions designated as legitimate, as well as the reading strategies needed to understand them—that appeared in the United States from the 1890s forward' (39–40). These 'apparatuses' include book-of-the-month clubs and smart magazines.

10. G.H. Douglas, *Smart Magazines: 50 Years of Literary Revelry and High Jinks at Vanity Fair, the New Yorker, Life, Esquire, and the Smart Set* (Hamden, CT: Archon Books, 1991), p. 4.

11. Hammill, *Sophistication*, p. 155.

12. See J. Radway, *A Feeling for Books: The Book-of-the-Month Club, Literary Taste, and Middle-Class Desire* (Chapel Hill: University of North Carolina Press, 1997). General studies on modern middlebrow fiction include J.S. Rubin, *The Making of Middlebrow Culture* (Chapel Hill: University of North Carolina Press, 1992) and R. Scholes, 'High and Low in Modernist Criticism', in *Paradoxy of Modernism* (New Haven: Yale University Press, 2006), pp. 3–32.

13. Douglas, *Smart Magazines*, p. 96.
14. See Keyser, *Playing Smart*, esp. pp. 1–6.
15. F. Crowninshield, 'In *Vanity Fair*' (Editorial), *Vanity Fair*, 1.3 (Mar. 1914): 15. Launched in October 1913, the magazine was titled *Dress & Vanity Fair* for the first four issues; Crowninshield came on board in 1914, dropping the emphasis on fashion and remaking the magazine with an emphasis on 'what people talk about' in the smart set.
16. In the May 1914 issue, similarly, the magazine declared itself 'unalterably opposed to gloom, and to gravity, and to all solemn and owlish attitudes of the mind', promising to provide a 'good measure of humor' (F. Crowninshield, 'In *Vanity Fair*' (Editorial), *Vanity Fair*, 1.5 (May 1914): 19).
17. Although space does not allow me to develop the point, it is worth noting that Huxley's was not the only dissonant voice in *Vanity Fair*: equally shrewd critics of modern society included the media critic and future Pulitzer-prize-winner Walter Lippmann, the novelist Theodor Dreiser, and the poet e. e. cummings.
18. L. Newton, 'Picturing Smartness: Cartoons in the *New Yorker*, *Vanity Fair*, and *Esquire* in the Age of Cultural Celebrities', *The Journal of Modern Periodical Studies*, 3.1 (2012): 64–92, at 73.
19. Originally published as 'Silence is Golden', *Vanity Fair*, 32.5 (July 1929): 72, 94. Keyser notes that, paradoxically, smart magazines at once appeal to the individuating quality of 'distinction' and urge consumers to conform to prevailing fashions and tastes (Keyser, *Playing Smart*, p. 22). In this respect, Huxley's individualism fits within *Vanity Fair*'s self-contradicting rhetoric.
20. In the 1920s, the advertisements comprised more than half of the magazine's contents: the March 1927 issue and October 1929 issues, for instance, by page count, comprised approximately 62 % and 67 % advertisements, respectively.
21. R. Ohmann, *Selling Culture: Magazines, Markets, and Class at the Turn of the Century* (London and New York: Verso, 1996), p. 215.
22. Tracy, 'Investing in "Modernism"', p. 17. On 'class publications', see Condé Nast's essay of the same name in *The Merchant's and Manufacturer's Journal* (June 1913): 3–11.
23. Published in *HCE2* as 'Comfort'. Originally published as 'The New Comfort', *Vanity Fair*, 28.2 (Apr. 1927): 62–3, 106.
24. Originally published as 'On Making Things Too Easy: How Modern Inventions and Distractions May Assist in Inducing Mental Decay', *Vanity Fair*, 25.5 (Jan. 1926): 66.
25. R. Marchand, *Advertising the American Dream: Making Way for Modernity, 1920–1940* (Berkeley, CA: University of California Press, 1985), p. 3.

26. Originally published as 'This Community Business', *Vanity Fair*, 33.4 (Dec. 1929): 62, 158.
27. The name 'lone individualist' forms part of the caption to 'This Community Business' (see *Vanity Fair*, Dec. 1929, p. 62). Mencken describes Huxley this way in the caption to Huxley's photograph in the April 1927 issue.
28. Originally published as 'Pleasures', *Vanity Fair*, 20.3 (May 1923): 40.
29. On Huxley's critical view of Dada art, see A. Young, *Dada and After: Extremist Modernism and English Literature* (Manchester: Manchester University Press, 1981), pp. 55–9. The shift from expensive tailored clothing to inexpensive, mass-produced fashions, readily available 'off the rack', evoked anxiety in the upper middle class about the lack of individuality and lack of differentiation from the masses. Men's ready-made fashions gained acceptance in America by the *fin de siècle*, and women's, in the early 1900s; in the more resistant English market, women's ready-made clothing only became widely acceptable after the First World War. See E. Ewing, *History of Twentieth Century Fashion* (Totowa, NJ: Barnes & Noble, 1986) and M. Gaipa, 'Accessorizing Clarissa: How Virginia Woolf Changes the Clothes and the Character of Her Lady of Fashion', *Modernist Cultures*, 4.1–2 (May 2009): 24–47.
30. See M. Horkheimer and T.W. Adorno, 'The Culture Industry: Enlightenment as Mass Deception', in *Dialectic of Enlightenment: Philosophical Fragments* (1947), ed. G.S. Noerr and trans. E. Jephcott (Stanford, CA: Stanford University Press, 2002): pp. 94–136. Adorno was skeptical, however, of Huxley's positing in *Brave New World* of an artistic and intellectual realm that transcended commercial culture. See *AHU*.
31. L. Frost, *The Problem with Pleasure: Modernism and its Discontents* (New York: Columbia University Press, 2013), p. 7 and p. 2.
32. Originally published as 'Recreations', *Vanity Fair*, 28.5 (July 1927): 34, 86.
33. Originally published as 'The Psychology of Suggestion', *Vanity Fair*, 24.6 (Aug. 1925): 58, 84.
34. R. Williams, 'Advertising: the Magic System', in *Problems in Materialism and Culture: Selected Essays* (London: Verso, 1985), pp. 170–95, at p. 185.
35. Williams, 'Advertising', p. 188.
36. Peter Firchow was among the first to make this link (see '*Brave New World* Satirizes the American Present, Not the British Future', in K. de Koster (ed.), *Readings on 'Brave New World'* (San Diego, CA: Greenhaven, 1999): pp. 77–85). A decade later, Huxley would, ironically, make his home in Los Angeles, drawn by the new age counterculture there.
37. Originally published as 'The Outlook for American Culture', *Harper's Magazine*, 155.20 (Aug. 1927): 265–72.

38. 'Fashions in Love', *Vanity Fair*, 31.24 (Dec. 1928): 73, 132, 134. Also published in *Vogue* (23 Nov. 1928): 85, 122.

39. Williams, 'Advertising', p. 187.

40. Eliot uses the phrase in his poem, 'Whispers of Immortality' (1918): 'Grishkin is nice [...] | Uncorseted, her friendly bust | Gives promise of pneumatic bliss' (l. 17 and ll. 19–20). Eliot seemingly plays on the first meaning of 'pneumatic' (relating to spiritual existence) as well as the second ('inflated'). See T.S. Eliot, 'Whispers of Immortality' (1918), in *The Complete Poems and Plays* (London: Faber and Faber, 1969), pp. 52–3, at p. 52.

41. For an analysis of *Brave New World* as a satire of ethnological tourism in the Southwest, see C. Snyder, '"When the Indian was in vogue": D.H. Lawrence, Aldous Huxley, and Ethnological Tourism in the Southwest', *Modern Fiction Studies*, 53.4 (Winter 2007): 662–96.

42. Frost, *The Problem with Pleasure*, p. 150.

43. See Snyder, '"When the Indian was in vogue"'.

CHAPTER 9

The Brave New World of Mothering

Kathryn Southworth

Brave New World (1932) is one of the most lucid and troubling fables about the appropriation of nature by science and one of the primary references for moral panics about the start of life and about test-tube fertilization and what it makes possible. The novel begins with the Director of Hatcheries and Conditioning introducing a group of students to the fertilization room, and it is specifically when the Savage sees its product, that is the workforce of cloned midgets, left-handers, and other engineered human machines, that Miranda's phrase is quoted in bitter irony and bound irrevocably in popular speech with the demonization of science. The tropes of *Brave New World* became so thoroughly naturalized in twentieth-century culture that today the novel does not need to be specifically mentioned for its cautionary tale to be evoked. For that reason alone, its context requires examination.

This chapter begins by exploring similarities to Huxley's exploration of artificial reproduction and mothering in the scientific debates and speculative fictions written before, during, and immediately after the publication of *Brave New World*. The pamphlet series *To-day and To-morrow* (1924–31), whose first volume was contributed by J.B.S. Haldane, establishes a context and model for Huxley's extrapolative fable, a context to

K. Southworth (✉)
Independent Scholar, London, UK

© The Editor(s) (if applicable) and The Author(s) 2016
J. Greenberg, N. Waddell (eds.), Brave New World: *Contexts and Legacies*, DOI 10.1057/978-1-137-44541-4_9

which women with family and other network connections with Haldane and Huxley make a distinctive contribution. In the wake of first-wave feminism, the pamphlets address the biological, social, and experiential reality and ideology of the nuclear patriarchal family. These works blend science-fiction and satire, imagining artificial technology not only as a realistic alternative to biological reproduction, but also a powerful trope to deconstruct the idea of the family and other categories of the 'natural'. After surveying these works this chapter then shows that as the scientific reality of artificial reproduction develops through the twentieth century, so does its potential as a trope for deconstruction, which undergoes a powerful explicit theorization in post-structuralism as the debate over reproductive technologies moves from '*in vitro*' to virtual: from biology to informatics.

Feminist theory and practice align with the scientific inroads into natural reproduction in different ways. Liberal feminists of Huxley's generation examine in some detail their potential to mitigate the more oppressive aspects of the patriarchal family and the social disadvantages of sexual reproduction. But in later decades both second-wave feminism and its literary manifestations bifurcate. On the one hand, essentialist and separatist feminists identify science with masculinity, following archetypal female models, such as Mary Shelley, while on the other postmodern theorists and novelists use science selectively and strategically to deconstruct oppressive categories and structures.

Huxley's novel satirizes not only *in vitro* fertilization but cloning, eugenics, the abolition of the family, and systematic conditioning. His World State has reduced human generation and nurturing to a technological production line in the name of efficiency, stability, and the elimination of unhappiness. To some of his intellectual circle this formulation was a reactionary betrayal of the progressive, enlightened project of modernity. One of the novel's starting points was Huxley's disdain for utopias he summed up as 'Wellsian', though the novel developed far beyond parody of the work he particularly disliked, *Men Like Gods* (1923; see *BNW* xx). Sorting out components of the rich mix of literary, intellectual, and social sources that determined *Brave New World* is not the purpose of this chapter, but I will look at the pamphlets of the 1920s and 1930s that explore the possibilities of biological technology for improving the human condition from its very start, in mothering. These pamphlets raise issues—such as sexual destiny and emancipation from it, the oppression of the nuclear family for women and children, and motherhood as a vocational choice—which, together with the way they have been imagined in these essays and fables, are central to later debates among feminist theorists and novelists in the 1970s and 1980s, although they are rarely referenced in these contexts.[1]

J.B.S. Haldane's *Daedalus; or, Science and the Future* (1924)—which was based on a lecture he gave at Cambridge to the 'Heretics' club in February 1923 and on a paper he wrote in 1912—raised questions about the potential of science to promote human happiness, particularly through biological intervention in birth outside the womb (ectogenesis), eugenic selection, and genetic engineering. Having discussed the work of H.G. Wells, Haldane concluded that 'the biologist is the most romantic figure on earth at the present day.'[2] A series of responses followed. Bertrand Russell's *Icarus; or, The Future of Science* (1924) was less sanguine, suggesting that science would be used oppressively to promote the power of dominant groups, an argument whose pessimism infuriated some of the left-wing intelligentsia just as *Brave New World* was to do, yet anticipates those feminists of the 1980s for whom advances in reproductive medicine were sex, class, and race battles.

Published that same year, Anthony Ludovici's *Lysistrata; or, Woman's Future and Future Woman* (1924) was a Nietzschean rant against the 'body-despising values' (*WFFW* 92) of modern life. He argued that the human species was falling behind because the masses lacked vitality and because many who were kept alive should never have been born. The most natural, 'once beautiful and enthralling' (*WFFW* 44) functions of gestation, parturition, and lactation had become 'things of ugliness and pain' (*WFFW* 44) and what was 'ecstasy' (*WFFW* 53) to other races had become despised in European culture. Ludovici foresees a future in which women will overrun all industries since modern technological processes will destroy the need for skills. Men will be superfluous even for procreation, since fertilization will be performable in a surgery. Women desiring natural fertilization will be despised and finally science will be required to invent extracorporeal gestation, at which point 'the Feminist ideal of complete emancipation from the thraldom of sex will be realized' (*WFFW* 84).[3] Ludovici warns, as dystopian writers generally do, that although his nightmare vision seems fantastical, it represents only the further growth of existing tendencies. Indeed, unpleasantly eugenist and supremacist as its ideology may be, the work has some thematical resonances with radical feminism later in the century, as we shall see.

A direct rebuttal to Ludovici was Dora Russell's *Hypatia; or, Women and Knowledge* (1925), but her subsequent, more substantial work *The Right to Be Happy* (1927) contains chapters on sex and parenthood and the rights of children, chapters which are more especially pertinent to the feminist debate on mothering. She concedes that the status of the mother has fallen below that of independent women socially, economically, and intellectually. Guardians of children, she argues, need to have sexual and economic freedom to carry out their responsibilities effectively, and women can bring about more change through maternity and child nurture than through any other achievement in the arts and sciences. Freud's influence, she believes, has generated an anxiety that parenthood can lead to dangerous neuroses. Her ideas overlap with those of *Brave New World*, where the Controller will tell how Our Freud revealed the appalling dangers of family life, full of every kind of 'perversion' from sadism to chastity, madness, and suicide. He will evoke a picture of the 'home' of the past, 'reeking with emotion[s]' (*BNW* 31), with mothers maniacally brooding like a cat that could say '"my baby"', over and over again' in the 'unspeakable agonizing pleasure' of breast feeding (*BNW* 32). Ludovici described motherly love as a perversion of sexual devotion to a mate. Russell, while also believing maternal love can be unbalanced, urged that mothers should be paid by the state in recognition of their important role and educated to perform it effectively, rather than have the mothering role be left to the state, such as in the Soviet Union (or in *Brave New World*).

Vera Brittain's witty pamphlet *Halcyon; or, The Future of Monogamy* (1929) takes the form of a dream vision ostensibly appearing to a female professor in a chair founded by Baron Morris of Cowley (anticipating Huxley's Ford).[4] For Brittain, technology is no panacea in the realm of mothering. She imagines the first ectogenetic girl being brought to 'birth' in a lab in 1971 but portrays such children suffering psychologically from lack of individual parental affection, and, despite being raised from 'the best stock', dying at around the age of five. Brittain imagines the removal and growth of fertilized embryos 'for convenience', but the babies are then returned to their biological mothers to induce lactation. On the whole, Brittain's pamphlet seems to serve a broadly liberal feminist agenda similar to Russell's, imagining a modestly utopian future in which the majority of wives would no longer be slaves or toys, and sex is no longer a humiliating concession for economic security.[5]

Charlotte Haldane's position is paradigmatic of the paradoxes inherent in the relationship between feminism and science. An admirer of H.G. Wells's novels, Charlotte set up the Science News Service in 1925 and in 1926 married J.B.S. Haldane, whom she made legendary through her journalism. Her later career saw her act as Britain's first female front-line war correspondent and spanned a range of socialist political activities, together with biography and fiction writing.[6] Her novel *Man's World* (1926) depicts a future centuries hence, developing and challenging J.B.S.'s *Daedalus* (1924). Charlotte Haldane's title suggests that her book is satirical and dystopian, a critique of scientific hubris presented through a female prism; certainly the character Bruce, who represents J.B.S., is an unpleasantly patronizing figure. Nevertheless, while more sceptical than her husband's work in anticipating the promises of scientific advances, Haldane's text is less satirical than Huxley's was to be.

In Haldane's New World State women are classified by their biological roles. They are either sterilized and able to take on a range of employment, or they are members of the cadre of Mothers, whose Council wields considerable power. The traditional family has been outgrown 'as government outgrew empire and thought outgrew religion' (*MW* 77). The society has experimented with ectogenesis and anticipates the development of a 'World Mother', a queen termite human from whom the future race will be descended (see *MW* 78). For the moment, elite women pride themselves on being 'vocational mothers' (*MW* 23) with a mission to be 'perfect vessels' (*MW* 68) and to safeguard the genetic stock, in contrast to the 'dirty, bestial', and haphazard 'breeding of the past' (*MW* 148). They distinguish themselves from the women of earlier times, who were either reluctantly forced into motherhood by custom or whose neurotic attachment to their children harmed them both. Though Haldane never complained in print that her work had been appropriated, there are many specific parallels with *Brave New World*, including state nurseries, cinemas akin to the feelies, a cult of youth and beauty, and a questioning of the social order by outsiders who have been inadequately conditioned. Like Bernard, the feminized male character, Christopher, resents the prioritizing of community over the individual, and, like the Savage, sees merit in mortification of the flesh. He dies in the manner of Icarus, seeking transcendence. Rationality has created its own limits because, as Mustapha Mond recognizes in quoting Newman, against the ideal state you can only appeal to God.

However, for feminists *Man's World* has a theoretical dimension lacking in Huxley's novel, since the pseudoscience of sex selection enables some examination of sex and gender as determinants. That said, in *Brave New World* women who are not sterile have to practise birth control and must subdue their maternal instincts pharmacologically, while gender is unproblematized, with no distinction otherwise made in the conditioning of girls and boys or their attitude to sexuality. In *Motherhood and its*

Enemies (1927) Haldane argued strongly for vocational maternity and suggested that women's emancipation did not involve ignoring difference. She saw that the 'dream vision' of a baby entrapped women, but argued for empowering them as mothers through reform in child-rearing. Haldane rejected alternative fantasies and 'half-baked eugenical schemes' as potentially abusive on racial and class grounds.[7] This defence of the basic biological model of motherhood, socially recuperated by ameliorating social and political changes, enables us to understand the ideological position of her novel as essentially liberal feminist.

Naomi Mitchison, J.B.S.'s younger sister, was an even earlier contributor to the Haldane scientific circle. She conducted genetic experiments with him on small mammals, publishing her first scientific paper on colour inheritance in rats. Despite her understanding of biology, she said she was ignorant of birth control. Marie Stopes was a regular visitor to the household and Mitchison had heard of something called the 'Malthusian capsule', presumably an early form of pessary. She writes in her autobiography of the deep excitement at meeting her brother's friends, especially Aldous Huxley.[8] James Watson's account of the discovery of DNA, *The Double Helix* (1968), is dedicated to Mitchison, 'daughter, sister and mother of distinguished scientists', who helped edit the book.[9] Mitchison went on to be a literary author rather than a scientist, producing over 90 books in an astonishing variety of genres. However, it was not until the latter half of the century that her feminism and interest in biology came together in the science-fiction novels *Memoirs of a Spacewoman* (1962) and *Solution Three* (1975), which was dedicated to Watson, and her work constitutes a bridge of sorts between the early-century debates among the Haldane-Huxley circle and the late-century flourishing of women's science fiction (SF) that would take up the implications of those debates.[10]

The protagonist of *Memoirs of a Spacewoman* searches for signs of other species while also bearing children, the two activities being symbolically related. The space travellers represent a commitment to species understanding, development, and change which enables them to explore their relationship with science and their own maternal instincts. *Solution Three* is more clearly reminiscent of Huxley but is also inspired by contemporary embryology. The novel is set in a future society which seems to have solved problems of overpopulation and aggression through subscription to 'The Code', a genetic model that produces 'admirably alike' babies; any children of traditional marriage are monitored suspiciously. These clones are carried by women described as 'nests', since their own genetic material has been eliminated from the babies; they give love to the children but only until the end of babyhood, when the latter are removed by 'The Watchers', never to be seen again. There are, as is often the case in utopian/dystopian fables, disordered deviants who cannot help their own damaging 'possessive thoughts', and who secretly marry to bring up their own children. Moreover, The Code cannot prevent the clones from developing individual differentiating characteristics, and the scene seems set for a further development in the understanding of a good society and a good species, one which values diversity.

So far in this chapter I have avoided interrogating the taxonomies of literary genres and used the terms 'utopian' and 'dystopian' loosely and virtually synonymously. The literary texts discussed here can all be located somewhere in the romance–science fiction spectrum and are best thought of as speculative or extrapolative fiction because of their ideological designs on the reader. However, as we move into second-wave feminism, and its use of the science fiction mode to explore mothering, we enter a more self-conscious and contested theoretical realm. For my purposes, three types of feminism can be distinguished. First, critical feminism seeks equal rights for men and women, and in its approach to literature, critiques oppressive patriarchal representation; it distinguishes between the real biological difference of sex and the insidious social differentiation and conditioning of gender. It can be seen as a development of earlier liberal feminism and its metaphor might be the female eunuch. Second, essentialist feminism assumes a real difference between male and female, literally and symbolically and, in its approach to literature, privileges writing by and about women: its literary mode is the separatist female utopia and early gothic fiction; its metaphor could be the nature goddess. Third, deconstructive criticism interrogates boundaries and categories including gender, race, and species, as well as categories of natural and made: its characteristic form is cyberpunk. Its metaphor is the cyborg and its politics radical socialism.

Shulamith Firestone's *The Dialectic of Sex: The Case for Feminist Revolution* (1970), dedicated to Simone de Beauvoir, is one of the earliest of radical feminist manifestos, and constitutes an important source for the speculative fiction of the next decade and more. Indeed, Firestone anticipates and inspires, directly or indirectly, writers who are clearly deconstructionists. Mobilizing Marx and Engels, and claiming the personal as political, Firestone seeks to recuperate science and technology for the liberation of children and of women. She argues that women will never be free from sexual and economic oppression until the biological tyranny of reproduction 'set up by nature and reinforced by man' (*DS* 15) is overcome by technology, and proposes that images of parthenogenesis, artificial wombs, and cloning break taboos around the unnatural and appear anti-motherhood. Baby factories may seem dystopian, and in the hands of our present-day society it is difficult to see them being used non-oppressively: 'We are all familiar with the details of Brave New World [*sic*]: cold collectives, with individualism abolished, sex reduced to a mechanical act, children become robots, [...] rows of babies fed by impersonal machines, eugenics manipulated by the state [and so on]' (*DS* 188). Nevertheless, what is required, Firestone urges, is an honest re-examination of motherhood itself. She suggests that the 'maternal instinct' is not inevitable or insurmountable since having children is a displacement activity used to bolster the ego. For her, pregnancy is 'barbaric' (*DS* 180) and the cult of natural childbirth 'reactionary hippie-Rousseauean Return-to-Nature' (*DS* 181).

Firestone argues that human evolution and technological development have now reached a point at which in some countries the preconditions for feminist revolution exist. With the discovery of DNA, humanity has begun to outgrow nature; full mastery of the reproductive process is in sight, enabling children to be born to both sexes or independently of either, breaking both the 'tyranny' of the biological family and 'the Great Father', Freud. The nuclear family household is a major agent of repression, intensifying 'the psychological penalty of the biological family' (*DS* 10). Any programme for feminist revolution must also redress the oppression of children. Children would be better served by households who are selected to rear children and they should be allowed to learn what interests them. Reviewing alternative experiments in child-rearing and education, such as the kibbutz movement or schools like Summerhill (the independent British boarding school founded in 1921), Firestone argues that their limited success can be explained by their clinging to strong sex role models (*DS* 196–7).

In advancing her 'utopian speculation' Firestone recognizes that such futures are impossible to imagine from our current perspective. She looks to culture as the dynamic between the scientific and aesthetic modes through which the limitations of contingent reality may be overcome, and complains: '[w]e haven't even a literary image of this future society; there is not even a *utopian* feminist literature yet in existence' (*DS* 203). This observation was scarcely true at the time (1970), although, as Tom Moylan has observed, in the twentieth century 'utopian writing came upon hard times' and was dominated by dystopias.[11] Writers subsequently

THE BRAVE NEW WORLD OF MOTHERING 157

rose to Firestone's challenge, so much so that this chapter becomes particularly selective at this point.

Joanna Russ, another feminist lamenting the lack of women in SF, took up the challenge herself, since the form represents the perfect medium to explore 'innate' values and 'natural' arrangements. Russ's *The Female Man* (1975), written in 1970, is modernist and radical in its literary form as much as its utopian and dystopian content, resisting linearity and closure and challenging 'natural' realist techniques and characterization in its fracturing of identity and narrative coherence. The text is playful and self-referential, mirroring the openness of the imagined utopian society of Whileaway, where sophisticated technology is combined with a libertarian pastoral setting and social networks are loose associations of like-minded individuals who rear children on large communal farms. The narratives of four characters whose names all begin with 'J' are braided together. For each of them, Whileaway represents praxis, a challenge to transform their lives and the lives of others, whereas its dark side—the dystopian, authoritarian, militarized Manland—represents the consequence of not doing so.

More so than any other writer, Marge Piercy in *Woman on the Edge of Time* (1976) has engaged with Firestone's challenge to reconsider motherhood and to embrace the liberating potential of technology. In the utopian society of Mattapoisett, reproduction and child-rearing are divorced from sexual difference and gender differences are minimal. Babies gestate in tanks like Huxley's bottles, are 'born' according to group planning and are reared by small kinship teams of 'comothers' who are not 'sweet friends' who might entangle them in 'love misunderstandings' (*WOET* 74). The words 'father' and 'mother' have been consigned to history, although the genetic origins of children are identifiable and important. The time visitor, Connie, is repelled by the sight of a gestating foetus in the brooder. Seeing men breastfeed babies, she has to confront her own taboos: these women 'had abandoned to men the last refuge of women', surrendered 'the last remnants of ancient power' (*WOET* 134).

Connie's host and guide, Luciente, explains (in language reminiscent of Firestone) that this is the price for genuine equality:

> 'It was part of women's long revolution. When we were breaking all the old hierarchies. Finally there was one thing we had to give up too, the only power we ever had, in return for no more power for anyone. The original production: the power to give birth. Cause as long as we were biologically enchained, we'd never be equal. And males never would be humanized to be loving and tender. So we all became mothers.' (*WOET* 105)[12]

Although Connie may reflect the instinctive response of the reader, she is an unreliable witness, a woman who clings particularly to the ideal of personal motherhood because, abused by her pimp and betrayed by her brother, she has been declared an unfit mother and has had her womb removed. A Chicana woman, a victim of racism and sexism, it is no wonder she initially hates the 'bland bottleborn monsters of the future, born without pain, multi-coloured like a litter of puppies without the stigmata of race and sex' (*WOET* 106). While this attitude is entirely plausible in terms of psychological realism, the ideology of the novel requires that finally Connie becomes entirely persuaded that what she wants for her own daughter is what Luciente's society offers.

The Mattapoisett society is, in a planned and meaningful fashion, highly technically developed in communications, the arts, textiles, and, not least, genetics. Luciente is a plant geneticist and babies are deliberately designed to serve social engineering purposes, for instance to diversify the population without creating a homogenized 'thin gruel' (*WOET* 104), such as the gametes of *Brave New World*. This idea is developed further in C.J. Cherryh's later trilogy, *Cyteen* (1988), in which colonists seek to establish digital recordings of gene sets so that no genetic material can be lost and to create, in their Huxley-like birthing tanks, the 'azi', a designer people selected from genetically mixed batches.[13] However, even in Mattapoisett society genetics is not without controversy. Its rulers only screen for birth defects and genes linked with disease susceptibility, whereas the Shapers want to breed for selected traits. Mixers, on the other hand, deem this an abuse of power and place their trust in chance, though in special cases a dead person may be honoured by having specific 'genetic chances' selected for reuse or to be 'born again' (see *WOET* 298–9). Nevertheless, genes are not thought to be important determinants once 'negative' ones have been 'weeded out'. This debate and the 'enhancement' tricks of the alternative dystopian future society presented in the novel are juxtaposed. Women selected for the sex trade, because they 'naturally' have brain defects from nutritional deficiencies in the womb, are consigned after use to organ banks: human commodification at its most obvious (see *WOET* 324).

Piercy's instantiation of Firestone's ideas did not end with this novel. In her later science fiction work *He, She and It* (1991), or *Body of Glass* (1992) as it was published in the UK, Piercy further deconstructs biological categories. Firestone had imagined pregnancy becoming a tongue-in-cheek archaism. In *He, She and It*, the central character, Shira, is considered deviant by her employer, one of the multinational corporations which control all aspects of the environment and their employees' lives, because she has, like Huxley's Linda but from choice, conceived and born a child naturally. Ironically, Shira goes on to co-create a totally manufactured being, the cyborg Yod, who is both brother and father to her natural child. Yod talks to Shira of 'human specs' and is corrected for mistaking metaphorical language for reality, since humans 'are not engineered or built but born' (*HSI* 91). Yet 'specifications' aptly describe unique patterns of DNA, which is information, and everything in the novel refutes the apparent difference between engineered creations and natural ones.[14] Yod speaks of previous cyborgs of the lab as 'brothers' and addresses Avram, his designer, as 'Father' (*HSI* 93)—though he is later at pains to point out that this is a deliberate strategy to create an emotional bond with Avram, to prevent his destroying him. However, as Avram's natural son, Gadi, tells Shiva, he was himself a test-tube baby: perhaps the five years spent trying to conceive him made Avram think of easier ways to create life, and thus to make a more obedient version of himself (*HSI* 154).

Yod's experience of laboratory creation and his final assassination of Avram and destruction of his lab suggest not so much *Brave New World* as Mary Shelley's *Frankenstein* (1818).[15] Indeed for feminist critics and authors of the second wave, it was Shelley's novel rather than Huxley's which most powerfully spoke of the male appropriation of the mysteries of creation and pointed to male fear of the female power of gestation and birth. Feminist theorists and utopian novelists might re-appropriate the creative act by the invention of a utopian space, a new world. To quote Jean Pfaelzer:

> Women's space: the gap, the rupture, the enclosure, the absence of female inscription in discourse and history. Utopian space: no place, the inversion, the hole in history which signifies and allows for the fantasy and the wish.[16]

Pfaelzer finds in French discourse theorists a significant utopian element, particularly in their view that 'reading and writing are subversive activities', quoting Hélène Cixous's observation that women's sexuality of repetition makes them 'the beginning of a new history, or rather a process of becoming'.[17] For Cixous, the utopian genre, whether it satirizes the status quo or anticipates future developments and potential praxis, is empowering in invoking a creation myth in which woman can be progenitor or destroyer. However, Pfaelzer asks whether, in setting their utopias in wildernesses, on islands, or in otherwise distant places, feminists are subverting or perpetuating their marginality. While Piercy merges genders, the frequency of separatist, mono-gendered utopias in the period suggests that the problem of gender is not easily resolvable. The essentialist dilemma will be explored further below when the 'politics' of the cyborg trope begin to take over from the eunuch of critical feminism and the remote goddess of separatism.

Much of feminist science fiction of the 1970s and some of the 1980s imagines men and women living as virtually separate races.[18] Reproduction is usually parthenogenic, bizarrely so in Susie McKee Charnos's *Motherlines* (1978), the second volume of the *HOLDFAST* series, in which the process is initiated by coupling with a stallion. Indeed, separatist utopias are unconvincing as models in their essentialist presentation of gender distinctions and symbolic representations of difference. For instance, in Sally Miller Gearhart's *The Wanderground: Stories of the Hill Women* (1979) men inhabit the cities and their violence is exemplified by rape, but outside the city, in the 'women's realm' of nature, their technologies do not work and they cannot get erections. In Pamela Sargent's *The Shore of Women* (1986) the Mothers of the women enclaves conceive by conditioning men to believe they are called to receive mystical favours of the Goddess, but instead subject them to a form of rape: they unwittingly donate semen while tied up, connected to tubes and subjected to pornographic films. As one of Sargent's characters says: "'It seemed uncomfortably close to what men had done to women in the past'", and she criticizes the closed culture which denies the possibility of something more, presumably a less sexually differentiated future.[19]

However, the momentum of 1970s utopian feminism was difficult to sustain. The 1980s was characterized by a backlash associated with neo-conservative politics, a backlash exemplified in a particularly visceral form by Margaret Atwood's dystopia *The Handmaid's Tale* (1985). Atwood warns that modern Western women skate on thin ice and, imagining what a totalitarian USA would look like, focuses on reproduction control, making herself a rule to include in the novel nothing that has not already actually been done. In her invented society, Gilead, an oppressive fundamentalist patriarchal regime enforces rigid gender roles wherein women with functioning ovaries are forced to be 'handmaids', a primitive form of surrogacy on the biblical model of Genesis. They dress in red, like 'walking wombs', with their reproductive capacity amounting to their sole identity, and are at the centre of a regressive quasi-female culture which valorizes the 'natural'. Birthing is a woman-only, collective affair that is entirely separated from technology and uses a traditional birthing stool; it is a public and dramatic event in a world where fertility has been severely compromised. In some respects the birth scene is a dream of 1970s feminism, of Kitzinger and home births rather than the lonely and alienating and technological experience of hospital delivery.[20] Though (male) doctors are waiting in reserve, they are only admitted in an emergency. As one of the establishment cadre of Aunts (a group reminiscent of Charlotte Haldane's elite) points out, in the past men were in charge. She shows the Handmaids a film of the 'olden days', with a powerless pregnant woman wired up to a machine, invaded by electrodes, a man with a searchlight between her legs. After one Birth Day in Gilead, the main character Offred confronts the irony of the feminist past, telling her own mother, who wanted a female culture, that there is one now—and it isn't what she meant. Atwood's novel, as she was to say of Huxley's, is a 'double-sided' (*BNW* xvi) work, in her case implicating utopian thinking in her unequivocal dystopia. It can be read as an endorsement of Firestone's argument about women's physical, political, and economic vulnerability as a reproductive vessel and as a warning against complacency.

However, most feminists did not respond as enthusiastically as Firestone might have wished to the plethora of reproductive technologies which began to emerge around this time, and there was strong suspicion that such technologies represented a threat to women's autonomy rather than a potential tool for overcoming patriarchal structures. The first baby actually to be conceived by *in vitro* fertilization was born in 1978 in the UK. In 1984 the Warnock Commission published the report which brought about a licensing system for IVF and set a 14-day limit for experimentation on 'spare' embryos. A variety of 'infertility' treatments became available and the development of techniques began to raise the possibility of making children with two genetic mothers or none. More immediately, IVF demonstrated the practical separability of fertilization and gestation and again opened up the debate about what this meant for the concept of 'motherhood'—and, indeed, whether as a unified concept it still made any sense.

Gena Corea charts the history of medical developments which literally and metaphorically opened up the womb to investigation and pathologized it.[21] In 1970, Gerald Leach talked of the womb as 'the most hazardous environment in which humans have to live.'[22] In 1974 Joseph Fletcher welcomed the prospect of an 'open window' on the womb to facilitate the work of placentologists, embryologists, and fetologists.[23] In 1984 Frederick Leboyer in *Birth without Violence* presented the womb as a prison where children are potential victims of, among other dangerous effects, drug abuse, alcohol, malnutrition, and malformations from mothers who contract German measles.[24] But if artificial wombs to protect developing life would have to wait a little longer, human surrogacy at least meant that children could be born quite independently from their genetic parents. While the father's role in the process had always been abstract and difficult to verify, now the mother's could be also. Indeed, the laws of different countries would decide differently about who was 'the' mother: the genetic mother, the gestational mother, or the nurturing mother. In the notorious 'Baby M' case in the USA, a baby was taken by a court from a woman's breast because the baby's genetic father had a better claim to it—a legal judgement which privileged the more removed, patriarchal 'ownership' of genetics over the immediate relationship of nurturing. On the other hand, however, Phyllis Chesler asked in a collection of essays based on the case whether compartmentalizing 'mother' into different functions might be welcomed, enlarging and enhancing the experience and opening it up to single and married, fertile and infertile, men as well as women. The question posed was: would the ability to 'let go' of such bonds 'free us to control our destiny more scientifically' and to clear up the 'imperfect mess'?[25] A contrary view celebrating the natural, holistic experience was passionately expressed in one contribution to a collection of essays published in 1984 as *Test-Tube Women: What Future for Motherhood?*:

> We have considered mothering to be the process of pregnancy, of labour, of nurturance; a mutual experience involving the giving of life, the physical changes, the growth, the movement inside, the physical pushing of another being into the world, the nursing and feeding. More than the donation of a complement of chromosomes, this has to be mothering.[26]

Indeed, since this was at least theoretically possible, could a genetic mother who had never actually been born be in any meaningful way described as 'mother'?

The new technologies clearly had the potential to commodify not only babies but also wombs, with the inevitable exploitation of the poor and racial minorities who might 'rent' them out. 'Infertility' itself became something of a new epidemic. Susan Faludi, in what she described as the 'backlash' or 'undeclared war against women', pointed out that professional women were demonized for delaying and therefore potentially failing to have children, and that the definition of infertility in France had been reduced from five years trying for a child to only one, creating needless anxiety and medical intervention.[27] Even before IVF, when the practice was often to implant multiple embryos to increase the chances of successful pregnancy, there were problems with the dosage of fertility drugs which could lead to multiple births. Doctors were described as early as 1972 as behaving 'like sorcerers' apprentices'.[28]

The Bokanovsky process of *Brave New World* represents the full-blown version of such 'sorcery'. Fertilized ova from excised ovaries are put in incubators, where the Alphas and Betas remain until bottling. Ova for Gammas, Deltas, and Epsilons have their development arrested, and respond by budding and dividing up to a practical limit of 96, 'not in [the] piddling twos and threes' of the 'old viviparous days' (*BNW* 4), as the Director gloats. Fay Weldon in *The Cloning of Joanna May* (1989) was to have the doctor who produced four clones explain that the technique was a comparatively archaic and simple parthenogenesis and extra-uterine conception, rather than the swopping of nuclei and shuffling of genes, so he was only able to divide one egg into four. Weldon adds: 'Then the clones despised him for a failure in ambition' (*CJM* 233).

IVF also brought forward the prospect of cloning humans. Although Dolly the sheep was not created until 1996, cloning had been a topic in science fiction for some time, allowing interesting exploration of the traditional debate about nurture and nature. In Cherryh's *Cyteen* (1988), children are 'conceived' in gene batches and gestated in a bio-plasmic environment which duplicates the womb in movements, sounds, and chemistry.[29] Most of the resulting babies are assigned a 'maman' who may raise 50 children at once but they are mostly conditioned, as in *Brave New World*, by tape-learning. However, the alpha class of 'azi' are designer jobs, and when the leader of Reseune state, Ariane Emory, is murdered, she is genetically replicated and 'resurrected', the new Ariane being tutored by a tape left by her mother.

Cloning as a trope in fiction also enabled writers to pursue questions of individual uniqueness, of the power of science as an agent of male chauvinism, and of the problems in differentiating the natural from the 'man'-made. Fay Weldon in her particular combinations of feminist, gothic, and realist fiction had already tackled the conventional identification of women and nature in *Praxis* (1978), in which it is said that 'Nature our Friend is an argument used, quite understandably, by men'.[30] *The Cloning of Joanna May* (1989) moves the argument nearer to science fiction and postmodern territory. Rejecting Huxley's assumption that women 'natu-rally' want children, Joanna asks herself whether the maternal instinct is not just a socially determined 'performance' (*CJM* 155). Discovering that her nuclear physicist husband, Carl, has had her cloned, Joanna and her clones use their collective female power transgressively to triumph over him and his technology.

Not only motherhood but womanhood itself was under ontological attack throughout this period and had been since at least 1949, when Simone de Beauvoir initiated the distinction between sex and gender in suggesting that one is not born but, rather, becomes a woman. In her exploration of the debate in feminist theory between essentialist and con-structivist ideas, Diana Fuss identifies the strategy of avoiding essential-ism by shifting the categories from single to plural, for instance 'women's histories' rather than 'woman's history': a coalition of affinity rather than identity. A particularly powerful attempt she explores to 'build unities rather than naturalize them' is the 'cyborg politics' of Donna Haraway.[31]

For Haraway there is not even such a state as 'being "female", itself a highly complex category constructed in contested sexual scientific dis-courses and other social practices' (*ACM* 107). Haraway's *Modest_Wit ness@Second_Millennium.FemaleMan_Meets_OncoMouse: Feminism and Technoscience* (1997) takes part of its title from Russ's influential novel in tribute to its deconstruction of gender categories.[32] A biologist, feminist, and cultural anthropologist, Haraway uses science fiction to explore moral and political issues in a fashion which is itself transgressive of disciplinary boundaries and academic conventions. Piercy paid tribute to Haraway in the preface to *Woman on the Edge of Time* and here Haraway returns the compliment, beginning *Modest_Witness* with an account of Piercy's char-acters from *He, She and It*—Nili and Riva (Shiva's mother)—the one a technologically enhanced and genetically engineered post-holocaust war-rior and the other a data pirate; she thus demonstrates 'the kinship of chip, gene, seed, bomb, lineage, ecosystem and database'.[33]

Haraway locates her work within 'the utopian tradition of imagining a world without gender' (*ACM* 104). She explodes boundary concepts, between species, nature, and technology (these categories all getting increasingly 'leaky' as our technology becomes ever more visceral and inti-mate), and between the physical and non-physical: machines being signals and organisms similarly strings of genetic coding. Haraway embodies these concepts in the cyborg (*ACM* 104), a creature not only of fiction but, in her account, of social reality. Haraway's 'cyborg semiology' eliminates feminist dilemmas around reproduction: sex roles, essential biological properties, and ideologies of the natural. Cyborgs regenerate and replicate from specifications: the reproductive matrix is no longer a relevant trope in this apotheosis of the postmodern.

The fiction and theory of cyberpunk may seem an unlikely legacy of Huxley's *Brave New World*, given its author's reputation as something of a mandarin. But Huxley's novel took part, as we have seen, in a volatile debate about the relations between science, science fiction, and feminism; and that debate, as it evolved through the years, responded to new reproductive technologies, developments in biological sciences, and progress in women's rights. In succeeding decades, consequently, female authors more and more turned to science fiction as an imaginative space in which to play out questions hinted at in the novels and pamphlets of a half-century before. The arc from Huxley and Haldane to Haraway is an unpredictable one, one that in many way upends Huxley's fears about the disappearance of the 'natural'. For as post-structuralist feminist theory aims not just to identify and explain, but to abolish gender, so cyberpunk moves beyond sex and the body itself to imagine, for better or worse, a brave new, post-human world.

NOTES

1. For a comprehensive survey of relevant twentieth-century imaginative literature see S.M. Squier, *Babies in Bottles: Twentieth-Century Visions of Reproductive Technology* (New Brunswick, NJ: Rutgers University Press, 1994).
2. J.B.S. Haldane, *Daedalus; or, Science and the Future* (London: Kegan Paul, Trench, Trubner & Co., 1924), p. 77.
3. Elise Schraner, in her review of Routledge's republication (as *To-day and To-morrow*) of the pamphlet series, criticizes the 'massive injustice to feminist studies' in Routledge's omission of rebuttals to Ludovici, such as Dora Russell's *Hypatia; or, Women and Knowledge* (1925). See E. Schraner, 'Review: The To-day and To-morrow Series', *Interdisciplinary Science Reviews*, 34.1 (Mar. 2009): 107–15, at 113.
4. V. Brittain, *Halcyon; or, The Future of Monogamy* (London: Kegan Paul, Trench, Trubner & Co., 1929), pp. 5–6 and p. 6.
5. See Brittain, *Halcyon*, pp. 76–8.
6. See J. Adamson, *Charlotte Haldane: Woman Writer in a Man's World* (Basingstoke, Hampshire: Palgrave Macmillan, 1998).
7. C. Haldane, *Motherhood and Its Enemies* (1927; Garden City, NY: Doubleday, Doran, & Co., 1928), p. 253.

8. N. Mitchison, *You May Well Ask: A Memoir 1920–1940* (London: Victor Gollancz 1979), p. 69.
9. J. Watson, *The Double Helix* (London: Weidenfeld and Nicolson, 1968), dedication.
10. N. Mitchison, *Solution Three* (New York: The Feminist Press, 1995), dedication.
11. T. Moylan, *Demand the Impossible: Science Fiction and the Utopian Imagination* (London: Methuen, 1986), p. 8. Other surveys of the utopian science fiction of the period include S. Lefanu, *In the Chinks of the World Machine: Feminism and Science Fiction* (London: The Women's Press, 1988). The postmodern period is covered by J. Wolmark, *Aliens and Others: Science Fiction, Feminism and Postmodernism* (Hemel Hempstead: Harvester Wheatsheaf, 1993).
12. A less radical call for a distribution of power in parenting was made by Nancy Chodorow in *The Reproduction of Mothering: Psychoanalysis and the Sociology of Gender* (Berkeley: University of California Press, 1978).
13. See also Octavia E. Butler's trilogy of novels about the human survivor Lilith and her rescuers, the gene-manipulating Oankali, which began with *Dawn* (1987). These novels focus on intra-species genetic changes, but the parallel with interracial marriage is obvious, especially when we consider Butler's primary fame as a writer about race, for instance in *Kindred* (1979). The Lilith novels—*Dawn* (1987), *Adulthood Rites* (1988), and *Imago* (1989)—are collected as *Lilith's Brood* (2000), formerly *Xenogenesis* (1989).
14. The difficulty of distinguishing between humans and their replicants was most famously explored by Philip K. Dick in *Do Androids Dream of Electric Sheep?* (1968), and especially by Ridley Scott in *Blade Runner* (1982).
15. Similarities with Huxley include the colour-coding of workers and the 'stimmy' films.
16. J. Pfaelzer, 'The Changing of the Avant-Garde: the Feminist Utopia', *Science-Fiction Studies*, 15.3 (Nov. 1988): 282–94, at 282.
17. Pfaelzer, 'The Changing of the Avant-Garde', 283.
18. An early twentieth-century example of parthenogenic reproduction can be found in Charlotte Perkins Gilman's *Herland* (1915).
19. P. Sargent, *The Shore of Women* (New York: Crown Publishers, Inc., 1986), p. 121.
20. Sheila Kitzinger was an activist for natural childbirth and prolific writer on the subject. Her autobiography *A Passion for Birth* was published posthumously in May 2015.
21. G. Corea, *The Mother Machine: Reproductive Technology from Artificial Insemination to Artificial Wombs* (London: HarperCollins, 1985), p. 250.
22. G. Leach, *The Biocrats* (Baltimore: Penguin, 1970), p. 161.
23. Corea, *The Mother Machine*, p. 258.

24. See F. Leboyer, *Birth without Violence* (London: Pinter & Martin, 1975).
25. See P. Chesler, *Sacred Bond: the Legacy of Baby M* (New York: Crown, 1988), p. 9.
26. J. Murphy, 'From Mice to Men? Implications of Progress in Cloning Research', in *Test-Tube Women: What Future for Motherhood?*, ed. R. Arditti, R.D. Klein, and S. Minden (London and Boston: Pandora Press, 1984), pp. 76–91, at p. 87.
27. See S. Faludi, *Backlash: The Undeclared War Against American Women* (New York: Crown, 1991).
28. N. Pfeffer, *The Stork and the Syringe: A Political History of Reproductive Medicine* (Cambridge: Polity Press, 1993), p. 148.
29. C.J. Cherryh, *Cyteen* (New York: Warner Books, 1988), p. 624.
30. F. Weldon, *Praxis* (London: Coronet, 1980), p. 147.
31. D. Fuss, *Essentially Speaking: Feminism, Nature and Difference* (New York: Routledge, 1989), p. 36.
32. D. Haraway, *Modest_Witness@Second_Millennium.FemaleMan_Meets_ OncoMouse: Feminism and Technoscience* (New York: Routledge, 1997), pp. 1–2.
33. Haraway, *Modest_Witness@Second_Millennium.FemaleMan_Meets_OncoMouse*, p. 2.

CHAPTER 10

Ethics in the Late Anthropocene

Keith Leslie Johnson

FLAT, DARK, MELANCHOLY

The satirical force of *Brave New World*—its cartoonish sci-fi anticipation of a controlled society—is greatly diminished for the twenty-first-century reader, who is surrounded by cruel evidence of its realization: narcotic bioregulation, hedonistic consumption, new apartheids, even the resurgence of eugenic protocols. Given the imminent horizon of these realizations, it becomes increasingly difficult to read the novel as a plea for some recuperation of humanist values or practices, even if that were Huxley's original intent. Rather, the question becomes how to read the novel *against* the humanist grain, to read it as an instance of what I call an 'ethics after people'—the form of relation that prevails under conditions of creaturely abjection, or life reduced to its material, protoplasmic essence. Such an ethics, one that did not particularly privilege certain relations (between humans, say) over others, would, on its face, seem very strange indeed and, in a way, not an ethics at all, at least not in the usual sense of rules or norms of behavior. Rather, it would be 'anti-normative' in at least two ways. Firstly, such an ethics would be allergic to the articulation

K.L. Johnson (✉)
Department of English and Film/Media Studies, The College of William and
Mary, Williamsburg, VA, USA

© The Editor(s) (if applicable) and The Author(s) 2016
J. Greenberg, N. Waddell (eds.), Brave New World: *Contexts and
Legacies*, DOI 10.1057/978-1-137-44541-4_10

of explicit codes of conduct; instead, it would attempt to describe the experience of confronting an other and the subsequent sense or intuition of implication, obligation, or indebtedness, prior to any question of what one *ought*.[1] Such an ethics would also be closer to the discourses of biology and ecology than law or theology. Anthropocentric ethics, for their part, are only as robust as the humanism that supports them. When that humanism is challenged, ethical standards can all too easily become eroded or perverted, and monstrous actions be justified. Writing in the wake of the First World War and during the rise of fascism across Europe, Huxley would have been only too aware of the fragility of ethical systems grounded in humanism. From our perspective, the challenge that *Brave New World* (1932) confronts is less how we might *redeem* the abject or reinstate humanism (for example, by treating *all* of the inhabitants of the Brave New World as humans, citizens, and stakeholders in a polity), than how we can ethically reconceive of life when it is recognized as a massive and *merely* biological phenomenon, when it is no longer 'propped up' by metaphysical fictions and conceits.

Why attempt such a reconception in the first place? Why not simply insist that humanist values be honored? We may respond that, as Mustapha Mond himself well knows, although humanist values are compromised, they are in fact preconditions for the Brave New World and its 'happy, hard-working, goods-consuming citizen[s]' (*BNW* 208). Secular humanist values like personal well-being, permissiveness and tolerance, moral objectivity (i.e. consequentialism), and the supremacy of empirical reason, not to mention such folderol as 'our destiny among the stars'—all these provide the mortar for the Brave New World. We cannot simply turn back the clock of human history to some arbitrary point before things went awry. Things didn't go awry. Huxley's 'bad utopia' is in fact a vision of what happens when everything goes according to plan. It isn't therefore enough to double-down on traditional verities; rather, to anticipate Huxley's later philosophy, we must imagine new and holistic modes of existence wherein humans are integrated into the system of nature in all its volatility.[2] In other words, the question is not how to preserve some fragile demesne for humanity but how to embrace life in its precarity.

The most recent name for this precarity is the *Anthropocene*. This term, originally coined by Eugene Stoermer, an environmental biologist, and popularized by Paul Crutzen, a Nobel Prize-winning atmospheric chemist, has come to signify the ecological impact of human technology since, roughly, the Industrial Revolution. As this impact has been primarily negative—impeding or deranging natural processes, exhausting resources, toxifying the atmosphere, and so on—the Anthropocene era designates the paradoxical cost of our scientific ingenuity: namely, our impending extinction, an eventuality we contemplate even as the Brave New Worlders do not. As a consequence, the profound material imbrication of living and non-living things comes sharply into relief; where once were hierarchies, now there are suddenly chains of dependency and mutual ramification. Ontology itself, the way we understand the nature of being, is somewhat *flattened*: the qualitative differences between kinds of beings (that separate kings from kumquats) are diminished when we stop thinking of beings as discrete and self-enclosed and start thinking of them in terms of energy flows, say—or to put it less obscurely, elements of a larger ecological system.[3] As far as kumquats are concerned, the belly of a king may simply be a stage on life's way. It isn't that ontological distinctions are no longer possible, but less and less are they cut and dried and less and less still do they sustain or justify strong ethical divisions.

In bygone times, ethical divisions were keyed to fairly stringent ontological categories: divinity, for example, partook more fully of Being than humanity, as humanity did relative to animality, and animality relative to vegetality, and vegetality relative to minerality. One's obligations were consequently intensified the higher one ascended the *scala naturae* or 'Ladder of Nature' imagined by scholastic philosophers in order to square classical thought with biblical revelation. When Albertus Magnus referred to humans as the 'most perfect of animals', he was echoing Galen, who was in turn echoing Aristotle.[4] There is in this line of thinking (particularly in its shifting senses of 'perfection') an equation, more or less, of physiological and moral complexity: the difference between *Paracoccus* and Paracelsus is measured not only in terms of the gap between prokaryotic and eukaryotic organisms, but in the latter's capacity for virtue, what the Swiss mystic considered one of the 'four pillars' of his art.[5] Conscience, then, becomes essentially the opposable thumb of the soul, an aspect of humanity that lifts it from the welter of animal life, an idea that persists long after its scientific basis is discredited. There is, historically, a strong correlation between our images of the biological and moral orders: under Ernst Haeckel's *Stammbaum des Menschen* lies the ghostly outline of Ramon Llull's *Arbor moralis* (Figs. 10.1 and 10.2). So deeply rooted is the idea that it can be found even in modern, secular ontologies from which divinity has ostensibly been pruned. The philosopher Martin Heidegger's famous apothegm, 'the stone is worldless, the animal poor in

Fig. 10.1 'Arbor moralis', Ramon Llull, *Arbor scientiae venerabilis et caelitus illuminati Patris Raymundi Lullii …: liber ad omnes scientias utilissimus* (Lyon: Guilhelmi Huyon, & Constantini Fradin, 1515)

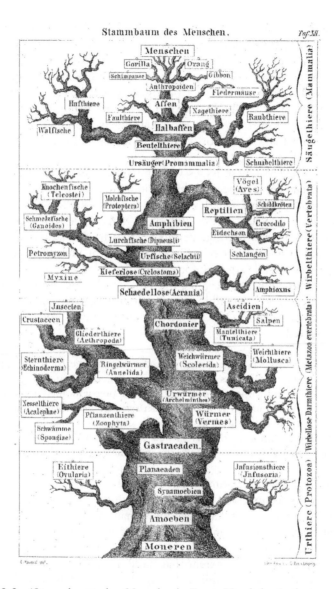

Fig. 10.2 'Stammbaum des Menschen', Ernst Haeckel, *Anthropogenie oder Entwickelungsgeschichte des Menschen. Gemeinverständliche wissenschaftliche Vorträge über die Grundzüge der menschlichen Keimes-und Stammes-Geschichte.* (Leipzig: Engelmann, 1874)

world, and man world-forming', represents precisely this kind of super-imposition of metaphysics and natural science.[6] Heidegger provisionally defines the notion of *world* as the 'accessibility of beings', a capacity for relation to others: at its lowest threshold, this might mean something as simple as *irritability* in the strict biological sense, but at its uppermost, one imagines, sits the Buddha, a kind of infinite being-for-others.[7] In a way, though, the Anthropocene moots all this hairsplitting. Its most saturnine truth is that, in the not-too-distant future, man and stone may be equally worldless.

For the Huxleys, these issues were rather a personal affair; the family tree linked them, either directly or indirectly, to eminent Victorians like Sir Francis Galton, Charles Darwin and his 'bulldog' T.H. Huxley, and Matthew Arnold.[8] These and other figures helped establish the terms by which we conceptualize our relation to the natural world and, by extension, the prospect of its loss. Our current understanding of the Anthropocene is still largely informed by attitudes a century-and-a-half old, and in that sense we are, like the Huxleys themselves, strange post-Victorian creatures, susceptible to technological optimism and pessimism in equal measure. In his 1957 essay, 'Transhumanism', Aldous's brother Julian observed:

> It is as if man had been suddenly appointed managing director of the biggest business of all, the business of evolution—appointed without being asked if he wanted it, and without proper warning and preparation. What is more, he can't refuse the job. Whether he wants to or not, whether he is conscious of what he is doing or not, he is in point of fact determining the future direction of evolution on this earth. That is his inescapable destiny, and the sooner he realizes it and starts believing in it, the better for all concerned.[9]

This, we might say, is a somewhat sunnier vision of the Anthropocene, sanguine in its technocratic conflation of industry, science, and environment. Aldous, for his part, harbored more than a little ambivalence toward his intellectual forebears (and siblings!), and his vision of the ecological future, *his* Anthropocene, is consequently less triumphant. It is, in fact, a nightmare precisely to the extent that the Brave New World has achieved the position described by Julian: 'a world controlled by man.'[10] It is a nightmare precisely in its vision of Nature conceived as resources to be managed, Nature as zoned variously for habitation, industry, agriculture, recreation, and incarceration (e.g. Malpais and the dissident isles).

At the same time, we can't but countenance the *other* side of Aldous's ambivalence, the side that brings him into parallel with Julian: namely, his endorsement of eugenics, of sterilization for the 'sub-normal', of class segregation, and so on. This 'hidden Huxley', as David Bradshaw styles him, is very far indeed from the acid-tripping hoot owl of the hippie generation.[11] *That* Huxley, the one who in *The Perennial Philosophy* opined that '[i]t is by losing the egocentric life that we save the hitherto undiscovered life which [...] we share with the divine Ground'—a sort of first principle of the Age of Aquarius—is, remarkably, the same Huxley who in *Literature and Science* (1963) catechizes, with equal piety, that '[s]cience is a matter of disinterested observation, unprejudiced insight, and experimentation, [and] patient ratiocination within some system of logically correlated concepts' (*HCE6* 126).[12] It isn't that the ideas themselves are antithetical so much as the temperaments we imagine could support them. The mystic and the positivist are equally improbable in the Anthropocene, or anyway mirror images of a dangerous faith—to find them both in one and the same figure not only courts paradox, but confirms it.

Brave New World, therefore, no less than its author, embodies the fraught double-message of the Anthropocene: mastery and mortification. Our heightened awareness of precarity, of our contingent relation to the environment, of the need for renewed scrutiny of ecological assumptions—these inform our sense of the stakes of the novel. Because whatever else it is, the Anthropocene potentially heralds the dawn of radical ecological consciousness, a more palpable sense of living and non-living things in relation to each other, and a recalibration of values and priorities: an ethics *after* people. Setting aside the novel's aesthetic and historical merits—elucidated by other critics, and worthier—and declining also to defend the novel in terms of its predictive accuracy—too often a journalistic garnish—I'd like to consider how the novel, as a purely speculative mode, helps us to suss out the meaning of our moment, particularly its ethical meaning, in which ecology is (seemingly more than ever) implicated.

The kernel of what I'm calling 'ethics after people', to indicate the extension of moral consideration beyond the human sphere, was, ironically enough, proposed in the early Anthropocene by the very thinker whose utilitarian philosophy would, via John Stuart Mill and Henry Ford, shape Huxley's Brave New World: Jeremy Bentham. In an oft-cited footnote to *An Introduction to the Principles of Morals and Legislation* (1789), Bentham radically reframes the question of what morally qualifies a creature for protection under the law. Imagining a day when 'the rest of animal creation may acquire the rights which never could have been withholden from them but by the hand of tyranny', he asserts that the fundamental criterion is not whether animals can reason or speak, but '[c]an they *suffer?*'[13] The ecocritic Lawrence Buell places this passage alongside Darwin's discussion, nearly a century later, of 'sympathy beyond the confines of man [...] extended to all sentient beings' as evidence of a burgeoning ethics after people.[14] For Bentham and Darwin, such an ethics proceeds by a democratization of feeling, qualified by the capacity for suffering or sentience. Fellow-feeling is no longer an idiosyncrasy of humankind, let alone its sovereign province, but part, we might say, of an ecological outlook.

Far from a sense of general weal, however, such an outlook can't help but be bleak in the Anthropocene, where Nature is a site of ongoing spoliation. In her recent *cri de coeur*, 'Anthropocene, Capitalocene, Plantationocene, Chthulucene: Making Kin' (2015), Donna Haraway asserts that 'to live and die well as mortal critters' in the Anthropocene vitally involves gestures of recuperation as well as 'mourning irreversible losses'; indeed for her 'flourishing cannot grow from [...] failure to become-with the dead and the extinct'.[15] It isn't just that humanity can no longer watch the drama of Nature unfold from the loges of moral and biological superiority, but that we must linger at a death scene in which we are both actor and spectator. Ecology in the Anthropocene is a *dark* ecology, and dark ecology, as Timothy Morton argues, is a 'melancholy ethics', at the center of which is 'the contingent and necessarily queer idea that we want to stay with a dying world'.[16] In other words, the endpoint of 'extensionist thinking' *à la* Bentham and Darwin entails two admissions: firstly, that humans are de-essentialized, rather than the measure of all things; and secondly, that we're all in the soup.[17] If humans are de-essentialized, our humanity reduced to something historically contingent, then that means we are a site of construction—'"the much more interesting world"', as Mr Foster enthuses, '"of human invention"' (*BNW* 10).

But this contingency was already the lesson of Darwin before it was the premise of Huxley (see my endnote 3). In the absence of essence, better living in the Brave New World is accomplished through basic chemistry and psychology: alcohol and pituitary in the 'blood-surrogate', immunization, and exposure to toxic substances on the one hand; hypnopaedia and behavioral conditioning on the other. The efficacy of these measures in the Brave New World seems, if anything, to confirm a bald materialism, the notion that human life (even in its 'nobler' moral and aesthetic dimensions) is reducible to metabolism, to glands, hormones, and enzymes. Far from a rejection of secular humanism and its emphasis on the inner life, the core ethical principle of the Brave New World—compulsory and, essentially, 'neural' happiness—seems a horrid literalization of Satan's quip, in *Paradise Lost*, that '[t]he mind is its own place', as if the lessons of Quixote and Hamlet in turn, their humanist insistence on the power of the mind to trump the circumstances of the flesh, were less refuted than intensified, compressed, and reintroduced in easy-to-swallow tablet form.[18] The Brave New World is therefore not a break with modernity as handed down from Cervantes, Shakespeare, and Milton, but its full flower. If we regard it with no small dismay, we are only reacting to possibilities inherent to the humanist world-picture. *Brave New World* imagines an endpoint of humanism, at once logical and inimical, wherein all 'are physico-chemically equal' (*BNW* 63); wherein Nature exists solely as a backdrop for 'country sports' (*BNW* 18); wherein sublimity can be measured in grams of *soma* (*BNW* 47). This is the meaning of the Anthropocene, the irony of our 'ascendance': our ontology, our ecology, our ethics are at last revealed in all their flatness, darkness, and melancholy.

THE OLD VIVIPAROUS DAYS

On its surface, *Brave New World* seems primarily interested in hierarchy, not flatness; radiance, not darkness; vivacity, not melancholy. Its society is striated by class and occupation; everything in it, we are told, is clean and bright; and its people contented and death-averse. Patrick Parrinder notes, however, that '[w]hile Huxley's New Worlders have done everything possible to break their links with the human past', that very past 'comes back to haunt them'.[19] We, in effect, are their bogeymen. The 'old viviparous days' (*BNW* 4), in the Director's quaint parlance, is shorthand not only for a disavowed biological past (i.e. sexual reproduction), but an ethical one as well, when human relations were organized according to kinship and obligations according to ontology. If the Anthropocene ultimately puts paid to certain ancient prejudices about where humans fit into the grand pecking order, those prejudices nonetheless persist, if only to be burlesqued, in the Brave New World: the haunting works both ways. So while the Brave New World is superficially hierarchical, bright, and pleasant, those aspects only serve to point up darker thematic and symbolic realities—its own and ours, 'the monstrosity of a world', as Peter Firchow writes, 'that is in many ways the mirror image of our own, and that, because of this similarity, we may be in danger of accepting'.[20] Just as the Brave New Worlders disavow their human past, we disavow our post-human future.

Reproduction is the initial site of both disavowals: viviparity in the case of the Brave New Worlders, ectogenesis in our own.[21] Each represents for the other an assault on human dignity, either a reminder of our basic animal nature or a vision of our supersession by technology. As early as his first novel, *Crome Yellow* (1921), Huxley submitted ectogenesis to satiric scrutiny. Ectogenesis was rather in the air it seems, a subject of general scientific and philosophical interest. J.B.S. Haldane's *Daedalus; or, Science and the Future* (1924) and J.D. Bernal's *The World, the Flesh, and the Devil* (1929), both published in the influential *To-day and To-morrow* series (1924–1931), are routinely cited in connection with *Brave New World*, though clearly Huxley had considered the matter for some years prior.[22] The pontificating character of Mr Scogan (loosely based on Bertrand Russell, whom Huxley met while living and working at Garsington Manor during the First World War) imagines 'vast state incubators' in which 'rows upon rows of gravid bottles will supply the world with the population it requires' (*CY* 23). Reproduction having been rationalized, '[t]he family system', he continues, 'will disappear [and] society, sapped at its very base, will have to find new foundations' (*CY* 23). The caste system he envisions filling the void, in which 'human beings will be separated out into distinct species' (*CY* 124)—namely 'the Directing Intelligences, the Men of Faith, and the Herd' (*CY* 125), each bred specifically to the purpose—uncannily anticipates the social structure of the Brave New World and explicitly positions humanism as a fantasy for duping the masses, convincing them that 'they are happy, that they are tremendously important beings, and that everything they do is noble and significant', restoring them 'to the centre of the universe and [...] to pre-eminence on the earth' (*CY* 126). Against the enlightened sobriety of the Directing Intelligences, the lives of the Herd, however deluded, will pass 'in a rosy state of intoxication from which they will never awake' (*CY* 127), a 'lifelong bacchanal' (*CY* 127) of not so much sensual as emotional gratification.

The Director's sneering allusion to the 'old viviparous days' in *Brave New World* is but an echo of Mr Scogan's indictment of 'Nature's hideous system' (*CY* 23): sexual reproduction as a scene of animadversion to which Huxley returns in *Ape and Essence* (1948), whose characters, devil-worshipping post-nuclear mutants, pray on the one hand for 'detumescence' (*AE* 27 *et passim*) and engage on the other in massive seasonal mating rituals (*AE* 111). In each case, Huxley presents what Theodor

Adorno calls 'organized orgiastics' (*AHU* 103), an ironical image of licensed and mandatory transgression. In Huxley's fictions sexuality ceases to be subversive when it is decoupled from reproduction ('civilization is sterilization'; *BNW* 94); and promiscuity is in fact the basis for social stability ('everyone belongs to everyone else'; *BNW* 34). The reader may be forgiven for not quite knowing what sexual attitudes are being lampooned: bourgeois heteronormativity or Bloomsbury Group libertinism? According to Adorno, Huxley correctly identifies 'the contradiction that in a society where sexual taboos have lost their intrinsic force [...], pleasure itself degenerates to the misery of "fun"', but finds himself thereby roundly on the side of repression, 'fail[ing] to distinguish between the liberation of sexuality and its debasement' (*AHU* 103). For all its 'shocking' permissiveness, the Brave New World defines sexuality only in the narrowest, most conventional terms: even masturbation and homosexuality are, it would seem, like vivipary, relics of a former, barbaric age (*BNW* 27).

Caught in his own kind of gender trouble, Huxley doesn't quite know how to tackle the 'problem' of Woman or sexuality in general. Considering the limitations of Huxley's thought in this respect, June Deery concludes 'that [he] sins more by omission than intention', a victim of his class, certainly, but also a delicate disposition, capable of addressing sexual politics in the delivery room, but not the bedroom.[23] While he could acknowledge, apropos of D.H. Lawrence, that the latter had struck upon 'the best possible solution' when it came to depicting sexual experience, namely 'a soaring lyrical eloquence, firmly anchored [...] to the most uncompromisingly explicit of four-letter words', Huxley could not bring himself to utter it, referring euphemistically to the 'Saxon tetragrammata' (*HCE6* 103). The Brave New World is likewise shot through with Victorian artifacts of this sort, not least of which is the coy term 'pneumatic'—applied to sofas, shoes, and women alike to indicate comfort, voluptuousness, and (in the latter case) sexual buoyancy. Detached from its reproductive destiny or burden, the female body is repurposed for recreation. In a certain light, this can't be but liberating. As Elizabeth Grosz points out, patriarchal ideologies typically function by asserting that 'women's oppression is, at least to some extent, biologically justified insofar as women are less socially, politically, and intellectually able to participate as men's equals when they bear or raise children'[24]; ectogenesis would on this score seem to vitiate the ideological basis for oppression. But is that the case in the Brave New World? Do its women seem the equals of its men? Though they no longer bear children, I would contend that they are in fact more profoundly bound than ever to an abjected notion of the female (reproductive) body, subject to ever more minute, specific and, above all, *compulsory* gynecological ministrations—the whole raft of hormones, extracts, and whatnot that comprise the Pregnancy Substitute and Malthusian drill. What appears at first as a dampening or flattening of sexual ontology—remove childbirth from the equation and men and women differ at only the most minor level of plumbing—winds up reinforcing gender difference. Barring Dr Wells, Fanny and Lenina's physician, men of the Brave New World seem scarcely aware of contraception, let alone endocrinology.

The erasure of female biology in *Brave New World* tends in fact to reinforce the sexist view that women's bodies require more policing than men's because 'women are somehow more biological, more corporeal, more natural than men'[25]; the novel's women are surrounded by constant reminders of their disavowed biology, their lockers and medicine cabinets full of 'boxes and labelled phials' (*BNW* 32), substances perpetually to be swallowed and injected. Ovaries are routinely excised 'for the good of Society, not to mention [...] a bonus amounting to six months' salary' (*BNW* 3). Here is a denial of Woman masquerading as liberation, just as 'pneumatic' is derogation masquerading as compliment. It seems to fill the gap of the disavowed and pornographic term 'mother' with the equally pornographic image of the female body as a sex pump—in the process displacing the figurative etymological sense of *pneuma* as 'spirit' or 'soul' for its literal sense as 'wind' or 'air': woman as an empty thing, a figure of hollowness or negativity fully in line with sexist denials of female interiority and substance. The pneumatic women of *Brave New World* are figured in terms of readiness-to-hand, an unreflective, instrumental relation, but the very terms of the figuration entail what Parrinder means by haunting. A ghost, or anyway a spirit, peeks out from the sex machine.

If the repressed truth of a woman's body returns in this subtle way (and in a less-than-subtle way in the form of Linda, an actual mother), then the more general truth of the human body does as well. Secreted within attitudes toward sexuality and reproduction are attitudes about ecology as well—the body as an evolutionary document. Vivipary is not unique to humans or even, for that matter, animals; certain plants can exhibit forms of vivipary. It is a condition which links us to other living things, that provides a reminder of our shared evolutionary heritage, an affective ground for sympathy. The Brave New World rejects the implications of this biological heritage in lieu of a technological one, trading one kind of flatness for another—a kind of smearing or indistinction between humans, whether the 'uniform batches' of '[s]tandard men and women' (*BNW* 5) touted by the director or the 'nightmare of swarming indistinguishable sameness' (*BNW* 183–4) from which John Savage recoils. 'Everybody belongs to everybody else' is not just a sexual slogan, but a genetic truth, thanks to Bokanovsky and Podsnap. But in the language of the Brave New World, even its silly hit song, 'Bottle of Mine', one glimpses the specter, if only at a figurative level, of a more expansive ecology in which helicopters buzz like insects, buildings resemble mushrooms, clouds bulge like athletic torsos, and humans scuttle about like ants (*BNW* 52–4) or dart like fish (*BNW* 175), in which fetuses 'ripen' (*BNW* 3) and 'bud' (*BNW* 3) like fruits. In this uncanny way there persist images of interconnectedness which, far from eliding difference, generate an ever more intense apprehension of immanent, inscrutable, pervasive otherness. Indeed, for Huxley humans are practically others to themselves, a 'race of multiple amphibians, uneasily living at one and the same moment in four or five different and disparate universes' (*HCE6* 131).

ETHICS AFTER PEOPLE

Otherness, not to put too fine a point on it, is inimical to the World State, a fact writ large in its motto COMMUNITY, IDENTITY, STABILITY. It therefore approaches otherness (that is, strangeness and difference) with suspicion. The IDENTITY of the State motto is not personal but communal, and therefore any assertion of individuality is considered adversarial to all. At the same time, the stability of the community requires occasional exposure to otherness, if only to reassert its commitment to identity. As Huxley's contemporary Carl Schmitt put it:

> The political enemy is the other, the stranger; and it is sufficient for his nature that he is, in a specially intense way, existentially something different and alien, so that in the extreme case conflicts with him are possible. These can neither be decided by a previous determined general norm nor by the judgment of a disinterested and neutral party.[26]

In other words, the Brave New World cannot quite exist without its savages. Malpais is not permitted owing to the State's benignity, but to structural necessity: between Mustapha Mond and John there can be no détente, a situation the former seems to understand perfectly and which the latter grasps only belatedly and to his despair. The World State can only function by a kind of push-pull of unity and apartheid, the consolidation of its population under various political rubrics: its caste system as well as its extra-juridical zones like the dissident isles.

But there are other ways of viewing the other and the stranger that don't inscribe them straight away as political enemies. There are, primordially, the ethical other, from whom issues a ceaseless call for acknowledgment, and, not unrelated, the ecological other, what Timothy Morton calls the 'strange stranger'.[27] To encounter the other as the strange stranger is to be attuned to the entanglement of living and non-living things: 'Nothing exists all by itself, and so nothing is fully "itself"', Morton writes; as a consequence, existence becomes perceived not as an abstract plane or billiard table across which we and all other things carom, but as a 'mesh' of irreducible interconnections.[28] Not IDENTITY, but co-implication. When we contemplate living and non-living things as aspects of the mesh, they become very strange, their boundaries more difficult to discern. They are other, but not wholly separable from us.

The ideology of the World State, and the humanism that subtends it, prepares the Brave New Worlders for a confrontation with the other only as an enemy and not a strange stranger. The state, Huxley wrote in *An Encyclopædia of Pacifism*, is 'a community organized for war', and given that definition it shouldn't surprise us that modern political life is for him overdetermined by an essential enmity.[29] Such an enmity takes the form, in *Brave New World*, of a shallow fascination with John Savage, one that does not seek a real encounter with otherness, but an ultimately comforting and harmless caricature, essentially consigning him to his 'long night of pain' (*BNW* 216). Whereas for John the night, its fears and perils, are part of the ritual maturation and a fact of ethical life, for the Brave New Worlders the night is merely a time for sexual carousal and hypnopaedic reinforcement. There is, in this visceral rejection of the night, something more than a little suggestive of the metaphorics of Emmanuel Levinas, for whom the night signified the sort of ambient background of anonymous being through which the ethical subject wanders, insomniac, like John a '[b]enighted fool' (*BNW* 221) in a kind of waking nightmare.[30] The Brave New Worlders prefer to live in 'happy ignorance of the night' (*BNW* 67); when it is experienced, it is only ever 'depressing' (*BNW* 65) or, worse, a horrible 'rushing emptiness' (*BNW* 78).

If we concede that a failure to confront the night is also, at some figurative level, an ethical failure, a denial of otherness, then what is the alternative? In *Brave New World*, it is, apparently, abjection, a subhuman or animalized existence in the Reservation (*BNW* 93–4). But this is an example of what I've been pointing out as the bad wiring between humanist ethics and the novel. For George Woodcock, *Brave New World* presents the reader with an ethical dilemma—submit to the world of Mustapha Mond or fight for the world of John Savage—where the choice is obvious: 'The anti-individualist tendencies latent in our society have to be opposed by the poetic primitivism of the savage, who alone, since he is the only character conscious of tragedy, can embody the tragic possibilities of man's future'.[31] To the modern reader, however, it may well seem that Mustapha Mond is, if anything, *more* conscious of tragedy than is John Savage, who remains blinkered by naïve romanticism. It is only Mond who grasps both sides of the situation and thus understands the terms of the dilemma; and this is partly why his disquisition is quite strangely, given our sense of Huxley's ostensible thesis, more persuasive than John's flimsy protestations. Mond has, by his own lights, made the more difficult choice and opted for 'a harder master [...] than truth', namely 'other people's happiness' (*BNW* 200). Is this not, as William Blake put it, 'the most sublime act', putting the needs of others before one's own? Because John too, as a humanist, accepts happiness as an ethical good, he finds it difficult to refute the Controller and is forced instead to concede, awkwardly, to the agonies of old age, disease, and torture (*BNW* 212). But this whole dilemma is conditioned by its humanist frame, which countenances happy abjection and doleful dignity as the only options. If in the Anthropocene we jettison the frame or find it no longer tenable, what other possible choices emerge? Is there a way to split the difference, as it were, between Mond and the Savage, or to conjure up new options altogether?

Huxley himself tried to do as much in his final novel, *Island* (1962), as well as in his psychedelic and mystical writings. These later efforts stemmed from his growing sense that 'any attempt to influence humanity outside a moral ambiance inspired by mystical religion was a futile palliative'.[32] In the Anthropocene, however, primitivist or mystical retrenchment is no longer an option, nor is (continued) techno-optimism. What seems to be needed is an ecologically inflected ethics, an ethics after people, which can rebut instrumentalist rationality without falling back on a specious otherworldliness; which can utilize and promote scientific knowledge, even disturbing knowledge, to the betterment of species rather than to maintain the illusion of human exceptionality and privilege.

The ontology of the Anthropocene, I have suggested, is relatively flat: obviously there exist differences between human and non-human beings, but these increasingly seem a matter of degree rather than kind. Everywhere we see continua, rather than exclusive categories: many ethologists and linguists, for example, nowadays assert that animal communication systems are effectively language; and the idea of 'minimal cognition', a notion of plant-intelligence, is slowly gaining traction among theoretical biologists.[33] For some, these ideas seem to threaten or undermine the possibility of human meaning; for others, they create a more profound sense of intimacy with the natural world. And along with that intimacy comes a premonitory consciousness, a dark ecology. For Nature is not a harmonious, self-sustaining system designed to promote the comfort of all creatures; it is also violent and chaotic. The ties that bind us to one another are therefore tinged with a melancholy born of our fragility and finitude. Whatever narratives we tell ourselves to elevate humanity above baser creatures, at the end of the day we persist within and subsist upon the same commonwealth of nutrients, to which we inevitably return in death, becoming literally a geologic factor in the perpetuation of life.

To deny this represents what McKenzie Wark, after Karl Marx, calls a 'metabolic rift', like the charnel houses of the Brave New World that harvest trace elements from crematory smoke, preventing them from returning to renew 'the molecular flows out of which our shared life is made and remade'.[34] The Anthropocene is a series of metabolic rifts that are at one and the same time ecological and ethical. The vital question we must ask ourselves, and which *Brave New World* helps us to think, is what kind of ethics survives the dismantling of humanism and its false dilemma of freedom or happiness, what kind of ethics can usher us past these metabolic rifts and into a Brave New World worthy of the name? Though Huxley's novel is generally read as a defense of humanism in the face of rampant technological will, it actually stages an ethical failure. In the terms of that failure, however, we can perhaps see hints of a future that is, in the words of Nicolas Berdiaeff, *moins 'parfaite' et plus libre.*

NOTES

1. The student of philosophy will no doubt recognize here the stamp of Emmanuel Levinas (1906–1995), whose concepts are being used in a way somewhat contrary to his intent. As a committed humanist, Levinas would find the coinage 'ethics after people' nonsensical. Only on a very few occasions did he hint at the possibility of an ethics extending beyond humans (for example, in 'The Name of the Dog, or Natural Rights', an essay about his incarceration in a Nazi prison camp and the stray dog who befriended

him and his fellow inmates), but that has not prevented others from using his ideas as the foundation for a non-anthropocentric ethics. See, for example, D. Perpich, *The Ethics of Emmanuel Levinas* (Stanford: Stanford University Press, 2008), particularly Chap. 2.

2. We shall have to bracket here a parallel reading of Huxley's *Island*, whose 'mysticism', while fascinating and clearly preferable to the 'humanism' of *Brave New World*, is also fundamentally compromised. It is, to my thinking, a wrong step in the right direction. Further, I am not entirely convinced it represents Huxley's attempt at describing a cultural program or antidote to modernity, as is implied, for example, in Jeffrey J. Kripal's glancing assessment in 'Brave New Worldview', *Chronicle of Higher Education*, 55.16 (12 Dec. 2008): B7–B9. Jerome Meckier, having earlier argued that 'in *Island* […] Huxley offers his own version of the future' (see *Aldous Huxley: Satire and Structure* (London: Chatto & Windus, 1969), p. 175), has more recently concluded that the novel actually articulates Conradian despair, a culminating vision of existence as a 'routine of successive agonies in the bargain basement' (*I* 318); see J. Meckier, 'Conradian Reminders in Aldous Huxley's *Island*: Will Farnaby's *Moksha*-Medicine Experience and "The Essential Horror"', *Studies in the Novel*, 35 (Spring 2003): 44–67. For a more positive assessment of the novel's utopian possibilities, see W.M. Curtis, 'Rorty's Liberal Utopia and Huxley's *Island*', *Philosophy & Literature*, 35.1 (Apr. 2011): 91–103.

3. According to Manuel de Landa, it is Charles Darwin who laid the foundation for this kind of thinking by breaking with the Platonic/Aristotelian notion of species as 'eternal archetypes', by instead seeing them as historical; the biologist Michael Ghiselin, he continues, extends Darwin's logic by seeing species as '*individuals*, not kinds' (Manuel de Landa, *Intensive Science and Virtual Philosophy* (New York: Continuum, 2002), p. 46). The upshot of this conceptual extension is that 'while an ontology based on relations between general types and particular instances is *hierarchical*, each level representing a different ontological category (organism, species, genera), an approach in terms of interacting parts and emergent wholes leads to a *flat ontology*, one made exclusively of unique, singular individuals, differing in spatio-temporal scale but not in ontological status' (De Landa, *Intensive Science*, p. 47). Our discussion here will take up how Huxley's novel allows us to think about the fate of ethics within such an ontology.

4. See Albertus Magnus, *Questions Concerning Aristotle's 'On Animals'*, trans. I.M. Resnick and K.F. Kitchell, Jr (Washington, DC: The Catholic University of America Press, 2008), pp. 16–17; Galen, *On the Usefulness of the Parts of the Body (Peri Chreias Morion. De usu partium)*, trans. M. Tallmadge May (Ithaca, NY: Cornell University Press, 1968), vol. 2, p. 630; and Aristotle, *Politics*, trans. B. Jowett, in *The Basic Works of*

Aristotle, ed. R. McKeon (New York: Random House, 1941), pp. 1113–1316, at 1.1253a. Aristotle adds an important, and for our purposes highly relevant, caveat: 'man, when perfected, is the best of animals, but, when separated from law and justice, he is the worst of all' (ll. 31–2).

5. The others, 'encompassed and sustained [by virtue]', being philosophy, astronomy, and alchemy (Paracelsus [Theophrastus Bombastus von Hohenheim], *Essential Theoretical Writings*, ed. and trans. A. Weeks (Leiden: Brill, 2008), p. 75). Linking high and low, ethical virtue for Paracelsus is associated with mercury, as the soul with sulfur, and the flesh with salt. If his cosmos (or grand ecology) is not quite 'flat' in the sense I've suggested, there is nonetheless a strong connection between the mineral and spiritual. Each 'layer' of ontology, from the grossest to the most sublime, is implicated in all the others.

6. M. Heidegger, *The Fundamental Concepts of Metaphysics: World, Finitude, Solitude*, trans. W. McNeill and N. Walker (Bloomington, IN: Indiana University Press, 1995), p. 185.

7. Heidegger, *The Fundamental Concepts of Metaphysics*, p. 198.

8. Francis Galton (1822–1911), an extraordinary polymath who made major contributions to multiple fields (several of which—e.g. meteorology and psychometrics—he essentially founded himself), is nowadays primarily known for his dubious ideas about eugenics, a term he coined in *Inquiries into Human Faculty and Its Development* (1883). The illustrious career and legacy of Charles Darwin, half-cousin to Galton, needs no dilation here, nor does that of T.H. Huxley, whose famous debate with Bishop Wilberforce greatly established the validity of evolution in the Victorian mind. The estimable poet and critic Matthew Arnold, Aldous Huxley's great-uncle, is not typically counted among this company, but Sylvia Bailey Shurbutt has argued persuasively that his complex attitudes toward Nature should be regarded as an important corrective to lingering Romanticism. See, S.B. Shurbutt, 'Matthew Arnold's Concept of Nature: A Synthesist's View', *Victorian Poetry*, 23.1 (Spring): 97–104. After a decent interval, these branches once again converge with the marriage of Angela Huxley, Aldous's half-niece, to George Pember Darwin, son of Charles Galton Darwin and great-grandson of Charles Darwin.

9. J. Huxley, 'Transhumanism', in *New Bottles for New Wine* (New York: Harper & Row, 1957), pp. 13–17, at p. 14. R.S. Deese contends that, despite Julian's anthropocentrism, 'his work with [various conservation agencies] should rank him as one of the pioneers of the more biocentric environmentalism that emerged in the sixties and seventies' (R.S. Deese, *We Are Amphibians: Julian and Aldous Huxley on the Future of Our Species* (Oakland: University of California Press, 2014), p. 148). Deese notes the further irony that it is in fact Aldous, darling of the Deep

Ecology movement, who remains indebted to 'the old, Fabian vision of a society ruled by technical experts' (ibid.).

10. J. Huxley, *What Dare I Think? The Challenge of Modern Science to Human Action and Belief* (London: Chatto & Windus, 1931), p. 42.
11. See *HH*, particularly Bradshaw's introduction and preludial essays on the influence upon Huxley of H.L. Mencken and H.G. Wells. Bradshaw presents the (often odious) material within a loose narrative framework of philosophical evolution, acknowledging that while 'the liberal-humanist does not emerge unscathed [...], it may well be that the Huxley who surfaces is a figure even more deserving of our attention' (*HH* xxiii). See also D. Bradshaw, 'Huxley's Slump: Planning, Eugenics and the "Ultimate Need" of Stability', in J. Batchelor (ed.), *The Art of Literary Biography* (Oxford: Clarendon Press, 1995), pp. 151–71. This and similar archival work by James Sexton and Robert S. Baker has proven an important counter to stereotypical portraits of Huxley as pacific doomster and spirit-guide. By contrast, Nicholas Murray's biography characterizes Huxley's writings on eugenics as little more than a 'brief flirtation' (*MAH* 200), chalking them up, in fact, to his catholic mind, for which no idea, on its face, was out of bounds.
12. A. Huxley, *The Perennial Philosophy* (London: Chatto & Windus, 1946), p. 124.
13. J. Bentham, *An Introduction to the Principles of Morals and Legislation* (1780; Oxford: Clarendon, 1907), p. 311n.
14. See L. Buell, *Writing for an Endangered World* (Cambridge, MA: Harvard University Press, 2001), pp. 224–8. The cited passage is from Darwin, *The Descent of Man, and Selection in Relation to Sex* (1871; rpt. Princeton, NJ: Princeton University Press, 1981), vol. 1, p. 101. The only real difference, I suppose, between Buell's 'nonanthropocentric ethics' (*Writing for an Endangered World*, p. 227) and 'ethics after people' is that the latter is articulated specifically in the shadow, if only fictive, of human extinction.
15. D. Haraway, 'Anthropocene, Capitalocene, Plantationocene, Chthulucene: Making Kin', *Environmental Humanities*, 6 (2015): 159–65, at 160–61.
16. T. Morton, *Ecology without Nature: Rethinking Environmental Aesthetics* (Cambridge, MA: Harvard University Press, 2007), p. 186 and p. 185.
17. Buell, *Writing for an Endangered World*, p. 225.
18. J. Milton, *The Complete English Poems*, ed. G. Campbell (London: Everyman's Library, 1992), p. 156.
19. P. Parrinder, 'Robots, Clones, and Clockwork Men: The Post-Human Perplex in Early Twentieth-Century Literature and Science', *Interdisciplinary Science Reviews*, 34.1 (Mar. 2009): 56–67, at 65.
20. P. Firchow, *The End of Utopia: A Study of Aldous Huxley's 'Brave New World'* (Lewisburg, PA: Bucknell University Press, 1984), p. 80.

21. Among journalists and bloggers of a futurist bent, there has been in recent years renewed interest in ectogenesis as an imminent reality. See, for example, I. Zoltan, 'Artificial Wombs Are Coming, but the Controversy is Already Here', *Motherboard* (4 Aug. 2014). Available at http://motherboard.vice.com/read/artificial-wombs-are-coming-and-the-controversys-already-here (accessed 11 Oct. 2015); D. Warmflash, 'Artificial wombs: the coming of motherless births?', *Genetic Literacy Project* (12 June 2015). Available at http://www.geneticliteracyproject.org/2015/06/12/artificial-wombs-the-coming-era-of-motherless-births/ (accessed 11 Oct. 2015); R. Salam, 'The end of pregnancy: And the inevitable rise of the artificial womb', *Slate* (23 Oct. 2014). Available at http://www.slate.com/articles/news_and_politics/culturebox/2014/10/ectogenesis_the_end_of_pregnancy_and_the_inevitable_rise_of_the_artificial.html (accessed 11 Oct. 2015).

22. For an insightful discussion of Huxley's intellectual debts, particularly to Haldane, whose ideas Huxley may have encountered via Julian as earlier as 1919, see Firchow, *The End of Utopia*, pp. 40–5.

23. J. Deery, 'Technology and Gender in Aldous Huxley's Alternative(?) Worlds', *Extrapolation*, 33.3 (Fall 1992): 258–73, at 271.

24. E. Grosz, *Volatile Bodies: Toward a Corporeal Feminism* (Bloomington: Indiana University Press, 1994), p. 16.

25. Grosz, *Volatile Bodies*, p. 14.

26. C. Schmitt, *The Concept of the Political*, trans. G. Schwab (Chicago: University of Chicago Press, 1996), p. 27.

27. T. Morton, *The Ecological Thought* (Cambridge, MA: Harvard University Press, 2010), p. 40 *et passim*.

28. Morton, *The Ecological Thought*, p. 15 and p. 28.

29. A. Huxley (ed.), *An Encyclopædia of Pacifism* (London: Chatto & Windus, 1937), p. 76.

30. See, for example, E. Levinas, *Existence and Existents*, trans. A. Lingis (The Hague and Boston: Martinus Nijhoff, 1978), pp. 53–5. For further commentary on this 'nocturnal' reading of Levinas, see T. Sparrow, *Levinas Unhinged* (Winchester: Zero Books, 2013).

31. G. Woodcock, *Dawn and the Darkest Hour: A Study of Aldous Huxley* (London: Faber and Faber, 1972), p. 180.

32. Woodcock, *Dawn and the Darkest Hour*, p. 223.

33. See M.D. Hauser, N. Chomsky, and W.T. Fitch, 'The Faculty of Language: What Is It, Who Has It, and How Did It Evolve?', *Science*, 298 (22 Nov. 2002): 1569–79; and P.C. Garzón and F. Keijzer, 'Plants: Adaptive Behavior, Root-Brains, and Minimal Cognition', *Adaptive Behavior*, 19.3 (June 2011): 155–71.

34. M. Wark, *Molecular Red: Theory for the Anthropocene* (London: Verso, 2015), p. xiii.

CHAPTER 11

'My Hypothetical Islanders': The Role of Islands in Aldous Huxley's *Brave New World* and *Island*

Jerome Meckier

Brave New World (1932), Aldous Huxley's best-known satirical novel of ideas, appears at times to be the victim of insufficient thought. For example, in a society whose religio-economic basis is Fordism, the ever more expedient mass production of people and goods, no one bothers to explain the absence of automobiles. None of the central characters—Bernard Marx, Helmholtz Watson, Lenina Crowne, and surely not John the Savage—has seen a 'flivver'; only the Director of Hatcheries and Conditioning (DHC) mentions it (*BNW* 37).[1] Assembly lines remain for other purposes, but cars are inexplicably extinct. The Savage's ability to parse Shakespeare boggles the mind. *The Complete Works* is a strange birthday present from Popé, who is not plausible as a book lover. An autodidact just turned 12, John instinctively knows that the 'enseamed bed' and 'nasty sty' (*BNW* 113) in

This essay is reprinted from the *Aldous Huxley Annual*, 12–13 (2012–2013): 319–40 by permission of the author and its editors. It has been shortened and reformatted.

J. Meckier (✉)
Department of English, University of Kentucky (Emeritus), Lexington, KY, USA

© The Editor(s) (if applicable) and The Author(s) 2016
J. Greenberg, N. Waddell (eds.), Brave New World: *Contexts and Legacies*, DOI 10.1057/978-1-137-44541-4_11

Hamlet are 'about Linda and Popé' (*BNW* 114). Huxley was too preoccupied with 'the application to human beings of the results of future research in biology, physiology and psychology' (*BNW* xliv) to avoid small failures of the imagination. When the Savage disrupts the *soma* distribution at the Park Lane Hospital for the Dying and the Deputy Sub-Bursar decides to call Helmholtz Watson for help, he looks up a number 'in the telephone book' (*BNW* 186). In A.F. 632, the Brave New World still relies on directories and rotary telephones.

Islands pose a bigger problem. Scattered throughout the novel, they are employed effectively but not consistently. Samoa, the Trobriands, Iceland, Cyprus, St Helena, the Marquesas, and the Falklands are all variations on the theme of separation, but is island exile punishment or reward? Iceland is a threat to Bernard Marx as is St Helena for an unnamed biologist, but for a special group of Alphas, Cyprus was a reward that turned sour; for Helmholtz Watson, the Falklands are a banishment that could be a blessing. Not until Pala in Huxley's last completed novel, *Island* (1962), did he spell out once and for all the role of an island in utopian fiction; it must be a necessarily isolated entity, as prescribed by Sir Thomas More, yet Huxley's perfect place cannot avoid an increasingly fatal inseparability.

Islands play a significant part in the history lesson that fills Chapter III of *Brave New World*. Mustapha Mond explains how 'Our Ford—or Our Freud' first revealed 'the appalling dangers of family life' (*BNW* 33), the plethora of complexes and neuroses it generates. Ever since, the Brave New World has abolished parenthood, decanting babies from bottles and educating its youth in state-run conditioning centers. An unidentified voice interrupts, mentioning simpler, saner solutions that prevail '"among the savages of Samoa, in certain islands off the coast of New Guinea"' (*BNW* 33). The voice points out that for Samoan children '[h]ome was in any one of twenty palm-thatched houses' (*BNW* 33). Able to move from family to family until comfortably situated, they are not subjected to 'every kind of perversion' (*BNW* 33) the way European youngsters were in pre-Freudian days.

Samoans have implemented something like the Mutual Adoption Clubs (MACs) that Huxley read about in Margaret Mead's *Coming of Age in Samoa* (1928).[2] Susila MacPhail describes them for Will Farnaby in *Island*. On Pala, 'everybody' in a club—15 to 25 couples—'adopts everyone else' (*I* 98). In such an 'open, unpredestined, inclusive family' (*I* 102), each child has dozens of parents to choose from. Neglect ceases to be a problem; abuse, incest, lust for the mother, and urges to kill the father disappear. To maintain a psychologically sound population, Samoans require only a few huts, not 'fifteen racks' of bottles on conveyors that travel '[t]wo thousand one hundred and thirty-six metres' around galleries on three floors (*BNW* 8). Instead of eliminating family, Samoan islanders have invented what Susila calls 'an entirely different kind' of it (*I* 98).

Similarly, the narrative voice in *Brave New World* continues, '[i]n the Trobriands conception was the work of ancestral ghosts; nobody had ever heard of a father' (*BNW* 33). Thanks to a comical superstition, these islanders are as immune as the Brave New Worlders to the Oedipus complex that torments John the Savage. To get rid of it, they need not apply the 'principle of mass production' (*BNW* 5) to biology. But Huxley does not explain why primitive phenomena such as thatched houses and belief in ghosts are still tolerated in parts of what is supposedly a World State.

Islands again become a concern in Chapter VI when the DHC threatens Bernard Marx with 'transference to a Sub-Centre'—preferably to Iceland (*BNW* 85). Only about 14,000 square miles smaller than Great Britain, Iceland seems large for a 'Sub-Centre'. Bad weather and involuntary isolation make a position there a terrible job. The DHC warns Bernard against further failure to maintain 'a proper standard of infantile decorum' after working hours (*BNW* 85). Iceland is clearly a negative place, ideal only for exile. Too uncivilized to be Sub-Centres, Samoa and the Trobriands were nevertheless used as positive locales, twin embarrassments that make the technologically proficient Brave New World seem primitive psychologically.

Initially 'undismayed', Bernard dismisses the DHC's warning as 'just a threat'; no one gets 'transferred for things like that', he rationalizes (*BNW* 85). Yet when he learns that the DHC has been '"looking out for someone to take [his] place"' (*BNW* 89), Bernard wails to Lenina, '"I'm going to be sent to Iceland"' (*BNW* 89). Huxley elaborates upon the DHC's warning in order to shatter Bernard's fragile bravado and expose his fundamental cowardice. Unlike Samoa and the Trobriands, however, Iceland reappears: in Chapter XVI, Bernard pleads with Mustapha Mond not to be sent there.

Chapter XII reinforces the idea of using islands for exile when the World Controller bans a paper titled 'A New Theory of Biology' (*BNW* 154). Its author posited 'some intensification and refining of consciousness' as the 'purpose' of earthly existence, a position that foreshadows the later Huxley's (*BNW* 154). By comparison, the Brave New World's *summum bonum*, 'maintenance of well-being' (*BNW* 154), seems shallow. Lest the biologist's heretical ideas unsettle the Brave New Worlders, his 'transference to the Biological Station of St Helena may become necessary' (*BNW* 154), Mond writes across the censored pages. Marx's potential exile sounded like a casual threat, no thought having been given to a society's systematic use of islands as a dumping ground for misfits and malcontents. Here that comic stroke has developed into an administrative policy for dealing with undesirables. But when as he composed the novel Huxley increased the role of islands, they had to accept gifted overachievers like the biologist, not just slackers like Bernard, while still remaining strictly punitive.

A British island of 47 square miles in the South Atlantic, St Helena was Napoleon's place of exile from 1815 until his death in 1821. For all its technological wizardry, the World State still falls back on a centuries-old method of isolating disruptive individuals. Although humane compared to solitary confinement or outright liquidation, island exile is hardly foolproof. Napoleon escaped from Elba, an Italian island in the Mediterranean, his first place of exile (1814–1815). That Mond bypasses Elba and selects St Helena straight off indicates a willingness to learn from past mistakes, even if Henry Ford maintained that history is bunk.

In Chapter XVI, prior to confessing that, as a young man, he narrowly avoided banishment to an island, Mustapha Mond gives Marx, Watson, and the Savage an account of 'the Cyprus Experiment' (*BNW* 196). On Cyprus, the Controller recalls, the Brave New World set up 'the only society of Alphas' in history (*BNW* 197) in the only utopian experiment ever conducted by a dystopia. The role that Cyprus plays in *Brave New World* differs substantially from the roles assigned to Samoa, the Trobriands, Iceland, and St Helena. Samoa and the Trobriands make the Brave New World's resort to elaborate mechanization look foolish. Iceland and St Helena both emphasize exile as punishment, but the latter specializes in ostracizing the Brave New Worlders whose excellence is unwanted, while the former appears to be reserved strictly for delinquents. Cyprus may have implanted in Huxley's mind the idea that an isolated island might be the perfect spot for utopia.

John inquires why the Brave New World does not '"make everybody an Alpha Double Plus"' (*BNW* 195). '"A society of Alphas"', Mond responds, '"couldn't fail to be unstable and miserable"' (*BNW* 195). On this point, he says, the Cyprus Experiment, a resounding failure, 'was convincing':

'The Controllers had the island of Cyprus cleared of all its existing inhabitants and re-colonized with a specially prepared batch of twenty-two thousand Alphas. [...] The result exactly fulfilled all the theoretical predictions. The land wasn't properly worked; there were strikes in all the factories; the laws were set at naught, orders disobeyed; all the people detailed for a spell of low-grade work were perpetually intriguing for high-grade jobs, and all the people with high-grade jobs were counter-intriguing at all cost to stay where they were. Within six years they were having a first-class civil war.' (*BNW* 196)

Although the long paragraph on the Cyprus fiasco seems pertinent to the discussion about islands in Chapter XVI, it remains a tour de force. Huxley takes a moment to ridicule implausible distributions of effort in the Wellsian utopia. In 'A Note on Eugenics', Huxley asked: where 'every individual is capable of playing the superior part, who will consent or be content to do the dirty work and obey?' (*HCE2* 284). He decided:

The inhabitants of one of Mr. Wells's numerous utopias solve this problem by ruling and being ruled, doing high-brow and low-brow work, in turns. While Jones plays the piano, Smith spreads the manure. At the end of the shift they change places; Jones trudges out to the dung-heap and Smith practices the A minor Etude of Chopin. An admirable state of affairs if it could be arranged. (*HCE2* 284)

But 'a state [...] of chronic civil war' (*HCE2* 284) is more likely, he predicted, because a 'state with a population consisting of nothing but these superior people could not hope to last for a year' (*HCE2* 285), an ominous forecast for any society of superiors such as Pala. The Brave New World's experiment on Cyprus confirmed the anti-Wellsian prophesies Huxley delivered five years earlier in *Proper Studies* (1927). Huxley's choice of details—'dung-heap' versus 'Chopin'—makes the idea of job rotation ludicrous. Which is more credible, Huxley asked Wells's admirers in 1932, cooperation between Jones and Smith or the Cyprus debacle?[3]

The failed experiment on Cyprus, Mond argues, justifies keeping 'eight-ninths' of the Brave New Worlders 'below the water-line' (*BNW* 197). A kind of floating island made of ice, Mond's 'iceberg' becomes Huxley's anti-Wellsian model for a perfectly organized society. The Cyprus community ridicules Wellsian job rotation within a World State that is already a complex refutation of Wells's. Nearly five centuries into its existence, the Brave New World implausibly considered abolishing its caste system with a universal upgrade on Cyprus. An all-Alpha society seems like a high-minded experiment in eugenics, an instance of benevolent social engineering: the 22,000 Alphas were 'specially prepared' (*BNW* 196). But one suspects that this experiment's failure was so predictable that the project was conducted to rule out alternatives to the status quo. In 1932, 'the Cyprus Experiment' was excellent satire that raised more questions about the role of islands in utopia than Huxley was prepared to answer. If Iceland and St Helena exist respectively for misfits like Bernard and over-achievers like the marine biologist, who does what Huxley called 'the dirty work' (*HCE2* 284) on either?

When the Palanese address the problem of high-brow, low-brow work, the solution is deceptively Wellsian. '"Changing jobs"', Dr Robert MacPhail emphasizes for Will Farnaby's edification, holds the key (*I* 167). '"[M]ost people like it better than doing one kind of job all their lives"' (*I* 167–8), he adds, which would be news to the Cyprians. The crucial difference is that the Palanese switch occupations willingly because they find changes therapeutic. 'Maximum efficiency' suffers in that everyone is always 'part-time' (*I* 167), Dr Robert admits, but 'human satisfaction' (*I* 168), all realize, takes precedence. Vijaya testifies that he enjoyed doing 'four months' in a 'cement plant', followed by 'six months in the jungle, as a lumberjack' (*I* 168). In his younger days, Dr Robert recalls, he '"did a stint at the copper smelters"', then worked on '"a fishing boat. Sampling all kinds of work—it's part of everybody's education"', he maintains; '"one learns an enormous amount […] about all kinds of people and their ways of thinking"' (*I* 168), provided, of course, this is society's agreed-upon goal. Evidently, the Controllers never thought to condition Cyprian Alphas to enjoy spells of menial labor. Vijaya and Dr Robert concur that physical toil benefits Pala's intelligentsia. Both have been out doing 'mus-cular work' (*I* 160) in the fields. '"In Pala"', explains Dr MacPhail, '"even a professor, even a government official, generally puts in two hours of dig-ging"' (*I* 161) every day. This sounds absurd until one compares diurnal digging with 'two rounds of Obstacle Golf' (*BNW* 47), the compulsory daily distraction for the Brave New Worlders.

When Mond tells Marx, Watson, and the Savage that in his youth, hav-ing conducted unauthorized physics experiments, he was 'on the point of being sent to an island' (*BNW* 199), Huxley confirmed the role of islands as a destination for the inconveniently talented. Bernard, in trouble for his part in the *soma* riot at the Park Lane Hospital, feels his old fears revive at the mention of islands. '"You can't send *me*. […] Oh, please don't send me to Iceland"' (*BNW* 199), he sobs, as if his Fordship knew the details of the DHC's earlier warning. Iceland remains for Bernard a geographical bugbear. But in Chapter XVI, the kind of island to which Mond was nearly sent sounds more exciting than the dead-end demotion proposed by the Director of Hatcheries and Conditioning. Because one can be dispatched to an island for displaying initiative and originality, the question again arises: which is an island exile after all—a reward or a punishment?

'"But *you* didn't go to an island"' (*BNW* 201), the Savage reminds Mond in Chapter XVI. The Controller admits that he regretfully sacrificed 'pure science' in exile for a position on the Controllers' Council (*BNW* 200). He makes transference sound more attractive than duty. Indeed, when Mond sentences Marx and Watson, being consigned to an island begins to seem like a blessing. Huxley alters banishment from the worst possible fate to a prize in disguise: '"punishment"', says Mond, that is '"really a reward"' (*BNW* 199). Watson will be 'sent to an island', the Controller decrees:

> 'That's to say, he's being sent to a place where he'll meet the most interest-ing set of men and women to be found anywhere in the world. [...] All the people who aren't satisfied with orthodoxy, who've got independent ideas of their own. Everyone, in a word, who's anyone. I almost envy you, Mr Watson.' (*BNW* 199–200)

Were it not for the 'almost', the reader might take Mond at his word and be envious also. Watson, he implies, is a privileged misfit. Earlier, he wasted no such sentiments on the marine biologist slated for St Helena. '"It's lucky"', Mond now muses, '"that there are such a lot of islands in the world. I don't know what we should do without them"' (*BNW* 201). Huxley, it seems, did not know exactly what to do with them; their role diversified as they multiplied.[4]

Mond offers Watson a choice of destinations: '"the Marquesas, for example, or Samoa"', both renowned for '"a tropical climate"' (*BNW* 201). Conceivably, Helmholtz is being awarded a vacation in paradise. He surprises Mond by choosing the equivalent of Iceland. When Mond asks, '"what about the Falkland Islands?"' Watson decides, '"Yes, I think that will do"' (*BNW* 202). He believes that he will 'write better' in bad weather. 'Officially' Mond disapproves of Watson's choice, but admires his 'spirit' (*BNW* 202). John the Savage is not so lucky. Mond denies his request to 'to go to the islands' (*BNW* 214) with Marx and Watson. When John's efforts to isolate himself in a Surrey lighthouse, in effect creating an island on land, fail dismally, the would-be islander commits suicide, the sole instance in *Brave New World* where *not* being sent to an island proves worse than being sentenced to one.

From the first, Huxley conceived of the novel's climax in Chapter XVII as a debate between opposing value systems: Mond represents the ideas of

H.G. Wells, Henry Ford, Freud, Pavlov, and Mond's namesake, the industrial magnate, Sir Alfred Mond; whereas John speaks for Shakespeare's conception of art and the life-worshipper's philosophy of D.H. Lawrence. However, in the spring and summer of 1931, between 27 May and 24 August, late in an extensive revision process, Huxley decided to bolster Watson's role as a potential third alternative to the 'insanity' of a Fordian utopia, on the one hand, and the 'lunacy' of an Indian village in Lawrence's beloved American southwest on the other (*BNW* xlii).[5] Thanks most likely to this revision, an island holds out to Watson a liberating opportunity for mental and spiritual advancement much as Pala in *Island* will prove rehabilitative for Will Farnaby.

In Chapter XVI, as it stands, Watson, Marx, and John are present at the start of the conversation with Mond. Then only Mond and the Savage talk in a section probably written *before* the chapter's opening pages. Huxley brought Watson and Marx back into the discussion for the chapter's third section, breaking up the talk with Bernard's hysterical collapse at the mention of islands.[6] Originally, on pages written earlier, Mond may have outlined 'the Cyprus Experiment' for the Savage's benefit only. That would explain why the account of this disaster jars against Mond's subsequent praise for Watson's upcoming destination. If a batch of specially prepared Alphas fared miserably on Cyprus, one wonders how a unit composed of disgruntled Alphas like Watson can do better on the Falklands. Possibly, Huxley wrote about Cyprus when parodying Wells was his top priority, that is, before Watson's prospects for enlightenment improved and the Falklands became more sanctuary than punishment.

The point to underline is that Huxley seems to have expanded the positive role of islands as Helmholtz Watson's importance to the novel increased. His burgeoning poetic urge presages spiritual growth. When Watson writes his first poem in Chapter XII, he embarks on the expansion of consciousness called for by the marine biologist.[7] The spectacle of Marx 'on his knees before the Controller', begging for 'another chance' (*BNW* 199), completed a key aspect of Huxley's revision process. Originally, the plot called for a rebellious Bernard, prompted by the Savage, to pose a real threat to the World State.[8] Now Marx collapses, and the Savage and Mond will argue to a standstill; only Watson still shows promise. In short, when Huxley proceeded to devastate Bernard and heroicize Helmholtz, he found island exile a useful vehicle for embarrassing the former and exalting the latter.

The narrative voice in *A Modern Utopia* (1905), presumably that of Wells's utopic alter ego, justifies his model society's reliance on 'islands of exile' (*MU* 103) to dispose of criminals and failures. He maintains that a modern utopia must 'purge itself' (*MU* 103). But Wells's alter ego reluctantly acknowledges that '"there is much dissatisfaction with our isolation of criminals upon islands"' (*MU* 186). When Huxley improved upon Wells's idea, he foresaw additional possibilities for islands depending on whether the malcontent was a scapegrace like Marx or, like Watson, a poet and nascent mystic. The inability to envision island exile as a complicated issue, Huxley implied, negated Wells as a practitioner of the discussion novel of ideas.[9]

When Huxley imagined Pala as an island, he resolved the separation issue posed by islands, the question of rewards versus punishment left unsettled in *Brave New World*. As the World State's opposite or 'reverse', Pala's policies systematically correct the former's mistakes.[10] Pala stands out as an alternative to the Brave New World's negative usage of Iceland and St Helena. Bypassing the Falklands, Huxley did not hesitate to choose a tropical setting for his ideal society. His final island depends for its appeal on a meticulous working-out of the Controller's guilty admiration for the 'most interesting' (*BNW* 199) islanders whom the soon-to-be exiled Watson is scheduled to meet. That is how the utopist wanted readers to regard the Palanese. To them, Miranda's outburst about 'beauteous mankind' (*BNW* 120, 184) applies straightforwardly.[11] In *Island*, Huxley changed the role of islands from that of a virtual penal colony into what Mond hints the Falklands may prove to be: the exceptional individual's only intellectual and spiritual haven in a mad world.

Pala resolves the counterpoint between primitivism and civilization that lies at the heart of *Brave New World*: Malpais versus Fordian London; a Lawrentian simple-lifer like the Savage versus a Wellsian Samurai such as Mond; native psychologists such as Samoans and Trobrianders versus Our Freud. In *Beyond the Mexique Bay* (1934), Huxley wished one could combine 'the virtues of primitives with those of the civilized', while exhibiting 'the vices of neither' (*HCE3* 576). The Palanese do this; they are Huxley's idea of noble savages. Only these islanders can be as rational and scientific as Wells's modern utopians, yet as natural and ritualistic as Trobrianders and Samoans. Thus Dr Robert MacPhail holds forth like a good technocrat on Pala's 'population policy' (*I* 89), which combines the latest techniques in experimental farming with universal birth control to produce better foods for a 'stable' population (*I* 90). At the same time, the initiation ceremony in Chapter X, where Palanese youth climb a mountain before ingesting the mind-expanding *moksha*-medicine, is the ideal community ritual. As a foretaste of enlightenment, it surpasses both the snake dance at Malpais in *Brave New World* and the Solidarity Service that Bernard Marx suffers through in Chapter V. As spiritually enlightened, technologically proficient primitives, Palanese islanders outstrip Wells's Samurai. They are not only Huxley's improvement on Lawrence's Indians of the North American Southwest, but also upon Samoans and Trobrianders; mentioned once and then largely forgotten, both receive their due in *Island* when Huxley ties up a loose end from *Brave New World*.[12]

Huxley strove throughout *Island* to be more consistent in his thinking about islands than he had been in *Brave New World*. With Pala, he scolded Wells for dealing in monolithic utopias.[13] Yet he also scoffed at Austin Tappan Wright's cult classic, *Islandia* (1942), for overestimating an island utopia's chances for survival. The challenge was to disown Wells's brand of utopia without seeming complicit with him when also parodying Wright—in effect cancelling both the World State and the island utopia. Huxley's solution was to present *Island* as a modification of Sir Thomas More's eponymous *Utopia* (1516): Pala is modern enough to offer a third alternative to Wells's scientific propaganda, on the one hand, and realistic enough to counter Wright's romantic fantasy on the other.

'No less than a planet', Wells pontificated, 'will serve the purpose of a modern Utopia. Time was when a mountain valley or an *island* seemed to promise sufficient isolation for a polity to maintain itself intact from outward force' (*MU* 15, italics added). Worldwide utopia, Huxley countered, almost certainly entails some measure of totalitarianism.[14] Authorities define perfection crudely and impose it on their charges. A small island, Pala is made up of even smaller constituencies.[15] In '"a federation of self-governing units"', Dr MacPhail explains, there is '"no place for any kind of dictator at the head of a centralized government"' (*I* 165).

Ranga, one of several islanders to engage Will Farnaby in expository conversations more like lectures, admits that Pala 'has been extraordinarily lucky' (*I* 88). Next-door-neighbor Rendang was overrun in turn by Arabs, Portuguese, Dutch, and English, but the Palanese escaped these 'infestations' (*I* 89) because their island was more difficult to reach. Consequently, Pala has not been victimized by planters and 'foreign administrators'; her soil has not been subjected to 'systematic exhaustion' (*I* 89). Still, Huxley's preference for an island utopia is compromised by Ranga's suspicion that Pala's survival has been a fluke. Huxley contends that Wells's demand for 'a planet' is dangerous to human liberty, yet he must attribute his ideal society's continued existence, her non-absorption into the so-called community of nations, mostly to luck. Nor, to recall Wells's words, can he "promise sufficient isolation [...] to maintain [Pala itself] intact' (see *MU* 15) from outsiders. In the closing chapter of *Island*, when Rendang annexes Pala, Wells's warnings turn out to be accurate. His World State is the best choice in *A Modern Utopia*, Huxley chided, because it is the only choice; in *Island*, however, the best choice does not remain viable for long. The novel reads like a requiem, a parody of the planetary World State that could also serve as a postmortem for the island utopia.

Although Mr Bahu's lecture-like talk with Will about Pala's status precedes Ranga's, it is the bleaker of the two assessments. Rendang's 'Voltairean' ambassador argues that Pala '"is out of context, [...] completely irrelevant to the present situation of the world in general"' (*I* 60). As long as it stayed 'completely off the map' (*I* 60), Pala could survive. That is, Bahu resumes, '"So long as it remains out of touch with the rest of the world, an ideal society can be a viable society. Pala was completely viable, I'd say, until about 1905. Then, in less than a single generation, the world completely changed"' (*I* 60), thanks to movies, cars, airplanes, and radio. '"By 1930 any clear-sighted observer could have seen that, for three quarters of the human race, freedom and happiness were almost out of the question. [...] What was once a viable ideal is now no longer viable"' (*I* 60), Bahu concludes.

The ambassador sums up viability the way Wells did: as a synonym for isolation. His choice of '1905' as the last time an island utopia stood a chance seems to validate the World State in *A Modern Utopia*, which was published that year. Picking '1930' as the cut-off date for the human race to be simultaneously free and happy, Bahu endorses *Brave New World*; published two years later, in 1932, it presented 'freedom and happiness' as one of life's fundamental counterpoints. In the novel's climactic debate, Mond champions happiness while John is willing to be unhappy if free. In *Island*, Huxley rejected Wells's call for global utopia only to appear to allow Pala to crumble in apparent accord with his rival's forecast.

Actually, Huxley's use of an island for utopia amounts to the conscientious revival of an anachronism whose time, he believed, had come again—in the real world Pala must be overcome, but in the realm of the imagination, in the genre of the utopia, an island could still function as the *hypothetical* alternative that utopia originally was meant to be. In 1962, Huxley returned utopian thinking to what it had been before 1905, when Wells got his hands on it. He charged Wells with replacing open-minded intellectual discussion with self-interested predictions: the future not only foreseen by H.G. Wells but also designed by him. *Brave New World* parodies the sort of utopia Wells wanted; *Island* attacks Wells's kind of utopian thinking.

To reorient twentieth-century literary utopianism, Huxley measured Austin Tappan Wright as well as H.G. Wells against Sir Thomas More. He contended that *Island* satisfies More's criteria in ways that Wells's *A Modern Utopia* and Wright's 1942 utopia *Islandia* do not. Huxley parodied Wright's first 500 pages by darkening the success for Islandia in remaining un-Westernized into catastrophe for Pala. When the latter is overrun by neighboring militaristic Rendang at the instigation of the West's oil companies, Huxley exposed Wright's naiveté to ridicule, much as he had earlier done with Wells's unacknowledged totalitarianism. Wells overlooked authoritarian propensities in planet-wide utopia; Wright seemed oblivious to an island utopia's fragility in an age of imperialism. At the start of the twentieth century, Islandia is threatened by imperialistic nations but survives; when multinational corporations endanger Pala in the 1950s, Rendang engulfs her.

In *Island*, Huxley risked seeming even less consistent about islands than he had been in *Brave New World*: first he preferred an island utopia to a planetary one, then he collapsed his island utopia for being vulnerable, just as Wells said anything smaller than a planet would be. Huxley was not contradicting himself, however. Although planet-wide utopia would be a genuine nightmare, a disaster that had to be forestalled, a utopia such as Pala had to remain imaginary, indeed, a daydream, because Huxley believed that ideals ought not to be presented as enduring entities. To Huxley's way of thinking, 'negative' utopia, thanks largely to Wells, had become a distinct possibility by 1932, whereas, 30 years later, 'positive' utopia was as impractical as ever.[16] The modern utopist's task, therefore, was to ridicule 'negative' utopias without deluding readers into expecting impossibly 'positive' ones.

In Wright's text, the character John Lang, recently graduated from Harvard, secures in 1907 an appointment as American Consul to Islandia, which is vaguely described as being situated on the northern portion of the Karain subcontinent in the southern hemisphere. For two years, the longest an outsider is allowed to visit, Lang will also operate as 'agent' for his uncle Joseph's company and for American 'commercial' interests in general (*WI* 25). They desire to sell the non-industrialized Islandians labor-saving equipment, such as agricultural implements and sewing machines. In return, American and European companies hope to investigate 'the possibilities of oil' (*WI* 300). Islandia has been given an ultimatum by the West: she must either ratify the Mora Treaty granting concessions to outside interests, as Lord Mora's pro-Western party wishes, or decide to keep her exclusionist laws in place, as Lord Dorn's followers recommend. If they do the latter, disappointed French and German concessionaires may goad their governments into invading.

At the start of *Island*, a freakish sailing accident washes Will Farnaby ashore on Pala so that he can infiltrate 'the Forbidden Island' (*I* 136) closed to all Westerners. Considerably older than Lang, the jaded, cynical Farnaby, ostensibly a journalist, is also a 'secret agent' (*I* 123) for Joe Aldehyde's Southeast Asia Petroleum, which covets the rights to Pala's rich oil deposits.[17] If Will can assist Pala's 'pro-oil minority' to reverse the island's policy of granting '[n]o oil concessions to anyone' (*I* 23), 'Uncle Joe' (*I* 116), as he calls his employer, will give him a year's sabbatical in which he can return to serious literature.

Lang and Farnaby both work for an avuncular businessman variously named Uncle Joseph, Joe Aldehyde (in *Island*), and 'Uncle Joe'. Thanks to Islandia, Lang begins to develop into the high-minded writer-journalist Huxley's Farnaby once was; he supplies American newspapers with even-handed articles about deliberations over the Mora Treaty. Joe Aldehyde in *Island* is greedier and less scrupulous than Lang's uncle, a not especially virulent caricature of America's burgeoning materialism at the start of the twentieth century. Farnaby and Lang both feel increasingly guilty about betraying their hosts. However, the latter's decision to resign as consul and his uncle's representative comes easier than Will's 'twinge of conscience' for 'plotting' to 'subvert' Pala (*I* 92). Wright has Lang choose the right side: Lord Dorn's policy triumphs without repercussions. In contrast, Farnaby helps to destroy Pala against the dictates of his conscience. Although he secedes from the pro-oil conspiracy he at first abetted, it succeeds despite his change of heart; his conversion cannot alter anything. Unlike Lang, Farnaby ultimately chooses the losing side, which Huxley implies, contrary to Wright, is what the right side often is.

In short, by an orderly vote of 23–11, Islandia's councilors turn down concession-seekers from France, Germany, and America. Islandia is allowed to remain isolated, unmolested. The island trades with no one; it accepts a maximum of 100 immigrants a year. In contrast, Mr Bahu—Rendang's ambassador is also a member of the pro-oil conspiracy—describes Pala 'as a small island surrounded by twenty-nine hundred million mental cases' (*I* 72). It is a doomed anomaly by the 1950s, fated to fall victim to the

West's imperialist greed. Which scenario, Huxley asked, is more likely: peaceful prosperity for Islandia or Rendang's annexation of Pala?

In the closing pages of *Island*, Dr Robert MacPhail, a Prospero figure who epitomizes Palanese values, is summarily shot by soldiers from Rendang. Will's future with Susila, Dr Robert's widowed daughter-in-law, the Miranda figure in Huxley's novel, remains uncertain. Wright's ending shows an American couple, Lang and Gladys Hunter, beginning a new life, Adam and Eve in the uncommercialized garden of *Islandia*. Anti-Miltonic to the core, Huxley depicts Will and Susila stranded in a lost paradise which Farnaby has helped to destroy. When *Island* was still a work-in-progress, Huxley knew that a utopia in the actual world could never succeed as well as Wright's: 'I'm afraid', he told the *Paris Review*, 'it must end with paradise lost—if one is to be realistic'.[18] Huxley felt that Wright allowed romantic fantasy to prevail in the face of harsh fact.

While Islandia will flourish forever, the island of Pala, from being the best place, turns into one of the worst. Pala submits to a faction that caters to the imperialist West's politicians, tycoons, generals, and moneylenders, whom Farnaby damns collectively as 'the cyanide of the earth' (*I* 87). Unlike Wright, Huxley realized that an island utopia can never be blameless; its goodness is an affront that neighbors will not abide. '*Too* good—that was their crime' (*I* 217), Will decides about the Palanese, using 'crime' ironically but not inadvisedly. Though entirely commendable, Pala nevertheless resembles the unsustainable private worlds that Huxley's eccentric characters are always setting up in order to reconfigure reality to suit themselves.[19] Where Lang becomes a staunch defender of Islandia, Farnaby, states Huxley, is 'the serpent in the garden'.[20] Poisonous imperialists, goodness as a reproach or insult, a remorseful, formerly serpentine protagonist—these are grave matters beyond Wright's ken, Huxley's parodic reworking seems to say.

On 11 June 1908, with Theodore Roosevelt in the White House and America the epitome of big business, John Lang records 'the most important event in Islandia's history' (*WI* 437). The vote pitting exclusionists, calling themselves Utopians, against the forces for change boils down to what Lang calls a 'test of a nation's right to be individualistic, to work out alone her own way of living, to refuse to yield to the new Western civilization, commercial and industrial, and to hold for itself material things, which other countries coveted, because the touch of the foreigners upon these things would endanger what she believed to be good' (*WI* 437). Pala fails this test in the 1950s because Huxley believed that Islandia should not have passed it so easily in 1908. Although vastly superior to Islandians intellectually and spiritually, the Palanese yield to 'Western civilization' and their island loses control of its materials. Bahu, one remembers, conceded Pala's viability 'until about 1905' (*I* 60). Wright grants Islandia three additional years before she is seriously threatened; then he extends her viability indefinitely. Pala lasts 50 years longer than Bahu's cut-off date, and for half a century after Wells predicted the advent of planet-wide utopia; but Pala's demise in the 1950s made Islandia's good fortune in 1908 seem like a stay of execution.

Huxley invented Pala, one must reiterate, simultaneously to resist Wells's idea of planetary utopia and to redo Wright's island utopia more realistically. Wells and Wright had both sinned against the cardinal rules for utopian fiction as exemplified in More's *Utopia*. They wrote utopias that the inventor of the genre would not have condoned: the former insisted on a planet instead of an island, whereas the latter posited an actual island instead of a purely conjectural one. Formerly called Abraxa, More's Utopia became an island because King Utopus, who gave the place its new name, dug up 15 miles of territory so that the sea could surround the land (*U* 56). Apparently, the King thought Utopia would be more secure reconfigured as an island. Following More, Huxley insisted in a letter (19 Jan. 1962) to Ian Parsons at Chatto & Windus that his last novel is really about 'the precariousness of happiness, the perilous position of any Utopian island in the context of the modern world' (*AHL* 928).

Island utopias become more secure in proportion to the difficulty in finding them. Not even More knew exactly where Utopia is located, most likely because it is a figment of his imagination. Raphael Hythloday, a seasoned mariner, told More about his journey to the island of Utopia in the New World, where he lived 'five years and more' (*U* 52). But Hythloday is even harder to find than his fabulous island because he, too, may be imaginary. More neglected to obtain latitude and longitude. Now it is rumored that Hythloday, whose name translates as 'expert in nonsense' (*U* xxii), has perished at sea.

Wells dodged the typography issue by presenting modern utopia as his better self's dream-vision. Nevertheless, the locus is clearly England in a future that Wells implies will materialize shortly. In her 'Afterword' to *Islandia*, Sylvia Wright tried to align John Lang with More's Hythloday, but the joke falls flat. Lang, she observes, assumed 'that everyone knows where [Islandia] is', so he never mentions 'latitude and longitude' (*WI* 944). Presumably, Pala lies somewhere in the vicinity of the Samoan and Trobriand islands mentioned favorably in *Brave New World*.[21] Of these three, only Huxley—not Wells or Wright—stressed his utopia's inaccessibility in More-like fashion. Pala's 'rockbound coast' has only one 'sandy beach' surrounded by steep cliffs (*I* 7). This is both the 'forbidden island' (*I* 22) and a very forbidding place. Swept ashore when his boat overturns, Will jokes that 'Providence was on [his] side' (*I* 50) but, as it turns out, not on Pala's.[22]

More's Utopia is nowhere to be found because he implied that the imagination is the ideal place for it. Though written in Latin, *Utopia* is famously founded on a Greek pun: if one spells the *u* in u-topus (place) as *ou*, it means 'no place'; if the *u* is *eu*, it means 'the good place'. More wished to suggest that 'the good place' must always be 'no place', a mental construct impossible, perhaps inadvisable, to attain. Huxley gave More's pun a cynical twist when he modeled the conclusion of *Island* after *Paradise Lost* (1674). He confirmed More in that, by the novel's end, 'the good place' is 'no place' again. The more Will Farnaby and the reader learn to appreciate Pala, the closer the novel inches towards the island's extinction. Indeed for the reader, Pala is becoming 'the good place' and 'no place' at the same time.

In *A Modern Utopia*, Huxley objected, the World State violates More's practice and intention twice over. Seen correctly it is not a fine place but an awful one, as the parodist revealed in *Brave New World*; moreover, instead of being nowhere, it was everywhere, not far off in time or space but proximate and imminent.[23] Wells had the audacity to call attention to its ubiquity by scornfully dismissing the More-like 'Nowheres'—Butler's *Erewhon* (1872), William Morris's *News From Nowhere* (1890)—on which premodern utopists wasted time and effort before Darwin 'quickened the thought of the world' (*MU* 11). In short, complained Huxley, Wells made utopia the inevitable product of a strictly scientific evolution that he was speeding up. As for Wright, he pretended Islandia actually existed; real countries—Germany, France, America—have consulates there. Islandia allegedly will continue to be a somewhere, a prospect Huxley considered escapist.[24]

Transforming 'no place' into every place or presuming that a romanticized best place could persevere indefinitely were, to Huxley's way of thinking, equally fatuous undertakings. 'From More to Bellamy', he lectured, 'from the Republic to the Phalansteries and the world of 1984, there is no utopian blue-print for a better world or an organized hell upon earth that could ever be fully actualized.'[25] This sweeping generalization implies two things: first, fabricating a perfect society should remain a literary exercise, an intellectual pastime, as it was for More, and not become a matter of community planning; secondly, human nature may be too complex to be fully subjected to any utopic scheme, whether agreeable or diabolical, despite Berdiaeff's warning in the epigraph to *Brave New World* that 'Utopias are realizable' and that twentieth-century 'life marches towards them' (*BNW* n.p.). Contrary to Wright and Wells, Huxley urged a return to a type of utopian speculation more in accordance with More's.

His classic island utopia, a forum for the discussion of ideas, may be regarded as 'a humorous, even satirical critique of European society' (*U* xxi). A playful venue, More's *Utopia* is best read as a series of suggestions rather than a warning, prediction, manifesto, or blueprint.[26] Yet no one did more than H.G. Wells to convert the literary utopia into a prophecy. More's communism, for example, sounds highly theoretical, but the Professor of Foresight, as Huxley disdainfully christened Wells, stands squarely behind the scientifically planned archetype of the welfare state outlined in *A Modern Utopia*.[27] Wellsian proposals are 'a soap-bubble' (*MU* 234) that eventually bursts, leaving him—i.e., his real self, not his utopian double—back in the England of 1905. But Wells's advocacy of his predictions and his confidence in their accuracy are never in doubt. Huxley described *Brave New World* 'as a parody' that 'got out of hand' once he began playing Wells's game by making predictions of his own.[28] Following many of the criteria for a perfect society set down in the opening pages of *A Modern Utopia*, he produced a 'negative Nowhere, a Utopia in reverse' very different from Wells's allegedly perfect society.[29] Huxley's return in *Island* to an island utopia amounts not just to a preference for island over planet, but also for More before Wells, classical utopia more than modern, and, above all, *hypothesis* over prediction. These preferences did not stop Huxley from issuing *Brave New World Revisited* in 1958 to show that his predictions from 1932 were unfortunately coming true daily. Nor was Huxley deterred from telling George Orwell that 'the nightmare' of *Brave New World* was more likely in the long run than that of *Nineteen Eighty-Four* (*AHL* 605). But *Island* is always a hypothesis, never a forecast except of Pala's inevitable demise.

Huxley knew the real problem facing the utopist: to develop just enough story to avoid seeming 'exceedingly didactic and expository' (*AHL* 875). The first half of *Islandia*, the tale of an island's struggle to remain independent from outside interests, supplied a plot Huxley could parody. He could dismiss Wright as a pseudo-Lawrentian reactionary. Not only is Islandia fantastic, it is also anti-progressive. In everything from agriculture to human relationships, the Palanese champion enlightened progress, indeed, progress towards enlightenment. They can do so because Huxley, like More but not Wright and more so than Wells, was a genuine polymath, a man for all seasons, a wide-ranging thinker equally well versed in philosophy, politics, economics, and the sciences, not to mention world literature and Eastern religions. In *Island*, Huxley wonders what a society would look like that adopted the lovemaking techniques of the Oneida community; applied W.H. Sheldon's science of human natures; practiced universal, state-supported birth control; made eugenic use of artificial insemination to upgrade the gene pool; revolutionized methods for teaching and farming; and subscribed to Vedanta's perennial philosophy with some Buddhist supplements. Compared with this eclectic recipe, its ingredients drawn from diverse fields, Wells's heavily scientific approach seems narrow and one-pointed, whereas Wright's emphasis on simplicity is revealed to be over-simplification.

In Huxley's final role for an island, Pala may be considered a kind of *hybrid*.[30] Clearly a good place, it abruptly ceases to be a place when Murugan and Colonel Dipa replace it with the 'United Kingdom of Rendang and Pala' (*I* 328). Utopia is nowhere not everywhere, no place not everyplace, Huxley tells Wells. It is imaginary, not real and definitely not indestructible, he cautions Wright. Yet Pala, as a synthesis of classical and modern, remains a blueprint of sorts: the Palanese are what human beings might be capable of becoming if they endeavored to live up to their potentialities and were permitted to do so, two unlikelihoods in Huxley's estimation.

Writing to Dr Humphry Osmond on 14 December 1960, Huxley referred to the Palanese as 'my hypothetical islanders' (*AHL* 899), a term one may also apply retrospectively to prospective islanders, malcontents such as Bernard Marx and Helmholtz Watson. Throughout *Brave New World*, Huxley pondered the usefulness of islands in utopian speculations. Finally, he settled on an island as his perfect place, provided it was imaginary or at least virtually inaccessible. Utopia, he decided, cannot be everywhere; nor can it ever be far enough from everywhere else. 'Hypothetical' remains the key word for the Palanese; they, not Wells's Samurai or Wright's Islandians, are the true successors to More's elusive Utopians.[31]

NOTES

1. 'Flivver' is slang for a small, old, and inexpensive auto.
2. See M. Mead, *Coming of Age in Samoa* (1928; New York: Dell, 1970), pp. 44–5 and J. Meckier, 'Coming of Age in Pala: The Primitivism of *Brave New World* Reconsidered in Huxley's *Island*', *Alternative Futures*, 1 (Summer 1978): 68–90, at 74.
3. Here the Controller, a caricature of Wells's idealized technocrats, such as the Samurai in *A Modern Utopia* (1905), seems to side with Huxley against Wells.
4. Islands for dissidents are 'powerful utopian elements' in Huxley's dystopia, Peter Firchow argues ('Brave at Last: Huxley's Western and Eastern Utopias', *Aldous Huxley Annual*, 1 (2001), pp. 153–74, at 157), but does not elaborate.
5. For details of Huxley's revision process, see J. Meckier, 'Aldous Huxley's Americanization of the *Brave New World* Typescript', *Twentieth-Century Literature*, 48 (Winter 2002): 427–60, at 446. See 'Helmholtz Watson's "Mental Excess": A Third Alternative', Sect. III of J. Meckier, 'Our Ford, Our Freud and the Behaviorist Conspiracy in Huxley's *Brave New World*', *Thalia*, 1 (Spring 1978): 35–59, at 46–55.
6. See Meckier, 'Aldous Huxley's Americanization', p. 449.
7. See J. Meckier, 'Poetry in the Future, the Future of Poetry: Huxley and Orwell on Zamyatin', *Renaissance and Modern Studies*, 28 (1984): 18–39, at 29–30.
8. See Meckier, 'Aldous Huxley's Americanization', 435.
9. In his introduction to his edition of *A Modern Utopia*, Mark R. Hillegas points out that Wells claimed to be combining the utopia with 'the discussion novel' developed by Peacock and Mallock (see H.G. Wells, *A Modern Utopia* (1905), ed. M.R. Hillegas (Lincoln: University of Nebraska Press, 1967), p. xxxiii).
10. Huxley told interviewers that Pala was 'a kind of reverse brave new world' (G. Wickes and R. Frazer, 'Aldous Huxley', in *Writers at Work: The 'Paris Review' Interviews Second Series* (New York: Viking, 1965), pp. 193–214, at p. 198). For a discussion of the reversals, see J. Meckier, *Aldous Huxley: Satire and Structure* (London: Chatto & Windus, 1969), pp. 199–205.
11. See W. Shakespeare, *The Tempest*, ed. V.M. Vaughan and A.T. Vaughan (London: Arden, 1999), V.i.181–4.
12. See J. Meckier, '*Brave New World* and the Anthropologists: Primitivism in A.F. 632', *Alternative Futures*, 1 (Spring 1978): 51–69 and Meckier, 'Coming of Age in Pala'.
13. According to Warren Wagar, whom Mark R. Hillegas quotes in his introduction, Wells's 'great contribution' to the utopian tradition was 'the concept of the World State' (see *A Modern Utopia*, ed. Hillegas, p. xi).

14. Robert S. Baker credited Huxley with detecting 'the political dystopia hidden within Wells's scientific utopia' (*Brave New World: History, Science, and Dystopia* (Boston: Twayne), p. 45).

15. For Donald Watt, 'an island' is one of the richest symbols in Huxley's last novel ('Vision and Symbol in Aldous Huxley's *Island*', *Twentieth-Century Literature*, 14 (Oct. 1968): 149–60, at 155). It symbolizes the isolation of the individual and of the Palanese as a society; but it also signifies a potential unity in that islands are connected beneath the sea.

16. Compared to 'utopia' and 'dystopia', the terms 'positive' utopia and 'negative' utopia seem redundant, but Huxley used them (see A. Huxley, 'Utopias, Positive and Negative' (1963), ed. J. Sexton, *Aldous Huxley Annual*, 1 (2001), 1–5, at 1).

17. The allusion to *The Secret Agent* (1907) is one of many to Conrad that add a sinister note not found in Wright. See J. Meckier, 'Conradian Reminders in Aldous Huxley's *Island*: Will Farnaby's *Moksha-Medicine* Experience and "The Essential Horror"', *Studies in the Novel*, 35 (Spring 2003): 44–67.

18. Wickes and Frazer, 'Aldous Huxley', p. 199.

19. See Meckier, *Aldous Huxley*, pp. 12–26.

20. Wickes and Frazer, 'Aldous Huxley', p. 199.

21. Firchow positioned Pala near the Andaman Islands in the Indian Ocean close to Sumatra, but suggested that Huxley actually had Bali in mind as a model ('Brave at Last', p. 172). Huxley told the *Paris Review* that Pala is 'an imaginary island between Ceylon and Sumatra' (Wickes and Frazer, 'Aldous Huxley', p. 198).

22. Will's allusion to Samuel Butler's *Erewhon*—'"Remember the beginning of *Erewhon*"', says Farnaby: '"As luck would have it, Providence was on my side"' (*I* 18)—deepens the irony. For the Erewhonians, Higgs's advent, which he considers providential for him, is a mixed blessing.

23. Firchow pointed out that classical utopias are set in 'no time' as well as in 'no place' (*The End of Utopia: A Study of Aldous Huxley's 'Brave New World'* (Lewisburg, PA: Bucknell University Press, 1984), p. 84). Starting with Wells, however, dates became increasingly important. Modern utopists presumed to tell readers not only *where* utopia would materialize but *when*.

24. The reviewer for *Time* magazine underlined Wright's 'desire for complete escape from the actual world' (R. Little, 'Daydream', *Time* (18 May 1942): 86). In *The New York Times*, *Islandia* was called 'a dream-compensation' for shortcomings in the American way of life (H. Strauss, 'A Novel That Casts a Spell', *The New York Times Book Review* (12 Apr. 1942): 1 and 22).

25. Huxley, 'Utopias, Positive and Negative', 3. In this lecture Huxley adopted a sarcastic tone towards both Wells and More. He ridiculed the World State in *A Modern Utopia* as a 'totalitarian' mistake ruled by 'a cross between the Boy Scouts and the Society of Jesus.' More's Utopia, he continued, 'is administered like an old-fashioned boarding school' (Huxley, 'Utopias, Positive and Negative', 4).

26. In his introduction, however, Richard Marius disparages critics who separate More's views from Hythloday's (*U* xxi).
27. For Baker, the Wellsian utopia is 'a form of prophetic history' (*Brave New World*, p. 25).
28. Wickes and Frazer, 'Aldous Huxley', p. 198.
29. Huxley, 'Utopias, Positive and Negative', 1.
30. Wells was fond of this term. In *A Modern Utopia*, he aimed for a 'hybrid' of fiction and essay (*MU* 8). Michael Szezekalla called Pala 'the hybrid civilization' of Huxley's 'literary imagination' ('The Scottish Enlightenment and Buddhism—Huxley's Vision of Hybridity in *Island*', in B. Nugel et al. (eds), *Aldous Huxley, Man of Letters* (Berlin: Lit Verlag, 2007): pp. 153–66, at p. 159); from its founding, it combined the fruits of two enlightenments: that of eighteenth-century Scotland, thanks to Dr Andrew MacPhail, and the Raja's Buddhist-Vedantic mysticism.
31. Huxley would have deplored J.W. Johnson's description of Islandians as an 'updated version of More's Utopians' (Johnson (ed.), *Utopian Literature: A Selection* (New York: Modern Library, 1968), p. 269). Naomi Jacobs considers *Islandia* an 'anticipation' of plotting strategies in subsequent utopias but does not include *Island* ('*Islandia*: Plotting Utopian Desire', *Utopian Studies*, 6 (1995): 75–89, at 80).

CHAPTER 12

'Words Without Reason': State Power and the Moral Life in *Brave New World*

Andrzej Gąsiorek

The two meanings of the word 'utopia' are so well known that they hardly require much commentary. But it is worth bearing in mind that because these meanings are intertwined the concept of utopia is always, in all its iterations, an unstable one. For on the one hand it denotes an ideal, a belief in perfectibility and thus a drive towards its realization, while on the other hand it secretes within itself a recognition that it posits an unattainable state: the optimistic hope for a flawless world is inseparable from the sharp sense that this is at best a problematic counterfactual and at worst a stark impossibility, a 'nowhere' that can exist solely in the minds of visionaries and fantasists. That inveterate theorizer H.G. Wells, whose *Men Like Gods* (1923) Huxley's *Brave New World* set out to parody, touched on this tension between the plausible and the unattainable in his earlier *A Modern Utopia* (1905): 'Our deliberate intention is to be not, indeed, impossible, but most distinctly impracticable, by every scale that reaches only between to-day and to-morrow' (*MU* 11–12). Utopian speculations are entangled with potentially dystopian consequences. The dream of an irreproachable life all too often is overtaken by the dread reality of an accursed existence.

A. Gąsiorek (✉)
Department of English Literature, University of Birmingham, Birmingham, UK

© The Editor(s) (if applicable) and The Author(s) 2016   211
J. Greenberg, N. Waddell (eds.), Brave New World: *Contexts and Legacies*, DOI 10.1057/978-1-137-44541-4_12

'The mind is its own place', Milton warns us, 'and in itself | Can make a heaven of hell, a hell of heaven.'[1]

What, then, does it mean to think utopianly? I shall make no overweening attempt at perfection in this chapter but will concentrate on those aspects of this vexed and vexing question that may help to make sense of the doubleness towards which I have gestured, taking *Brave New World* as my key focal point. To begin with, it is vital to hold on to an obvious, but easily forgettable, truth—the truth that Milton asserts so uncompromisingly: utopian schemes and their dystopian shadows originate in human minds. This is to say that any notion of the ideal is the result of *thought*, which is capable of conjuring up the most extraordinary chimeras. If we bear in mind that in philosophical terms idealism refers not only to a tendency to represent things in their perfect, unsullied forms, rather than as they are experienced noumenally, but also to the belief that the products of the mind constitute the world and that phenomena consist solely of ideas, then we may grasp why utopian thought is so often fantastical and why it so frequently shatters against the rocks of a stubborn material reality.

Wyndham Lewis convicted his younger utopian self in precisely these terms, and his words are relevant to the issue at hand:

> Almost, by nature, I am the pure revolutionary [...]. In me you see *a man of the tabula rasa*, if ever there was one [...]. My mind is *ahistoric*, I would welcome the clean sweep. I could build something better, I am sure of that, than has been left us by our fathers that were before us. Only I know this is quite impossible.
>
> This is the heart of what is, apparently, a political mystery—I have learnt my lesson, and, in spite of being the pure revolutionary, I am a bit of a realist too. Hence my extraordinary broadmindedness in politics, for instance. Otherwise I should be a man after Lenin's heart.[2]

Seeing himself as a revolutionary who is temperamentally like Lenin, he admits that what he wants in theory is a completely new beginning but that he has come to understand that this desire is an unattainable goal. As he ruefully acknowledges, this hard-won conclusion has made him a political realist.

The history of utopian speculation, going back at least as far as Thomas More, is full of impractical dreams and of warnings against the horrific nightmares that these dreams so frequently become when human beings try to put them into practice. So much so, indeed, that when we discuss utopia in its many forms we are almost inevitably drawn to the subject of dystopia. The first three decades of the twentieth century are particularly rich in utopian and dystopian reflections. This is almost certainly because the rapid changes brought about by processes of technologically driven modernization led to two twinned, but opposed, responses: on the one hand, a series of powerfully expressed hopes that the new future would transform the present in an entirely beneficent way, modernity ushering in a gleaming new age; on the other hand, a set of no less strongly articulated anxieties about the ways in which modernity in fact might produce the deepest forms of alienation. Adulation of technology vies with fear of it throughout the period, though the roots of both attitudes lie much further back in time.

Examples of utopian impracticality abound. D.H. Lawrence offers a useful approach to the issues I address in this chapter. For what drives Lawrence's utopian thinking around the time of the First World War is a desire to rediscover an essential bedrock of humanity. At the heart of his work is a radical purism, which is perhaps most clearly expressed by his alter ego Rupert Birkin in *Women in Love* (1920). Lawrence came to believe that the accoutrements of the past had to be sloughed off so that the individual could be reborn as a different kind of being. This line of thinking resulted in his ill-starred collaboration with Bertrand Russell and in the plan to create a utopian community abroad (Rananim). The idea for a new society that would be built far from an England Lawrence had come to detest already hints at the escapist nature of the Rananim scheme: its projection of an idealized 'somewhere' can be read as a kind of fantastical 'nowhere'. Lawrence wanted Rananim to be a self-sufficient commune of friends living abroad, but the impracticalities of the plan quickly became apparent, and the relationship between Lawrence and Russell collapsed. Huxley expressed his scepticism in a sardonic letter to Ottoline Morrell: 'What seems to me questionable is, are you going to hustle on the spring by going to Florida to immure yourself with one Armenian, one German wife and, problematically, one or two other young people? It may be possible that some Pentecostal gift of inspiration may descend, and I suppose it's worth risking failure for that possibility'.[3]

Insofar as the Rananim dream was predicated on the notion of escape—both from a place (England) and from a time (the present)—it reveals how indebted this kind of thinking is to the myth of a lost golden age, which, the would-be utopianist argues, only needs to be recovered for the world to be returned to its former glory. This structure of feeling is clearly at work in texts like Samuel Butler's *Erewhon* (1872), Richard

Jefferies's *After London* (1885), and William Morris's *News from Nowhere* (1890). For these writers, and for their twentieth-century counterparts, a pastoral way of life offered a beguiling alternative to what they saw as an inherently predatory capitalism. The attractions of agrarianism (which was understood in a wide range of ways) were widely canvassed in the 1920s and 1930s, the period in which Huxley emerged as a writer, and they feature prominently as an imaginative resource in the work of such figures as Mary Butts, T.S. Eliot, Ford Madox Ford, and W.B. Yeats. These writers urged a poetic return to the soil, offering critiques of industrial modernity from the standpoint of a nostalgic pastoralism, even if some of them knew (and sometimes acknowledged) that the world they longed for had been superseded by a technological age that was here to stay, a point that Orwell made in the second part of *The Road to Wigan Pier* (1937) and that Huxley echoed in *Ends and Means* (1937):

> But the problem of modern industry and finance cannot possibly be solved by setting up irrelevant little associations of handicraftsmen and amateur peasants, incapable in most cases of earning their livelihood and dependent for their bread and butter upon income derived from the hated world of machines. We cannot get rid of machinery, for the simple reason that, in the process of getting rid of it, we should be forced to get rid of that moiety of the human race whose existence on the planet is made possible only by the existence of machines. [...] Machine production cannot be abolished; it is here to stay. The question is whether it is to stay as an instrument of slavery or as a way to freedom. (*HCE4* 253)[4]

Like Orwell, Huxley well knew that the dream of a return to a pre-technological agrarian past was dewy-eyed idealism. That said, his political writing in the 1930s repeatedly returned to the possibility that loosely federated small communities might somehow resist the hegemony of modern industrial life. As he made clear in *Ends and Means*, Huxley sought to understand whether the relentless development of technology meant that human beings necessarily would be enslaved by it or whether it might yet liberate them.[5]

For Huxley, the machine was an ambiguous portent. It might, if developed in the right way, be an emancipatory force, but it could also be a threat to human life if it were permitted to dominate and control that life. In this respect, there are parallels between Huxley's twentieth-century concerns and the prescient warnings of the nineteenth-century Butler. In *Erewhon*, Butler's narrator refers to a book that had been written 'proving that the machines were ultimately destined to supplant the race of man, and to become instinct with a vitality as different from, and superior to, that of animals, as animal to vegetable life' (*E* 97). A corollary of this view is the fear, expressed later in *Erewhon*, that machines 'might cause a degeneracy of the human race, and indeed that the whole body might become purely rudimentary, the man himself being nothing but soul and mechanism, an intelligent but passionless principle of mechanical action' (*E* 224). The key point here is that if *Homo sapiens* is regarded as a kind of machine (and nothing other than that) then the way is opened up to a conception of the species that reduces it to pure corporeality, leaving consciousness entirely out of the equation. A later version of this anxiety appears in Lewis's *The Caliph's Design* (1919), which warns that under the conditions of modern technological life human beings might 'become overpowered by [their] creation, and become as mechanical as a tremendous insect world, all [their] awakened reason entirely disappeared.'[6] The opposition between a fully automated, and thus hive-like, society and one guided by purposive human agents chimes with Huxley's concerns; he and Lewis both feared that technology was taking control of human existence and, in doing so, was turning the individual into an adjunct of its all-embracing systems and structures. Huxley expressed his anxiety about this process in a postwar discussion of Maine de Biran, the philosopher who is referred to in the latter part of *Brave New World* (see *BNW* 204): 'What he did not perceive was the [...] insidious threat to the freedom and dignity of man inherent in the new techniques of production. [...] When a man is put in charge of a machine, or when he becomes part of some social or economic organization that is modelled upon the machine, he is compelled to be what it is not natural or normal for him to be. In more than moderate doses efficiency is incompatible with humanity' ('Variations on a Philosopher', 1950; *HCE5* 58).

The relevance of these anxieties to *Brave New World* hardly needs to be stressed. Among the many other things that it does, Huxley's text tries to imagine what could happen when an entire society is modelled on the logic of the machine, its subordinate parts (the people that live in it) existing to service its needs. John Stuart Mill's *On Liberty* (1859) offers an impassioned but also closely argued plea for individual autonomy and freedom of expression. Rejecting the notion of abstract rights that are derived a priori, Mill insists that the individual's liberty must be defended on the grounds of utility.[7] Famously, Mill asserts a single principle: that the 'only part of the conduct of anyone, for which he is amenable to society, is that which concerns others. In the part which merely concerns himself, his independence is [absolute]. Over himself, over his own body and mind, the individual is sovereign.'[8] At first glance, this seems straightforward enough. It proclaims the pre-eminence of the individual and describes social considerations as of secondary importance. In practice, however, things aren't that simple because a good deal hangs on how the phrase 'concerns others' is interpreted; the question of how we define and limit the scope of 'concern' (an alarmingly open-ended term) is a tricky one. Mill acknowledges as much when he writes that utility must be 'grounded on the permanent interests of a man as a progressive being' and then adds that in his view these interests 'authorise the subjection of individual spontaneity to external control, only in respect to those actions of each, which concern the interest of other people.'[9]

We might readily agree that the politics of *Brave New World* represent a parody of this caveat, but we would have to admit, I suggest, that they are derivable from the utilitarian position Mill develops in *On Liberty*. Huxley's future society is predicated on the need for stability above all else, and it holds that cohesion is maintained by giving all its members fixed roles and ensuring that these roles serve the good of the community to which their individual needs and desires perforce are subordinated. Mill would have been disturbed by a world in which it is suggested that '"[n]ot philosophers, but fret-sawyers and stamp collectors compose the backbone of society"' (*BNW* 2), but this world's insistence on stability and efficiency can be seen as one possible development of the argument that the polity should be organized in such a way that it can deliver the greatest good for the greatest number. In A.F. 632, after all, 'everyone belongs to everyone else' (*BNW* 34), and it is believed that '[w]hen the individual feels, the community reels' (*BNW* 81). This emphasis on the primacy of the collective trumps the individual's desire for autonomy precisely because it is feared that independence of mind and action inevitably will run counter to the interests of society at large.

Mill's *On Liberty* has the right to be called a utopian text, since it offers an idealized view of how the world would look if it were organized in the 'right' way. But it secretes within itself the seeds of its own destruction because its account of such key terms as 'interest' and 'concern' is so vague. As such, its ideas can be developed (deformed, one might say) in a direction that results in the crazed fantasies of the Brave New World's guardians. These fantasies, in turn, depend on a narrow understanding of what constitutes an ideal form of existence, since their exponents maintain

that anyone who has 'got too self-consciously individual to fit into community-life' (*BNW* 200) should be expelled from it. In the society of A.F.
632 the obsession with stability is inseparable from the conviction that
communal happiness is an overriding social and political good.

But happiness in Huxley's text is a distinctly odd phenomenon. It is seen
above all as conformity to a standardized type-life, every inhabitant existing not as a free-thinking individual but functioning as a fixed sprocket in
a constantly turning social wheel. Two strategies are deployed to prevent
dissatisfaction with this state of affairs: social conditioning and the promotion of pleasure. Conditioning takes the form of radical behaviourism,
while the exorbitation of pleasure reduces all leisure activities to the level
of physical sensation. Deliberately excluded from this state-sponsored version of a debased Epicureanism is access to intellectual and artistic pursuits
that might offer a different view of what makes for a flourishing human
life, since any such view inevitably would challenge the orthodoxies upon
which Huxley's futurist society depends.[10] 'All conditioning', we are told,
aims to make '"people like their unescapable social destiny"' (*BNW* 12),
while the endlessly running tap of pleasure ensures that, as Lenina blithely
puts it: '"I am free. Free to have the most wonderful time. Everybody's
happy nowadays"' (*BNW* 79).

Bernard Marx's response to this glib assertion is revealing: '"But
wouldn't you like to be free to be happy in some other way, Lenina?"'
(*BNW* 79). The force of this point is lost on Lenina, but it raises an obvious issue: can we really talk of 'liberty' when the form it takes is predetermined? If one is 'free' to be happy only in a way that has been decided in
advance, then in what sense is one really 'free'? Huxley's novel is preoccupied with this question. A key moment in the book occurs when John
the Savage rejects the state's vision of a controlled existence that is given
over to a permanently easeful life:

> 'I don't want comfort. I want God, I want poetry, I want real danger, I want
> freedom, I want goodness. I want sin.'
>   'In fact', said Mustapha Mond, 'you're claiming the right to be unhappy.'
>   'All right, then', said the Savage defiantly, 'I'm claiming the right to be
> unhappy.' (*BNW* 211–12)

This is a more profound objection to the ethos of the New World order
than that which is articulated by Bernard. For whereas Bernard talks of the
individual's right to choose an alternative kind of happiness (or pleasure),

the Savage suggests that a meaningful existence depends on the presence in it of pain and suffering, without which life is simply a flat panorama of the ever-same—a timeless limbo stretching out to eternity. Margaret Atwood connects this sense of pointlessness to the text's focus on endless consumption (a key feature of its reduction of everything to physical pleasure) when she observes that 'in a world in which everything is available, nothing has any meaning' (*BNW* xiv). In *Brave New World* John the Savage resists the evisceration of meaning that is the corollary of an endlessly commodified and pleasure-seeking world by insisting on the importance of suffering to human life, a point he underscores with a quotation from *Othello*: 'If after every tempest come such calms, may the winds blow till they have awakened death' (*BNW* 210).

From this perspective, meaning is inseparable from imperfection, a view that has implications not just for Huxley's text but for utopian thought more generally, since it suggests that the notion of an ideal (perfect) world is an oxymoron. But *Brave New World* makes a further point. By opposing the notion of happiness to the pursuit of truth and beauty, which it acknowledges is bound up with suffering and *consciousness* of suffering, the novel suggests that whereas universal contentment 'keeps the wheels steadily turning' (*BNW* 201), the arts and sciences are to be valued because they stimulate the mind and are potentially socially, culturally, and politically disruptive. As open-ended and speculative forms of inquiry, they implicitly raise questions about the nature of any given social order and by doing so open up the possibility that it might be organized differently. The novel further implies that, apart from the personal benefits that a rich inner life confers upon the individual, it may also be socially beneficial because it enables them to grasp that the dream of a perfectly ordered world, when implemented, will result in a deterministic horror show.

Brave New World challenges the myth that complete order is a valid political desideratum by means of the sublime. Halfway through the novel, Bernard and Lenina find themselves aboard a helicopter, with a heaving ocean beneath them. Roused by the roiling sea, Bernard orders Lenina to look at the scene below them, but she shrinks back:

> She was appalled by the rushing emptiness of the night, by the black foam-flecked water heaving beneath them, by the pale face of the moon, so haggard and distracted among the hastening clouds. 'Let's turn on the radio. Quick!' She reached for the dialling knob on the dashboard and turned it at random.

'... skies are blue inside of you,' sang sixteen tremoloing falsettos, 'the weather's always ...'

Then a hiccough and silence. Bernard had switched off the current.

'I want to look at the sea in peace,' he said. 'One can't even look with that beastly noise going on.'

'But it's lovely. And I don't want to look.'

'But I do,' he insisted. 'It makes me feel as though ...' he hesitated, searching for words with which to express himself, 'as though I were more *me*, if you see what I mean. More on my own, not so completely a part of something else. Not just a cell in the social body.' (*BNW* 78)

The sublime functions here as a rebuttal of the false idol of synthetic beauty that is upheld by the hapless Lenina. The thrilling agitation of the sea is opposed to the ersatz beauty of the radio tune in a specific way. It is associated with a uniqueness of identity ('as though I were more *me*') that enables the individual to see himself as an autonomous agent rather than as a unit in a larger communal organism ('just a cell in the social body'), terms that recall Lewis's observations in *The Caliph's Design*. The vision that gives rise to such thoughts is not one of order and symmetry but of energy and turmoil. The sublime functions here to challenge the smooth uniformity of a cellular social structure by introducing into it the disorder that frequently appears in nature and that, it is implied, solicits independence of mind. This disorder is then pitted against the 'happiness' that is maintained in the world of A.F. 632 by means of conditioning and *soma*.

Huxley's invocation of the sublime in this context is instructive. The pastimes that the New World's citizens are compelled to enjoy exist to serve physical pleasure, while the mind and its unpredictable creative achievements are systematically extirpated from social life. As Mustapha Mond remarks, 'the feelies and the scent organ' have replaced 'high art', and they exist solely to produce 'a lot of agreeable sensations' (*BNW* 194). The best way to understand what is at stake here is by way of Friedrich von Schiller's essay 'On the Sublime' (1801) and his insistence therein that 'reason and sensuousness' accord when human beings are in the presence of beauty but fly apart when they are confronted with the sublime, which throws them upon their inner resources. Schiller puts it as follows: 'The physical and the moral individual are here most sharply differentiated from one another; for it is precisely in the presence of objects that make the former aware only of his limitations that the latter is aware of his *power* and is infinitely exalted by the very same object that crushes the physical man to the ground.'[11] For Schiller, the physical individual is confined to a world of sensations whereas the free human being is released from that beguiling entrapment. Contemplation of the sublime liberates him, the 'grandeur outside him' functioning as 'the mirror in which he perceives the absolute grandeur within himself.'[12] What follows from this realization is a recognition of the value of intellectual independence, despite the fact that it brings with it both responsibility and anguish. Schiller is unequivocal, and his words speak to Huxley's concerns in *Brave New World*:

> To noble minds freedom, for all its moral contradictions and physical evils, is an infinitely more interesting spectacle than prosperity and order without freedom, when the sheep patiently follow the shepherd and the autonomous will reduces itself to an obedient cog in a machine. The latter makes of man a mere product of nature's ingenuity and her fortunate subject; but freedom makes him a citizen and co-regent of a higher system in which it is incomparably more honorable to occupy the lowest rank than to lead the procession of the physical order.[13]

For Schiller, an ordered and prosperous society that is imposed from above turns people into the playthings of a system they don't understand and cannot change, whereas an autonomous life encourages them to become moral agents with the capacity to face existence in all its ambiguous, and at times horrific, splendour. Translated into the idiom of *Brave New World*, what we have here is social predestination versus the freely chosen life. Schiller's sublime confronts human beings with imperfection and then incites them to defy it. The Savage is responding to this version of the sublime when he speaks of 'living dangerously' and wonders if the exposure of 'what is mortal and unsure to all that fortune, death and danger dare' (*BNW* 211) might not make for the best kind of life. This way of thinking has Nietzschean overtones, calling to mind the German philosopher's concept of the Dionysian state, a fully conscious affirmation of the *terribilità* of existence: 'I promise a tragic age: the highest art in saying Yes to life, tragedy, will be reborn when humanity has weathered the consciousness of the hardest but most necessary wars *without suffering from it*.'[14]

There is another significant aspect of the sublime that is pertinent to *Brave New World*. Towards the end of the novel, Mustapha Mond turns to several religious works in order to suggest that, contrary to the physicalist philosophy of the utopia he controls, a deity of some kind might well exist but that this possibility is deliberately denied by the New World's rulers in the name of social stability and a life given over to sensation rather than thought. God, we are told, '"isn't compatible with machinery and scientific medicine and universal happiness"' (BNW 207). The Savage's rejection of this way of thinking, which is shared to a degree by Helmholtz and Bernard Marx, goes hand in hand with his exaltation of a tragic view of life, which for him is inseparable from belief in a presiding deity.[15] He ends his life as a hermit who turns his back on the society presided over by Mond, and his self-flagellating final days are those of an anchorite who strives 'to escape further contamination by the filth of civilized life' in an attempt 'actively to make amends' (BNW 218). Explicitly rejecting Mond's naturalist and sensationist perspective, the Savage draws in a rather muddled way on religious ideas, Shakespeare, and an idealist tradition that runs from Plato and the Neoplatonists through to Schopenhauer. For what follows the Savage's claim that he desires tragedy is his withdrawal from life and his attempt to atone for it by means of ascetic self-purification. Schopenhauer, we might recall, claimed not only that our sense of the tragic exposes the meaninglessness of existence but also that it leads to 'the deeper insight that what the hero atones for is not his own particular sins, but original sin, in other words, the guilt of existence itself'.[16] This way of thinking can lead to the rejection of the world in its entirety (the Savage's response) or to mystical speculations about a non-material *telos* and a transcendent reality (which Mond touches on towards the end of the novel). Both of these alternatives resist the Brave New World's emphasis on the community rather than the individual and, in different ways, offer an alternative to its technocratic materialism.

Theodor Adorno took Huxley to task for what he saw as *Brave New World*'s internal contradictions. Writing from a broadly Marxist perspective, he objected that Huxley's anti-behaviourist emphasis on consciousness reified the mind and ignored the importance of social change: '"Intensification and refinement of consciousness" or "enlargement of knowledge" flatly hypostatize the mind in opposition to praxis and the fulfilment of material needs' (AHU 108). This reading of *Brave New World* imposes a dichotomy upon the text that is too clear-cut, since the book doesn't unequivocally oppose 'mind' to 'praxis' but explores how the former can be destroyed by means of extreme behaviourist techniques allied to a technocratic utilitarianism. When Adorno argues that Huxley leaves no 'room for a concept of mankind that would resist absorption into the collective coercion of the system', he concludes that a 'construction which simultaneously denounces the totalitarian world-state and glorifies retrospectively the individualism that brought it about becomes itself totalitarian' (*AHU* 114). This is an ideological criticism that scants the complexities and ambiguities of *Brave New World*; it derides the text for its refusal to point to the politics Adorno espouses and ends by accusing it of bourgeois quietism.

Adorno's insistence that what 'must be attacked is the socially dictated separation of consciousness from the social realization its essence requires' leads him not only to hypostatize consciousness (note the recourse to the language of 'essence') but also to mistake the nature of the genre to which Huxley's dystopian satire belongs.[17] Such satire makes a particular state of affairs grotesque by means of exaggeration in order to highlight its most salient characteristics; it does not typically offer a solution to the evils it identifies but traduces them, the better to expose them to ridicule. Huxley explained in his later reflections on the novel that in it the 'standardization of the human product has been pushed to fantastic, though not perhaps impossible, extremes' (*BNW* xlix). It is only indirectly, by implying that an alternative scale of values exists, that Huxley's satire invites the reader to think critically about the society that is being lampooned. In the case of *Brave New World*, there is also another issue to consider. The novel discloses its scepticism about the monologic arrogance of utopian thought by mocking the abstractions upon which the world of A.F. 632 is built, starting with 'COMMUNITY, IDENTITY, STABILITY' (*BNW* 1) and ending with 'civilization is sterilization' (*BNW* 94). Huxley uses these phrases to suggest that the ideology behind them necessarily will be hostile to human autonomy and will suppress the freedom of thought upon which purposeful agency depends, for if social stability is a state's highest good then any challenge to it is bound to be disallowed, as Mustapha Mond makes clear: '"We don't allow [science] to deal with any but the most immediate problems of the moment. All other enquiries are most sedulously discouraged"' (*BNW* 200).[18]

The rationale for this strategy has been provided earlier on when Mond privately admires the elegance of a scientific paper but refuses to allow it to be published on the grounds that it is subversive and might lead 'the more unsettled minds among the higher castes' to 'lose their faith in happiness as the Sovereign Good and take to believing, instead, that the goal was somewhere beyond, somewhere outside the present human sphere' (*BNW* 154). *Brave New World* does not, finally, plump for this alternative view of meaning and purpose, which Huxley would embrace later in his life, as he made clear in a series of lectures delivered in 1959.[19] There is an unresolved tension in *Brave New World* between two different responses to the problem of existence. Dissatisfaction with a supremely efficient but deterministic society takes two dominant forms: on the one hand, a call for an intense, possibly even violent, life in which passion and suffering are the key loci of value; and, on the other hand, an orientation of the self towards a transcendent metaphysical reality. This latter perspective looks to a realm of meaning and purpose that lies beyond material life; it proposes a way of thinking that would become increasingly important to Huxley but that remains undeveloped in *Brave New World*, which alludes to the Bible, Thomas à Kempis's *The Imitation of Christ*, William James's *The Varieties of Religious Experience*, Maine de Biran's *Journal Intime*, and John Henry Newman's *Parochial and Plain Sermons*, using the latter two texts to allude to the possible existence of 'some other standard than ours' (*BNW* 208).[20] The novel takes the logic of a thoroughly mechanized society run on behaviourist principles and given over to relentless consumption to an extreme point, in contrast to which it posits the possibility of a non-material *telos*.[21]

In his introduction to the novel David Bradshaw has pointed out that much of what went into *Brave New World* was based on Huxley's initial experiences of America, which were recounted in *Jesting Pilate* (1926). In this travelogue's concluding remarks Huxley suggested that America is presiding over 'a revaluation of values, a radical alteration (for the worse) of established standards' (*HCE2* 555). Tracing this change back to the development of the scientific outlook in the nineteenth century, Huxley suggested that it had produced a naturalistic (materialist) understanding of life that was inseparable from democratic thought and that could be seen in its purest form in America. Huxley argued that the highest human values were knowable by means of intuition, whereas arguments based on 'scientific materialism [...] must infallibly end in a denial of the real existence of values.' These values, he made clear in *Jesting Pilate*, depend on a religious conception of life: 'the established spiritual values are fundamentally correct and should be maintained' (*HCE2* 564). He contrasted this conviction with 'a stupid materialism that would deny the very existence of values' (*HCE2* 565), a point that is expressed in *Brave New World* with reference to Newman and Biran.

Huxley provides no decisive answers to the questions about meaning that he poses in *Brave New World*. But he indicates what is at stake in them by presenting a future world that has altogether denied the value of consciousness and that sees human life in terms of collectivized productivity buttressed by the satisfaction of physical desires (a lubrication of the social machine that keeps it running smoothly).[22] The novel suggests that to live in a world whose citizens are not permitted to ask questions about its purpose or to think in terms of different conceptions of the good is to inhabit a helot state of a particularly invidious kind. Rejecting Adorno's doubts about the value of consciousness (prior to its realization in social forms), *Brave New World* suggests that utopian schemes that suppress independence of mind will destroy the individual autonomy and agency that a society requires if it is not to become a dystopian hell. For Huxley, centralized control by a ruling cadre was a disaster, as he made clear in texts like *Ends and Means* (1937) and *After Many a Summer* (1939). Later in his life he described this form of political power as a 'third revolution [...] which will subvert the individual in the depths of his organic and hyper-organic being' in order to 'bring his body, his mind, his whole private life directly under the control of the ruling oligarchy' ('Variations on a Philosopher'; *HCE5* 108–9), a process that he described as 'the most important and the most terrible fact in human history' (*HCE5* 109).

Huxley saw the relationship between the individual and the state as an intractable problem. He observed in *Themes and Variations* (1950) that 'the conflict between what is good for a psycho-physical person and what is good for an organization wholly innocent of feelings, wishes, and ideas, is real and seems destined to remain forever unresolved' (*HCE5* 65).[23] What he favoured was not a utopian alternative to the dystopia he described in *Brave New World* but a more modest, more piecemeal understanding of social advance. The 'most valuable ideals', he argued in *Proper Studies* (1927), 'are possible, but unrealizable' ('A Note on Ideals'; *HCE2* 275). Huxley suggested that when such ideals are viable but unachievable then 'the incentive to pursue them never fails' (*HCE2* 275), and this led him to conclude that these ideals encourage human beings cautiously to improve their circumstances without enticing them to imagine that those circumstances can be perfected. 'The best', Huxley pithily remarked, 'is ever the enemy of the good' ('A Note on Eugenics', 1927; *HCE2* 285).

NOTES

1. J. Milton, *The Complete English Poems*, ed. G. Campbell (London: Everyman's Library, 1992), p. 156.
2. W. Lewis, 'A Letter to the Editor', *Twentieth Century Verse*, 'Wyndham Lewis Double Number', 6/7 (Nov./Dec. 1937): n.p.
3. O. Morrell, *Ottoline at Garsington: Memoirs of Lady Ottoline Morrell, 1915–1918*, ed. R. Gathorne-Hardy (London: Faber and Faber, 1974), p. 80.

4. See also G. Orwell, *The Road to Wigan Pier* (1937; Harmondsworth: Penguin, 1979), p. 192.
5. For an account of the wider context, see M.J. Wiener, *English Culture and the Decline of the Industrial Spirit, 1850–1980* (Cambridge: Cambridge University Press, 1982).
6. W. Lewis, *The Caliph's Design: Architects! Where is Your Vortex?* (1919), ed. P. Edwards (Santa Barbara: Black Sparrow Press, 1986), p. 76.
7. Thus Mill: 'I regard utility as the ultimate appeal on all ethical questions' (J.S. Mill, *Utilitarianism, On Liberty, and Considerations on Representative Government*, ed. H.B. Acton (London: J.M. Dent, 1976), p. 74).
8. Mill, *Utilitarianism, On Liberty, and Considerations*, p. 73.
9. Mill, *Utilitarianism, On Liberty, and Considerations*, p. 74.
10. Debased because Epicurus saw happiness as the absence of pain and ridiculed the idea that it lay in the pursuit of sensual pleasure. See Epicurus, *The Extant Remains*, ed. and trans. C. Bailey (Oxford: Clarendon Press, 1926), pp. 87–93.
11. F. Schiller, *Naïve and Sentimental Poetry and On the Sublime*, trans. J.A. Elias (New York: Frederick Ungar, 1980), p. 200.
12. Schiller, *Naïve and Sentimental Poetry and On the Sublime*, p. 203.
13. Schiller, *Naïve and Sentimental Poetry and On the Sublime*, p. 206.
14. F. Nietzsche, *On the Genealogy of Morals and Ecce Homo*, trans. and ed. W. Kaufmann (New York: Vintage, 1959), p. 274.
15. See the whole of Chapter XVIII, but especially the Savage's suggestion that divine perfection is the ground of meaningful human activity: '"God's the reason for everything noble and fine and heroic"' (*BNW* 209).
16. A. Schopenhauer, *The World as Will and Representation: Vol. 1*, trans. E.F.J. Payne (New York: Dover, 1969), p. 254.
17. We should note that Huxley later took the novel to task for not giving John the Savage a third option: a decentralized, semi-anarchist community that would use technology to serve people's needs rather than to enslave them (*BNW* xliii).
18. This is where the ideology of *Brave New World*'s technocrats is coterminous with that of behaviourism. See especially B.F. Skinner, *Beyond Freedom and Dignity* (1971; London: Jonathan Cape, 1972), Chap. 1.
19. See A. Huxley, *The Human Situation: Lectures at Santa Barbara, 1959*, ed. P. Ferrucci (London: Chatto & Windus, 1978), pp. 212–15.
20. Maine de Biran is quoted thus: 'we feel the need to lean on something that abides, something that will never play us false—a reality, an absolute and everlasting truth' (*BNW* 206). For a long essay on Biran, see 'Variations on a Philosopher' (*HCE5* 34–124).
21. For Huxley's hostility to a life given over to the pursuit of physical sensations, see 'Varieties of Intelligence' (1927), which appeared in *Proper Studies* (*HCE2* 175–6).

22. Writing approvingly about the power of the social environment over the individual, Skinner asks: 'Is man then "abolished"? Certainly not as a species or as an individual achiever. It is the autonomous inner man who is abolished, and that is a step forward' (Skinner, *Beyond Freedom and Dignity*, p. 215).
23. For Huxley's scepticism about premature conclusions, see his claim that 'any theory which is to cover all the human facts must necessarily be absurd, since the facts contradict one another and yet co-exist' ('A Note on Dogma', 1927; *HCE2* 247).

BIBLIOGRAPHY

Adamson, J. (1998), *Charlotte Haldane: Woman Writer in a Man's World* (Basingstoke: Palgrave Macmillan, 1998).

Adamson, M., and Moore, R.I. (1934), *Technocracy: Some Questions Answered* (New York: Technocracy Inc.).

Adorno, T.W. (1942), 'Aldous Huxley and Utopia', in *Prisms*, trans. S. and S. Weber (1955; Cambridge, MA: MIT Press, 1967): pp. 95–118.

[Advertisement] (1933), 'The Wizard in the Wall', *Daily Mail* (20 Oct.): 19.

[Advertisement] (1936), 'Talbot "Ten"', *Daily Mirror* (6 May): 10.

Akin, W.E. (1977) *Technocracy and the American Dream: The Technocrat Movement, 1900–1941* (Berkeley, CA: University of California Press).

Alba, D. (2014), 'Sci-fi Author Neal Stephenson Joins Mystery Startup Magic Leap as "Chief Futurist"', *Wired* (16 Dec.); n.p. Available at http://www.wired.com/2014/12/neal-stephenson-magic-leap/ (accessed 11 Oct. 2015).

Albertus Magnus (2008), *Questions Concerning Aristotle's 'On Animals'*, trans. I.M. Resnick and K.F. Kitchell, Jr (Washington, DC: The Catholic University of America Press).

Aldridge, A. (1984), *The Scientific World View in Dystopia* (Ann Arbor, MI: UMI Research Press).

Amis, K. (1980), *Collected Poems 1944–1979* (Harmondsworth: Penguin).

Andreassi, J.L. (2013), *Psychophysiology: Human behaviour and Psychological Response*, 4th rev. ed. (Abingdon: Psychology Press).

[Anon.] (1933), 'Technocracy Idea is Old, says Soddy', *The New York Times* (8 Jan.): 23.

[Anon.] (2004), 'The Story Behind the Story', in *Aldous Huxley's 'Brave New World'* (Bloom's Guides), introd. H. Bloom and ed. A. Goodman (New York: Chelsea House): pp. 12–15.

© The Editor(s) (if applicable) and The Author(s) 2016   227
J. Greenberg, N. Waddell (eds.), Brave New World: *Contexts and Legacies*, DOI 10.1057/978-1-137-44541-4

Arciero, A. (2008), 'Some Kind of *Brave New World*: Humans, Society, and Nature in the Dystopian Interpretations of Huxley and Orwell', in D.G. Izzo and K. Kirkpatrick (eds), *Huxley's 'Brave New World'*: *Essays* (Jefferson, NC: McFarland, 2008): pp. 46–61.

Aristotle (1941), *Politics*, trans. B. Jowett, in *The Basic Works of Aristotle*, ed. R. McKeon (New York: Random House): pp. 1113–316.

Arlen, M. (1933), *Man's Mortality. A Story* (London: William Heinemann).

Atsusis, H. and Kebritchi, M. (2008), 'Examining the Pedagogical Foundations of Modern Educational Computer Games', *Computers & Education*, 51: 1729–43.

Atwood, M. (2007), 'Everybody is Happy Now', *The Guardian* (16 Nov.): n.p. Available at http://www.theguardian.com/books/2007/nov/17/classics. margaretatwood (accessed 11 Oct. 2015).

— (2011), *In Other Worlds: SF and the Human Imagination* (London: Virago).

Baker, R.S. (1990), *Brave New World: History, Science, and Dystopia* (Boston: Twayne).

— (1996), 'Aldous Huxley: History and Science between the Wars', *CLIO: A Journal of Literature, History, and the Philosophy of History*, 25.3: 293–300.

Barbarella (1968), dir. Roger Vadim (Dino de Laurentiis Cinematografica/ Marianne Productions).

Beaumont, M. (2005), *Utopia, Ltd.: Ideologies of Social Dreaming in England 1870–1900* (Leiden: Brill).

Bedford, S. (2002), *Aldous Huxley. A Biography* (Chicago: Ivan R. Dee).

Bellamy, E. (1888), *Looking Backward: 2000–1887*, ed. M. Beaumont (Oxford: Oxford University Press, 2007).

Bentham, J. (1780), *An Introduction to the Principle of Morals and Legislation* (Oxford: Clarendon, 1907).

Bergner D. (2013), *What Do Women Want? Adventures in the Science of Desire* (New York: Ecco).

Betjeman, J. (1958), *Collected Poems*, introd. The Earl of Birkenhead (London: John Murray).

Birnbaum, M. (2006), *Aldous Huxley. A Quest for Values* (Brunswick, NJ: Transaction Publishers).

Bradshaw, D. (1995), 'Huxley's Slump: Planning, Eugenics and the "Ultimate Need" of Stability', in J. Batchelor (ed.), *The Art of Literary Biography* (Oxford: Clarendon Press): pp. 151–71.

Brittain, V. (1929), *Halcyon; or, The Future of Monogamy* (London: Kegan Paul, Trench, Trubner & Co.).

Brooke, J. (1963), 'Obituary' (12 Dec.), in D. Watt (ed.), *Aldous Huxley. The Critical Heritage* (London and Boston: Routledge & Kegan Paul, 1975): pp. 462–5.

Brown, N.O. (1959), *Life Against Death. The Psychoanalytic Meaning of History* (Middletown, CT: Wesleyan University Press, 1985).

Buchanan, B. (2002), 'Oedipus in Dystopia: Freud and Lawrence in Aldous Huxley's *Brave New World*', *Journal of Modern Literature*, 25.3–4 (Summer): 75–89.

Buell, L. (2001), *Writing for an Endangered World* (Cambridge, MA: Harvard University Press).

Burdekin, K. (1934), *Proud Man*, ed. D. Patai (New York: The Feminist Press, 1993).

Butler, S. (1872), *Erewhon, or Over the Range*, ed. P. Mudford (London: Penguin, 1970).

Carey J. (1992), *The Intellectuals and the Masses: Pride and Prejudice among the Literary Intelligentsia, 1880–1939* (London: Faber and Faber).

Carey-Webb, A. (1999), 'National and Colonial Education in Shakespeare's *The Tempest*', *Early Modern Literary Studies*, 5.1 (May): 1–39.

Cherryh, C.J. (1988), *Cyteen* (New York: Warner Books).

Chesler, P. (1988), *Sacred Bond: the Legacy of Baby M* (New York: Crown).

Childs, D. (2001), *Modernism and Eugenics: Woolf, Eliot, Yeats, and the Culture of Degeneration* (Cambridge: Cambridge University Press).

Chodorow, N. (1978), *The Reproduction of Mothering: Psychoanalysis and the Sociology of Gender* (Berkeley: University of California Press).

Chomsky, N. (1988), *Language and Politics* (Montreal: Black Rose).

Clark, V. (1987), *Aldous Huxley and Film* (Metuchen, NJ: Scarecrow Press).

Clarke, T. and Pierson, R. (2015), 'FDA Approves "Female Viagra" with Strong Warning', Reuters (19 Aug.). Available at http://www.reuters.com/article/2015/08/19/us-pink-viagra-fda-idUSKCN0QN2BH20150819 (accessed 11 Oct. 2015).

Cobley, E. (2009), *Modernism and the Culture of Efficiency: Ideology and Fiction* (Toronto: University of Toronto Press).

Conole, G., et al. (2004), 'Mapping Pedagogy and Tools for Effective Learning Design', *Computers & Education*, 43: 17–33.

Corea, G. (1985), *The Mother Machine: Reproductive Technology from Artificial Insemination to Artificial Wombs* (London: HarperCollins).

Crowninshield, F. (1914), 'In *Vanity Fair*' (Editorial), *Vanity Fair*, 1.3 (Mar.): 15.

— (1914), 'In *Vanity Fair*' (Editorial), *Vanity Fair*, 1.5 (May): 19.

Curtis, W.M. (2011), 'Rorty's Liberal Utopia and Huxley's *Island*', *Philosophy & Literature*, 35.1 (Apr.): 91–103.

Darwin, Charles (1871), *The Descent of Man, and Selection in Relation to Sex*, vol. 1 (rpt. Princeton, NJ: Princeton University Press, 1981).

Davidson, J. (2009), *Breeding: A Partial History of the Eighteenth Century* (New York: Columbia University Press).

De Landa, M. (2002), *Intensive Science and Virtual Philosophy* (New York: Continuum).

Deery, J. (1992), 'Technology and Gender in Aldous Huxley's Alternative(?) Worlds', *Extrapolation*, 33.3 (Fall): 258–73.

— (1996), *Aldous Huxley and the Mysticism of Science* (New York: St. Martin's Press).

— (2005), '*Brave New World*, the Sequel: Huxley and Contemporary Film', in P.E. Firchow and H.J. Real (eds), *The Perennial Satirist: Essays in Honour of Bernfried Nugel* (Münster: Lit Verlag): pp. 183–200.

Deese, R.S. (2014), *We Are Amphibians: Julian and Aldous Huxley on the Future of Our Species* (Oakland: University of California Press).

Derbyshire, J. (2003), 'What Happened to Aldous Huxley?', *The New Criterion*, 21.6 (Feb.): 13–22.

Dewey, J. (1911), 'Education', in P. Monroe (ed.), *A Cyclopedia of Education*, Vol. II (New York: Macmillan, 1911): pp. 398–401.

— (1916), 'Nationalizing Education', in *The Essential Dewey – Vol. 1: Pragmatism, Education, Democracy*, ed. L.A. Hickman and T.M. Alexander (Bloomington, IN: Indiana University Press, 1998): pp. 265–9.

Diken, B. (2011), 'Huxley's *Brave New World* – and Ours', *Journal for Cultural Research*, 15.2: 153–72.

Dorrier, J. (2014), 'Virtual Reality May Become the Next Great Media Platform – But Can It Fool All Five Senses?', *SingularityHUB* (28 Sep.): n.p. Available at http://singularityhub.com/2014/09/28/virtual-reality-may-become-the-next-great-media-platform-but-can-it-fool-all-five-senses/ (accessed 11 Oct. 2015).

Douglas, G.H. (1991), *Smart Magazines: 50 years of Literary Revelry and High Jinks at Vanity Fair, the New Yorker, Life, Esquire, and the Smart Set* (Hamden, CT: Archon Books).

Dunne, M.W. (2013), *A Cold War State of Mind: Brainwashing and Postwar American Society* (Amherst, MA: University of Massachusetts Press).

Eliot, T.S. (1969), *The Complete Poems and Plays* (London: Faber and Faber).

Elsner, Jr., H. (1967) *The Technocrats: Prophets of Automation* (Syracuse, NY: Syracuse University Press).

English, D.K. (2004), *Unnatural Selections: Eugenics in American Modernism and the Harlem Renaissance* (Chapel Hill: University of North Carolina Press).

English, E. (2014), *Lesbian Modernism: Censorship, Sexuality, and Genre Fiction* (Edinburgh: Edinburgh University Press).

Epicurus (1926), *The Extant Remains*, ed. and trans. C. Bailey (Oxford: Clarendon Press).

Eordogh, F. (2014), 'When Porn and Virtual Reality Collide (NSFW)' *Gizmodo* (20 Nov.): n.p. Available at http://gizmodo.com/when-porn-and-virtual-reality-collide-nsfw-1660603261 (accessed 11 Oct. 2015).

Essid, J. (1993), 'No God but Electricity: American Literature and Technological Enthusiasm in the Electrical Age, 1893–1939', unpublished PhD thesis (Indiana University).

Ewing, E. (1986), *History of Twentieth Century Fashion* (Totowa, NJ: Barnes & Noble).

Faludi, S. (1991), *Backlash: The Undeclared War Against American Women* (New York: Crown).

Fenn, K., Nusbaum, H.C., and Margoliash, D. (2003), 'Consolidation During Sleep of Perceptual Learning of Spoken Language', *Nature*, 425: 614–16.

Firchow, P. (1972), *Aldous Huxley, Satirist and Novelist* (Minneapolis: University of Minnesota Press).

— (1984), *The End of Utopia: A Study of Aldous Huxley's 'Brave New World'* (Lewisburg, PA: Bucknell University Press).

— (1999), '*Brave New World* Satirizes the American Present, Not the British Future', in K. de Koster (ed.), *Readings on 'Brave New World'* (San Diego, CA: Greenhaven): pp. 77–85.

— (2001), 'Brave at Last: Huxley's Western and Eastern Utopias', *Aldous Huxley Annual*, 1: 153–74.

Fisher, R.T. (1963), *Classical Utopian Theories of Education* (New York: Bookman).

Flood, A. (2011), '*Brave New World* Among Top 10 Books Americans Most Want Banned', *The Guardian* (12 Apr. 2011): n.p. Available at http://www.the-guardian.com/books/2011/apr/12/brave-new-world-challenged-books (accessed 11 Oct. 2015).

Foucault, M. (1978), *The History of Sexuality – Volume I: An Introduction*, trans. R. Hurley (1976; New York: Vintage).

— (1991), *Discipline and Punish: The Birth of the Prison*, trans. A. Sheridan (1975; London: Penguin).

Fox, B.H., and Robbin, J.S. (1952), 'The Retention of Material Presented during Sleep', *Journal of Experimental Psychology*, 43.1: 75–9.

Frost, L. (2013), *The Problem with Pleasure: Modernism and its Discontents* (New York: Columbia University Press).

Frye, N. (1965), 'Varieties of Literary Utopias', *Daedalus*, 94.2 (Spring): 323–47.

Fuss, D. (1989), *Essentially Speaking: Feminism, Nature and Difference* (New York: Routledge).

Gaipa, M. (2009), 'Accessorizing Clarissa: How Virginia Woolf Changes the Clothes and the Character of Her Lady of Fashion', *Modernist Cultures*, 4.1–2 (May): 24–47.

Galen, *On the Usefulness of the Parts of the Body* (*Peri Chreias Morion. De usu partium*), trans. M. Tallmadge May (Ithaca, NY: Cornell University Press, 1968), 2 vols.

Garzón, P.C., and Keijzer, F. (2011), 'Plants: Adaptive Behavior, Root-Brains, and Minimal Cognition', *Adaptive Behavior*, 19.3 (June): 155–71.

Geoghegan, V. (1987), *Utopianism and Marxism* (London: Methuen).

Gilpin, L. (2014), 'The State of Women in Technology: 15 Data Points You Should Know', *TechRepublic* (8 July): n.p. Available at http://www.techrepub-lic.com/article/the-state-of-women-in-technology-15-data-points-you-should-know/ (accessed 11 Oct. 2015).

Godwin, W. (1797), *The Enquirer: Reflections on Education, Manners, and Literature* (London: G.G. and J. Robinson).

Goswami, U. (2004), 'Neuroscience and Education', *British Journal of Educational Psychology*, 74.1: 1–14.

Gottlieb, E. (2001), *Dystopian Fiction East and West: Universe of Terror and Trial* (Montreal: McGill-Queen's University Press).

Greenfield, J. (1974), *Wilhelm Reich vs. the U.S.A.* (New York: W.W. Norton).

Greenberg, D. (2016), *Republic of Spin: An Inside History of the American Presidency* (New York: W.W. Norton).

Griffith, R.M. (2004), *Born Again Bodies: Flesh and Spirit in American Christianity* (Berkeley: University of California Press).

Grosz, E. (1994), *Volatile Bodies: Toward a Corporeal Feminism* (Bloomington: Indiana University Press).

Hägglund, M. (2012), *Dying for Time: Proust, Woolf, Nabokov* (Cambridge, MA: Harvard University Press).

Haines, C.J. (2014), '5 Amazing Upcoming Virtual Reality Technologies (One For Each of Your Senses)', *Curiousmatic* (25 Mar.): n.p. Available at http://curiousmatic.com/5-amazing-upcoming-virtual-reality-technologies-one-senses/ (accessed 11 Oct. 2015).

Haldane, C. (1926), *Man's World* (New York: George H. Doran, 1927).

— (1927), *Motherhood and Its Enemies* (Garden City, NY: Doubleday, Doran, & Co., 1928).

— (1932), 'Dr. Huxley and Mr. Arnold' (23 Apr.), in D. Watt (ed.), *Aldous Huxley: The Critical Heritage* (London and Boston: Routledge & Kegan Paul, 1975): pp. 207–9.

Haldane, J.B.S. (1924), *Daedalus; or, Science and the Future* (London: Kegan Paul, Trench, Trubner & Co.).

Haldeman, J. (1974), *The Forever War*, introd. A. Roberts (London: Gollancz, 2009).

Halpin, D. (2003), *Hope and Education: The Role of the Utopian Imagination* (London and New York: Routledge-Falmer).

Hammill, F. (2010), *Sophistication: A Literary and Cultural History* (Liverpool: Liverpool University Press).

Haraway, D. (1997), *Modest_Witness@Second_Millennium.FemaleMan_Meets_OncoMouse: Feminism and Technoscience* (New York: Routledge).

— (2015), 'Anthropocene, Capitalocene, Plantationocene, Chthulucene: Making Kin', *Environmental Humanities*, 6: 159–65.

Hardy, T. (1895), *Jude the Obscure*, ed. D. Taylor (London: Penguin, 1998).

Hauser, M.D., Chomsky, N., and Fitch, W.T. (2002), 'The Faculty of Language: What Is It, Who Has It, and How Did It Evolve?', *Science*, 298 (22 Nov.): 1569–79.

Heidegger, M. (1995), *The Fundamental Concepts of Metaphysics: World, Finitude, Solitude*, trans. W. McNeill and N. Walker (Bloomington, IN: Indiana University Press).

Herzog, D. (2008), *Sex in Crisis: The New Sexual Revolution and the Future of American Politics* (New York: Basic Books).

Higdon, D.L. (2013), *Wandering into 'Brave New World'* (Amsterdam and New York: Rodopi).

Hillegas, M.R. (1967), *The Future as Nightmare: H.G. Wells and the Anti-Utopians* (New York: Oxford University Press).

Horan, T. (2007), 'Revolutions from the Waist Downwards: Desire as Rebellion in Yevgeny Zamyatin's *We*, George Orwell's *1984*, and Aldous Huxley's *Brave New World*', *Extrapolation*, 48.2 (Summer): 314–39.

Horkheimer, M. and Adorno, T.W. (1947), *Dialectic of Enlightenment: Philosophical Fragments* (1947), ed. G.S. Noerr and trans. E. Jephcott (Stanford, CA: Stanford University Press, 2002).

Howe, M.D. (1953, ed.), *Holmes-Laski Letters: The Correspondence of Mr. Justice Holmes and Harold J. Laski 1916–1935* (London: Geoffrey Cumberlege and Oxford University Press).

Huxley, A. (1920), *Leda* (New York: George H. Doran).

— (1921), *Crome Yellow*, introd. M. Bradbury, biog. introd. D. Bradshaw (London: Vintage, 2004).

— (1923), *Antic Hay* (London: Penguin, 1948).

— (1928), *Point Counter Point* (London: Chatto & Windus, 1933).

— (1932), *Brave New World*, introd. M. Atwood and D. Bradshaw (London: Vintage, 2007).

— (1936), *Eyeless in Gaza*, introd. D. Bradshaw (London: Vintage, 1994).

— (1937, ed.) *An Encyclopædia of Pacifism* (London: Chatto & Windus).

— (1946), *The Perennial Philosophy* (London: Chatto & Windus).

— (1948), *Ape and Essence*, introd. D. Bradshaw (London: Vintage, 1994).

— (1956), '*Brave New World*: A Musical Comedy', ed. B. Nugel, *Aldous Huxley Annual*, 3 (2003): 33–128.

— (1958), *Brave New World Revisited*, introd. D. Bradshaw (London: Vintage, 2004).

— (1962), *Island*, introd. D. Bradshaw (London: Flamingo, 1994).

— (1963), 'Utopias, Positive and Negative', ed. J. Sexton, *Aldous Huxley Annual*, 1 (2001): 1–5.

— (1969), *Letters of Aldous Huxley*, ed. G. Smith (London: Chatto & Windus, 1969).

— (1978), *The Human Situation: Lectures at Santa Barbara, 1959*, ed. P. Ferrucci (London: Chatto & Windus).

— (1994), *The Hidden Huxley*, ed. D. Bradshaw (London: Faber and Faber).

— (2000), *Complete Essays: Volume I, 1920–1925*, ed. R.S. Baker and J. Sexton (Chicago: Ivan R. Dee).

— (2000), *Complete Essays: Volume II, 1926–1929*, ed. R.S. Baker and J. Sexton (Chicago: Ivan R. Dee).

— (2001), *Complete Essays: Volume III, 1930–1935*, ed. R.S. Baker and J. Sexton (Chicago: Ivan R. Dee).

— (2001), *Complete Essays: Volume IV, 1936–1938*, ed. R.S. Baker and J. Sexton (Chicago: Ivan R. Dee).

— (2002), *Complete Essays: Volume V, 1939–1956*, ed. R.S. Baker and J. Sexton (Chicago: Ivan R. Dee).

— (2002), *Complete Essays: Volume VI, 1956–1963*, ed. R.S. Baker and J. Sexton (Chicago: Ivan R. Dee).

— (2007), *Selected Letters*, ed. J. Sexton (Chicago: Ivan R. Dee).

Huxley, J. (1931), *What Dare I Think? The Challenge of Modern Science to Human Action and Belief* (London: Chatto & Windus).

— (1957), 'Transhumanism', in *New Bottles for New Wine* (New York: Harper & Row): pp. 13–17.

Izzo, D.G. (2008), 'Introduction', in D.G. Izzo and K. Kirkpatrick (eds), *Huxley's 'Brave New World'*: *Essays* (Jefferson, NC: McFarland): pp. 1–9.

Jacobs, N. (1995), '*Islandia*: Plotting Utopian Desire', *Utopian Studies*, 6: 75–89.

Jäger, L. (2004), *Adorno: A Political Biography*, trans. S. Spencer (New Haven: Yale University Press).

Jaeger, G. (2001), 'The Palanese Way: Engaged Enlightenment in Aldous Huxley's *Island*', in C.C. Barfoot (ed.), *Aldous Huxley between East and West* (Amsterdam: Rodopi): pp. 113–30.

James, P.D. (1992), *The Children of Men* (London: Faber and Faber, 2010).

James W. (1910), 'The Moral Equivalent of War', in *Memories and Studies* (New York: Longmans, Green, and Co., 1911): pp. 265–96.

Jameson, F. (2005), *Archaeologies of the Future: The Desire Called Utopia and Other Science Fictions* (New York: Verso).

— (2009), 'Then You Are Them' [review of Margaret Atwood, *The Year of the Flood* (2009)], *London Review of Books*, 31.17 (10 Sep.): 7–8.

Johnson, J.W. (1968, ed.), *Utopian Literature: A Selection* (New York: Modern Library).

Keyser, C. (2010), *Playing Smart: New York Women Writers and Modern Magazine Culture* (New Brunswick: Rutgers University Press).

Kipling, R. (2013), *The Cambridge Edition of the Poems of Rudyard Kipling – Volume II: Collected Poems II*, ed. T. Pinney (Cambridge: Cambridge University Press).

Kracauer, S. (1927), 'The Mass Ornament', in *The Mass Ornament: Weimar Essays*, ed. and trans. Thomas Y. Levin (Cambridge, MA: Harvard University Press, 1995): pp. 75–86.

Kripal, Jeffrey J. (2008), 'Brave New Worldview', *Chronicle of Higher Education*, 55.16 (12 Dec.): B7–B9.

Kumar, K. (1987), *Utopia and Anti-Utopia in Modern Times* (Oxford: Blackwell).

Laver, J. (1961), *Between the Wars* (London: Vista Books).

Lawrence, D.H. (1993), *The Letters of D. H. Lawrence – Volume VII: November 1928–February 1930*, ed. K. Sagar and J.T. Boulton (Cambridge: Cambridge University Press).

Leach, A.F. (1915), *The Schools of Medieval England* (London: Methuen).

Leach, G. (1970), *The Biocrats* (Baltimore: Penguin).

Leboyer, F. (1975), *Birth without Violence* (London: Pinter & Martin).

Lefanu, S. (1988), *In the Chinks of the World Machine: Feminism and Science Fiction.* (London: The Women's Press).

Lepore, J. (2014), *The Secret History of Wonder Woman* (New York: Knopf).

Levinas, E. (1978), *Existence and Existents*, trans. A. Lingis (The Hague and Boston: Martinus Nijhoff).

Lewis, T. (2012), 'The Architecture of Potentiality: Weak Utopianism and Educational Space in the Work of Giorgio Agamben', *Utopian Studies*, 23.2: 355–73.

Lewis, W. (1932), *Doom of Youth* (London: Chatto & Windus).

— (1937), 'A Letter to the Editor', *Twentieth Century Verse*, 'Wyndham Lewis Double Number', 6/7 (Nov./Dec.): n.p.

— (1963), *The Letters of Wyndham Lewis*, ed. W. K. Rose (London: Methuen).

— (1986), *The Caliph's Design: Architects! Where is Your Vortex?* (1919), ed. P. Edwards (Santa Barbara: Black Sparrow Press).

Little, R. (1942), 'Daydream', *Time* (18 May 1942): 86.

Loeb, H. (1933), *Life in a Technocracy: What It Might Be Like*, introd. Howard P. Segal (Syracuse, NY: Syracuse University Press).

— (1946), *Full Production without War* (Princeton: Princeton University Press).

— (1959), *The Way It Was* (New York: Criterion Books).

'Lucio' [G. Phillips] (1933), 'Abracadabra', *The Manchester Guardian* (14 Jan.): 9.

Luckhurst, R. (2005), *Science Fiction* (Cambridge: Polity).

Ludovici, A.M. (1924), *Lysistrata; or, Woman's Future and Future Woman* (New York: E.P. Dutton, 1925).

Macleod, H. (2005), 'What Role Can Educational Multimedia Play in Narrowing the Digital Divide?', *The International Journal of Education and Development using Information and Communication Technology*, 1.4: 42–53.

Mannheim, K. (1929), *Ideology and Utopia: An Introduction to the Sociology of Knowledge*, trans. L. Wirth and E. Shils (New York: Harcourt, Brace & World, 1936).

Marchand, R. (1985), *Advertising the American Dream: Making Way for Modernity, 1920–1940* (Berkeley, CA: University of California Press).

Marcuse, H. (1955), *Eros and Civilization: A Philosophical Inquiry into Freud* (Boston: Beacon Press, 1966).

— (2003), *Herbert Marcuse: A Critical Reader*, ed. J. Abromeit and W.M. Cobb (London: Routledge).

Massó, G. (1972), *Education in Utopias* (New York: AMS Press).

Matz, A. (2014), 'Hardy and the Vanity of Procreation', *Victorian Studies*, 57.1 (Autumn): 7–32.

Mead, M. (1928), *Coming of Age in Samoa* (New York: Dell, 1970).

Meckier, J. (1969), *Aldous Huxley: Satire and Structure* (London: Chatto & Windus).

— (1978), '*Brave New World* and the Anthropologists: Primitivism in A.F. 632', *Alternative Futures*, 1 (Spring): 51–69.

— (1978), 'Coming of Age in Pala: The Primitivism of *Brave New World* Reconsidered in Huxley's *Island*', *Alternative Futures*, 1 (Summer): 68–90.

— (1978), 'Our Ford, Our Freud and the Behaviorist Conspiracy in Huxley's *Brave New World*', *Thalia*, 1 (Spring): 35–59.

— (1979), 'A Neglected Huxley "Preface": His Earliest Synopsis of *Brave New World*', *Twentieth-Century Literature*, 25.1: 1–20.

— (1979), 'Debunking Our Ford: *My Life and Work* and *Brave New World*', *South Atlantic Quarterly*, 78 (Autumn): 448–59.

— (1984), 'Poetry in the Future, the Future of Poetry: Huxley and Orwell on Zamyatin', *Renaissance and Modern Studies*, 28: 18–39.

— (2001), 'Prepping for *Brave New World*: Aldous Huxley's Essays of the 1920s', *Utopian Studies*, 12.2: 234–45.

— (2002), 'Aldous Huxley's Americanization of the *Brave New World* Typescript', *Twentieth-Century Literature*, 48 (Winter): 427–60.

— (2003), 'Conradian Reminders in Aldous Huxley's *Island*: Will Farnaby's *Moksha*-Medicine Experience and "The Essential Horror"', *Studies in the Novel*, 35 (Spring): 44–67.

— (2011), *Aldous Huxley, from Poet to Mystic* (Zurich: LIT Verlag).

Mencken, H.L. (1933), 'Old Dr. Scott's Bile Beans', *The American Mercury* (Apr.): 505–7.

Meynaud, J. (1964), *Technocracy*, trans. P. Barnes (New York: The Free Press, 1968).

Mill, J.S. (1976), *Utilitarianism, On Liberty, and Considerations on Representative Government*, ed. H.B. Acton (London: J.M. Dent).

Miller, C.C. (2014), 'Freezing Eggs as Part of Employee Benefits: Some Women See Darker Message', *The New York Times* (10 Oct.): n.p. Available at http://www.nytimes.com/2014/10/15/upshot/egg-freezing-as-a-work-benefit-some-women-see-darker-message.html?_r=0&abt=0002&abg=1 (accessed 11 Oct. 2015).

Miller, G. (2008), 'Political Repression and Sexual Freedom in *Brave New World* and *1984*', in D.G. Izzo and K. Kirkpatrick (eds), *Huxley's 'Brave New World': Essays* (Jefferson, NC: McFarland): pp. 17–25.

Milton, J. (1992), *The Complete English Poems*, ed. G. Campbell (London: Everyman's Library).

Mitchison, N. (1995), *Solution Three* (New York: The Feminist Press).

— (1979), *You May Well Ask: A Memoir 1920–1940* (London: Victor Gollancz).

More, T. (1516), *Utopia*, ed. R. Marius (London: J.M. Dent, 1994).

Morrell, O. (1974), *Ottoline at Garsington: Memoirs of Lady Ottoline Morrell, 1915–1918*, ed. R. Gathorne-Hardy (London: Faber and Faber).

Morris, W. (1890), *News from Nowhere*, in *'News from Nowhere' and Other Writings*, ed. C. Wilmer (London: Penguin, 2004): pp. 41–228.

Morton, T. (2007), *Ecology without Nature: Rethinking Environmental Aesthetics* (Cambridge, MA: Harvard University Press).

— (2010), *The Ecological Thought* (Cambridge, MA: Harvard University Press).

Moylan, T. (1986), *Demand the Impossible: Science Fiction and the Utopian Imagination* (London: Methuen).

Murphy, J. (1984), 'From Mice to Men? Implications of Progress in Cloning Research', in *Test-Tube Women: What Future for Motherhood?*, ed. R. Arditti, R.D. Klein, and S. Minden (London and Boston: Pandora Press): pp. 76–91.

Murray, N. (2003), *Aldous Huxley: An English Intellectual* (London: Abacus).

Nabokov, V. (1969), *Ada, or Ardor: A Family Chronicle* (New York: McGraw-Hill).

Nast, C. (1913), 'Class Publications', *The Merchant's and Manufacturer's Journal* (June): 3–11.

Newton, L. (2012), 'Picturing Smartness: Cartoons in the *New Yorker*, *Vanity Fair*, and *Esquire* in the Age of Cultural Celebrities', *The Journal of Modern Periodical Studies*, 3.1: 64–92.

Niethammer, L. (1992), *Posthistoire: Has History Come to an End?*, trans. P. Camiller (London: Verso).

Nietzsche, F. (1959), *On the Genealogy of Morals and Ecce Homo*, trans. and ed. W. Kaufmann (New York: Vintage).

Ohmann, R. (1996), *Selling Culture: Magazines, Markets, and Class at Turn of the Century* (London and New York: Verso).

Olsson, M. (2006), 'Totalitarianism and the "Repressed" Utopia of the Present: Moving beyond Hayek, Popper and Foucault', in M.A. Peters and J. Freeman-Moir (eds), *Edutopias: New Utopian Thinking in Education* (Rotterdam: Sense): pp. 99–124.

Orland, K. (2013), 'How Fast Does "Virtual Reality" Have to Be to Look Like "Actual Reality"?', *Ars Technica* (3 Jan.): n.p. Available at http://arstechnica.com/gaming/2013/01/how-fast-does-virtual-reality-have-to-be-to-look-like-actual-reality/ (accessed 11 Oct. 2015).

Orwell, G. (1937), *The Road to Wigan Pier* (Harmondsworth: Penguin, 1979).

— (1946), 'The Prevention of Literature', in *The Collected Essays, Journalism and Letters – Volume 4: In Front of Your Nose 1945–1950*, ed. S. Orwell and I. Angus (London: Penguin, 1970): pp. 81–95.

— (1946), 'Review [of *We* by E. I. Zamyatin]', in *The Collected Essays, Journalism and Letters – Volume 4: In Front of Your Nose 1945–1950*, ed. S. Orwell and I. Angus (London: Penguin, 1970): pp. 95–9.

— (1949), *Nineteen Eighty-Four*, introd. T. Pynchon (London: Penguin, 2003).

Ozmon, H. (1969), *Utopias and Education* (Minneapolis, MN: Burgess).

Paracelsus [Theophrastus Bombastus von Hohenheim] (2008), *Essential Theoretical Writings*, ed. and trans. A. Weeks (Leiden: Brill).

Parks, L. (1999), 'Bringing *Barbarella* Down to Earth: Astronaut and Feminine Sexuality in the 1960s', in H. Radner and M. Luckett (eds), *Swinging Single: Representing Sexuality in the 1960s* (Minneapolis: University of Minnesota Press): pp. 253–75.

Parrinder, P. (1997), 'Eugenics and Utopia: Sexual Selection from Galton to Morris', *Utopian Studies*, 8.2: 1–12.

— (2009), 'Robots, Clones, and Clockwork Men: The Post-Human Perplex in Early Twentieth-Century Literature and Science', *Interdisciplinary Science Reviews*, 34.1 (Mar.): 56–67.

— (2012), 'War is Peace: Conscription and Mobilization in the Modern Utopia', in D. Seed (ed.), *Future Wars: The Anticipations and the Fears* (Liverpool: Liverpool University Press): pp. 50–65.

Parsons, D. (1987), 'Dartington: A Principal Source of Inspiration Behind Aldous Huxley's *Island*', *The Journal of General Education*, 39.1: 10–25.

Partington, J.S. (2000), 'The Death of the Static: H.G. Wells and the Kinetic Utopia', *Utopian Studies*, 11.2: 96–111.

Peller, S. (2008), 'Laboring for a *Brave New World*: Our Ford and the Epsilons', in D.G. Izzo and K. Kirkpatrick (eds), *Huxley's 'Brave New World': Essays* (Jefferson, NC: McFarland): pp. 62–72.

Perpich, D. (2008), *The Ethics of Emmanuel Levinas* (Stanford: Stanford University Press).

Peters, M.A. and Freeman-Moir, J. (2006), 'Introducing Edutopias: Concept, Genealogy, Futures', in M.A. Peters and J. Freeman-Moir (eds), *Edutopias: New Utopian Thinking in Education* (Rotterdam: Sense): pp. 1–19.

Pfaelzer, J. (1988), 'The Changing of the Avant-Garde: the Feminist Utopia', *Science-Fiction Studies*, 15.3 (Nov.): 282–94.

Pfeffer, N. (1993), *The Stork and the Syringe: A Political History of Reproductive Medicine* (Cambridge: Polity Press).

Piercy, M. (1979), *Woman on the Edge of Time* (1976; London: The Women's Press).

— (1991), *He, She and It* (New York: Ballantine Books).

Pinker, S. (2002), *The Blank Slate: The Modern Denial of Human Nature* (London: Allen Lane).

Posner, R.A. (2000), 'Orwell versus Huxley: Economics, Technology, Privacy, and Satire', *Philosophy and Literature*, 24.1 (Apr.): 1–33.

Postman, N. (1985), *Amusing Ourselves to Death: Public Discourse in the Age of Show Business* (London: Methuen).

Radway, J. (1997), *A Feeling for Books: The Book-of-the-Month Club, Literary Taste, and Middle-Class Desire* (Chapel Hill: University of North Carolina Press).

Reich, W. (1933), *The Mass Psychology of Fascism*, trans. V. R. Carfagno (New York: Farrar, Straus and Giroux, 1970).

— (2003), 'Sexual Repression, Instinctual Renunciation, and Sex Reform', in J. Escoffier (ed.), *Sexual Revolution* (New York: Thunder's Mouth Press): pp. 578–98.

Rosenbaum, R. (1995), 'The Great Ivy League Nude Posture Photo Scandal', *The New York Times Sunday Magazine* (15 Jan.): 55–6.

Rosenfeld, I. (1988), *Preserving the Hunger: An Isaac Rosenfeld Reader*, ed. M. Shechner (Detroit, MI: Wayne State University Press).

Rosenhan, C. (2007), '"The Knowledge Economy": Aldous Huxley's Critiques of Universal Education', in B. Nugel, U. Rasch, and G. Wagner (eds), *Aldous Huxley, Man of Letters: Thinker, Critic and Artist*, Proceedings of the Third Aldous Huxley Symposium, Riga 2004 (Berlin: Lit Verlag): pp. 93–111.

Rubin, J.S. (1992), *The Making of Middlebrow Culture* (Chapel Hill: University of North Carolina Press).

Said, E. (1978), *Orientalism* (New York: Random House, 1978).

Salam, R. (2014), 'The end of pregnancy: And the inevitable rise of the artificial womb', *Slate* (23 Oct.). Available at http://www.slate.com/articles/news_and_politics/culturebox/2014/10/ectogenesis_the_end_of_pregnancy_and_the_inevitable_rise_of_the_artificial.html (accessed 11 Oct. 2015).

Sandberg, S. (2013), *Lean In: Women, Work, and the Will to Lead* (New York: Knopf).

Sargent, P. (1986), *The Shore of Women* (New York: Crown Publishers, Inc.).

Schiller, F. (1980), *Naïve and Sentimental Poetry and On the Sublime*, trans. J.A. Elias (New York: Frederick Ungar).

Schmitt, C. (1996), *The Concept of the Political*, trans. G. Schwab (Chicago: University of Chicago Press).

Schneiderman, H. (2012), 'Introduction', in A. Huxley, *Ends and Means: An Inquiry into the Nature of Ideals* (1937; New Brunswick: Transaction): pp. vii–xxvi.

Scholes, R. (2006), *Paradoxy of Modernism* (New Haven: Yale University Press).

Schopenhauer, A. (1969), *The World as Will and Representation: Vol. 1*, trans. E.F.J. Payne (New York: Dover).

Schraner, E. (2009), 'Review: The To-day and To-morrow Series', *Interdisciplinary Science Reviews*, 34.1 (Mar.): 107–15.

Scott, H. et al. (1933), *Introduction to Technocracy* (New York: John Day).

Seed, D. (2004), *Brainwashing: The Fictions of Mind Control* (Kent, OH: Kent State University Press).

— (2008), 'Aldous Huxley: *Brave New World*', in D. Seed (ed.), *A Companion to Science Fiction* (Oxford: Blackwell): pp. 477–88.

Segal, H.P. (1985), *Technological Utopianism in American Culture* (Chicago: University of Chicago Press).

— (2005), *Recasting The Machine Age: Henry Ford's Village Industries* (Amherst: University of Massachusetts Press).

— (2012), *Utopias: A Brief History from Ancient Writings to Virtual Communities* (Oxford: Wiley-Blackwell).

Self, W. (1997), *Great Apes* (New York: Grove).

Sellars, S., and O'Hara, D. (2012; eds), *Extreme Metaphors: Selected Interviews with J.G. Ballard, 1967–2008* (London: Fourth Estate).

Shakespeare, W. (1999), *The Tempest*, ed. V.M. Vaughan and A.T. Vaughan (London: Arden).

Shurbutt, S.B. (1985), 'Matthew Arnold's Concept of Nature: A Synthesist's View', *Victorian Poetry*, 23.1 (Spring): 97–104.

Silver, H. (1965), *The Concept of Popular Education: A Study of Ideas and Social Movements in the Early Nineteenth Century* (London: Methuen).

Sion, R.T. (2010), *Aldous Huxley and the Search for Meaning: A Study of the Eleven Novels* (Jefferson, NC: McFarland).

Sisk, D.W. (1997), *Transformations of Language in Modern Dystopias* (Westport, CT: Greenwood Press).

Skinner, B.F. (1971), *Beyond Freedom and Dignity* (London: Jonathan Cape, 1972).

Slade, G. (2006), *Made to Break: Technology and Obsolescence in America* (Cambridge, MA: Harvard University Press).

Smethurst, P. (2008), '"O brave new world that has no poets in it": Shakespeare and Scientific Utopia in *Brave New World*', in D.G. Izzo and K. Kirkpatrick (eds), *Huxley's 'Brave New World': Essays* (Jefferson, NC: McFarland): pp. 96–106.

Snyder, C. (2007), '"When the Indian was in vogue": D. H. Lawrence, Aldous Huxley, and Ethnological Tourism in the Southwest', *Modern Fiction Studies*, 53.4 (Winter): 662–96.

Sparrow, T. (2013), *Levinas Unhinged* (Winchester: Zero Books).

Spiller, E. (2009), 'Shakespeare and the Making of Early Modern Science: Resituating Prospero's Art', *South Central Review*, 26.1–2 (Winter–Spring): 24–41.

Squier, S.M. (1994), *Babies in Bottles: Twentieth-Century Visions of Reproductive Technology* (New Brunswick, NJ: Rutgers University Press).

Steel, E. (2015), 'Vice Uses Virtual Reality to Immerse Viewers in News', *The New York Times* (23 Jan.): n.p. Available at http://www.nytimes.com/2015/01/23/business/media/vice-uses-virtual-reality-to-immerse-viewers-in-news.html?_r=0 (accessed 11 Oct. 2015).

Stein, Z., et al. (2011), 'Ethical Issues in Educational Neuroscience: Raising Children in a Brave New World', in J. Illes and B. Sahakian (eds) *The Oxford Handbook of Neuroethics* (Oxford: Oxford University Press): pp. 803–22.

Strauss, H. (1942), 'A Novel That Casts a Spell', *The New York Times Book Review* (12 Apr.): 1 and 22.

Surette, L. (1999), *Pound in Purgatory: From Economic Radicalism to Anti-Semitism* (Urbana and Chicago: University of Illinois Press).

Surry, D.W., and Farquhar, J.D. (1997), 'Diffusion Theory and Instructional Technology', *Journal of Instructional Science and Technology*, 2.1: n.p. Available at http://www.southalabama.edu/coe/bset/surry/papers/dtit/dtit.htm (accessed 11 Oct. 2015).

Szezekalla, M. (2007), 'The Scottish Enlightenment and Buddhism – Huxley's Vision of Hybridity in *Island*', in B. Nugel et al. (eds), *Aldous Huxley, Man of Letters* (Berlin: Lit Verlag): pp. 153–66.

Tracy, D. (2010), 'Investing in "Modernism": Smart Magazines, Parody, and Middlebrow Professional Judgment', *The Journal of Modern Periodical Studies*, 1.1: 38–63.

Turner, C. (2011), *Adventures in the Orgasmatron: How the Sexual Revolution Came to America* (New York: Farrar, Straus and Giroux).

— (2013), '*Sex-Pol: Essays, 1929–1934* by Wilhelm Reich – Review', *The Guardian* (1 May): n.p. Available at http://www.theguardian.com/books/2013/may/01/sex-pol-essays-reich-review (accessed 11 Oct. 2015).

Varricchio, M. (1999), 'Power of Images/Images of Power in *Brave New World* and *Nineteen Eighty-Four*', *Utopian Studies*, 10.1: 98–114.

Verne, E. (1976), 'Literacy and Industrialisation: The Dispossession of Speech', in H.J. Graff (ed.), *Literacy and Social Development in the West: A Reader* (Cambridge: Cambridge University Press, 1981): pp. 286–303.

Waddell, N. (2012), 'Technocracy and the Fordian Arts: America, *The American Mercury*, and Music in the 1930s', in S. Haslam and S. O'Malley (eds), *Ford Madox Ford and America* (Amsterdam: Rodopi): pp. 167–80.

Wark, M. (2015), *Molecular Red: Theory for the Anthropocene* (London: Verso).

Warmflash, D. (2015), 'Artificial Wombs: the coming of motherless births?', *Genetic Literacy Project* (12 June). Available at http://www.geneticliteracyproject.org/2015/06/12/artificial-wombs-the-coming-era-of-motherless-births/ (accessed 11 Oct. 2015)

Watson, J. (1968), *The Double Helix* (London: Weidenfeld and Nicolson).

Watt, D. (1968), 'Vision and Symbol in Aldous Huxley's *Island*', *Twentieth-Century Literature*, 14 (Oct.): 149–60.

— (1975, ed.), *Aldous Huxley: The Critical Heritage* (London and Boston: Routledge & Kegan Paul).

Waugh, E. (1930), *Vile Bodies* (Boston: Little, Brown & Company).

Weeks, J. (2009), 'An "Untenable Illusion"? The Problematic Marriage of Freud and Marx', *Sitegeist: A Journal of Psychoanalysis and Philosophy*, 3 (Autumn): 9–26.

Weldon, F. (1980), *Praxis* (London: Coronet).

— (1989), *The Cloning of Joanna May* (London: Collins).

Wells, H.G. (1905), *A Modern Utopia*, ed. M.R. Hillegas (Lincoln: University of Nebraska Press, 1967).

— (1905), *A Modern Utopia*, ed. G. Claeys and P. Parrinder (London: Penguin, 2005).

— (1933), *The Shape of Things to Come*, ed. P. Parrinder (London: Penguin, 2005).

— (1938), 'Fiction About the Future', in *H.G. Wells's Literary Criticism*, ed. P. Parrinder and R.M. Philmus (Brighton: Harvester, 1980): pp. 246–51.

Wickes, G. and Frazer, R. (1965), 'Aldous Huxley', in *Writers at Work: The Paris Review Interviews Second Series* (New York: Viking): pp. 193–214.

Wiener, M.J. (1982), *English Culture and the Decline of the Industrial Spirit, 1850–1980* (Cambridge: Cambridge University Press).

Williams, L.R. (2005), *The Erotic Thriller in Contemporary Cinema* (Bloomington, IN: Indiana University Press).

Williams, R. (1985), *Problems in Materialism and Culture: Selected Essays* (London: Verso).

Witters, S.A. (2008), 'Words Have to Mean Something More: Folkloric Reading in *Brave New World*', in D.G. Izzo and K. Kirkpatrick (eds), *Huxley's 'Brave New World': Essays* (Jefferson, NC: McFarland): pp. 73–87.

Wodehouse, P.G. (1990), *Yours Plum: The Letters of P.G. Wodehouse*, ed. F. Donaldson (London: Hutchinson).

Woiak, J. (2007), 'Designing a Brave New World: Eugenics, Politics, and Fiction', *The Public Historian*, 29.3 (Summer): 105–29.

Wolmark, J. (1993), *Aliens and Others: Science Fiction, Feminism and Postmodernism* (Hemel Hempstead: Harvester Wheatsheaf).

Women in Technology Education Foundation (n.d.), 'WITEF Facts', *WITEF*: n.p. Available at http://www.womenintechnology.org/witef/resources (accessed 11 Oct. 2015).

Woodcock, G. (1972), *Dawn and the Darkest Hour: A Study of Aldous Huxley* (London: Faber and Faber).

Wright, A.T. (1942), *Islandia* (New York: Signet, 1958).

Young, A. (1981), *Dada and After: Extremist Modernism and English Literature* (Manchester: Manchester University Press).

Young, M. (1982), *The Elmhirsts of Dartington: The Creation of a Utopian Community* (Abingdon: Routledge & Kegan Paul).

Zoltan, I. (2014), 'Artificial Wombs Are Coming, but the Controversy is Already Here', *Motherboard* (4 Aug.). Available at http://motherboard.vice.com/read/artificial-wombs-are-coming-and-the-controversys-already-here (accessed 11 Oct. 2015).

INDEX

© The Editor(s) (if applicable) and The Author(s) 2016
J. Greenberg, N. Waddell (eds.), Brave New World: *Contexts and Legacies*, DOI 10.1057/978-1-137-44541-4

Skinner, Burrhus Frederic, *Walden Two*, 57
Smart Set, The, 129
Smith, George H., *Those Sexy Saucer People*, 79
Snowden, Edward, 69
Snyder, Carey, 63, 114
socialism, 33, 155
Socialist Society for Sex-Counseling and Sex-Research, 77
Soddy, Frederick, *Wealth, Virtual Wealth, and Debt*, 41
'soma' 1, 6, 21–2, 53, 56, 62, 70, 74, 75, 80, 81, 92, 98, 110, 122, 124, 133, 135, 139–41, 177, 190, 194, 219. *See also* pharmacology/pharmaceuticals
Spiller, Elizabeth, 62
St. Vincent Millay, Edna, 129
Stalin, Joseph, 6, 25, 121, 122
standardization, 5–7, 34–5, 38–9, 133–6, 143, 217, 222. *See also* Fordism, mass production
state power, x, 2, 4, 6, 11, 12, 46, 52, 56–8, 111–12, 120–123, 211–24
Statesman, the, 128
Stein, Gertrude, 130
Steinmetz, Charles, 39
Stephenson, Neal, *Snow Crash*, 82
sterilization, 91–2, 96, 116, 153, 175, 179, 222
Stock Market Crash of 1929, 34, 40
Stoddard, Lothrop, 113
Stoermer, Eugene, 171
Stopes, Marie, 154
Strachey, John St. Loe, 33
sublime, the, 12, 183, 218–20
Sullivan, John William Navin, vii
Summerhill School, 156
Sundance Film Festival, 82
Surry, D.W., 56

Swift, Jonathan, *Gulliver's Travels*, 8, 53, 99, 100

T
Tagore, Rabindranath, 62
Tantra, 74, 97–9, 101
Taylor, Fredrick, 39
Technical Alliance, 39
technocracy, 3, 31–9, 41–7, 58, 174, 197, 221. *See also* central planning, managerialism
Technocracy Movement, 7
Technocracy, Inc., 41
Technocracy: Some Questions Answered, 32
Test-Tube Women: What Future for Motherhood?, 162
Thomas à Kempis, *Imitation of Christ, The*, 223
Times Literary Supplement, 73
'To-day and To-morrow' (pamphlet series), 10, 149, 178
totalitarianism, 6, 25, 31, 64, 72, 76, 90, 92, 93, 96, 121, 135, 160, 198, 200, 221–2
Tzara, Tristan, 130

U
utilitarianism, 4, 12, 18–19, 34, 37, 47, 72, 175, 216, 221

V
Vadim, Roger, *Barbarella: Queen of the Galaxy*, 10, 79–80
Van Gogh, Vincent, 129
Vanity Fair (magazine), 11, 127–44
Veblen, Thorstien, 39
Vedanta, 97, 206